PRAISE FOR *DATA-DRIVEN CUSTOMER EXPERIENCE TRANSFORMATION*

'Mohammed Zaki specializes in using data and AI to analyse customer sentiment about products and services. This book is essential for those seeking competitive advantage through customer insights and modernizing their organization's approach.'
Ashish Gupta, Chief Growth Officer, Europe and Africa, Diversified Industries, HCLTech

'A must-read for any business serious about customer experience in the digital era. The book provides a practical guide for using data and AI to understand and delight your customers.'
Franziska Bell, a visionary tech executive previously at UBER, Toyota and BP

'Thought-provoking and practical in equal measures. Helps you cut through the noise surrounding AI and CX to decide where to focus for your business goals.'
Robert Bates, Head of Decision Sciences, Currys

'This publication represents a major leap forward in the professionalization of customer experience management. Zaki addresses the popular themes of our time, such as seamless omnichannel experiences and customer delight, and sets out practical, data-backed approaches to realize value in the real world, beyond the buzzwords. An essential handbook for all customer experience professionals'
Nicholas Clark, Partner and Associate Director, Service and Support Operations, Boston Consulting Group (BCG)

'A must-read for anyone that truly wants to understand how to delight their customers. Mohamed Zaki has been working in this field for over a decade and his hands-on, real-life experience shines through in this book. You will take away things that change your perspective on how to execute your customer strategy.'
Charlotte Mitchell, AI and Emerging Tech Capability Leader, PwC

'A detailed, practical and interesting examination of the opportunity digital technologies provide for creating differentiated customer experiences. The book usefully explores the role of data in driving solution efficacy and adoption as well as providing insight into the potential of AI.'
Robert Christmas, Head of Enterprise Process Design, AstraZeneca

'An insightful and timely guide for organizations striving to navigate the evolving landscape of customer engagement. By combining practical frameworks with data-driven strategies, Mohamed Zaki expertly addresses the integration of digital, physical and social dimensions to create seamless and impactful customer journeys. This book is invaluable for leaders seeking to drive sustainable growth through innovative, customer-centric approaches to experience design.'
Mohamed Elmasry, CEO, Tactful AI

'In an era where customer experience is the key differentiator, this book is an essential guide for leaders looking to harness data for meaningful impact. Mohamed Zaki masterfully bridges the gap between theory and practice, offering actionable insights to seamlessly integrate the digital, physical and social realms of customer journeys. Having led multiple experience-driven digital transformations, I see this book as an indispensable resource for businesses striving to lead with CX effectively.'
Gautam Jha, Founder, CXMi

'*Data-Driven Customer Experience Transformation* is really eye-opening. The book does a great job of making complex research digestible without oversimplifying it. It gives you concrete tools you can use right away while still diving deep into the theory behind them. Whether you're working in the field of CX or studying it, you'll get a lot out of this – it's rare to find a book that serves both audiences so well. If you're involved in customer experience and AI work, I'd definitely pick this up.'
Dr Jan Bluemel, Cofounder and CTO, Annex AI

'A practical guide for organizations and governments navigating digital transformation. The book is a blueprint for leveraging data-driven insights to optimize omnichannel strategies. Through well-researched case studies, Dr Zaki shows how digital technologies, AI and analytics reshape customer journeys. His ability to distil complex concepts into actionable strategies makes this work indispensable for business leaders, policymakers and CX professionals. It will shape the way businesses and governments design, manage and measure customer and citizen interactions.'

Hassan Al-Ibrahim, Managing Founder, Local Context Consulting Services and a public sector adviser

Data-Driven Customer Experience Transformation

Optimize your omnichannel approach

Mohamed Zaki

KoganPage

First published in Great Britain and the United States in 2025 by Kogan Page Limited

Kogan Page
Kogan Page Ltd, 2nd Floor, 45 Gee Street, London EC1V 3RS, United Kingdom
Kogan Page Inc, 8 W 38th Street, Suite 90, New York, NY 10018, USA
www.koganpage.com

EU Representative (GPSR)
Authorised Rep Compliance Ltd, Ground Floor, 71 Baggot Street Lower, Dublin D02 P593, Ireland
www.arccompliance.com

Kogan Page books are printed on paper from sustainable forests.

ISBNs
Hardback   978 1 3986 1742 1
Paperback   978 1 3986 1739 1
Ebook   978 1 3986 1743 8

British Library Cataloguing-in-Publication Data
A CIP record for this book is available from the British Library.

Library of Congress Control Number
2024060495

Typeset by Integra Software Services, Pondicherry
Print production managed by Jellyfish
Printed and bound by CPI Group (UK) Ltd, Croydon CR0 4YY

To my father, El Sayed Helmi, who passed away when I was just 12 years old. This is a tribute to your soul, a reflection of the strength and values you left behind.

To my mother, Wegdan Elbahi, whose unwavering inspiration and guidance have shaped me into who I am today. Your love and wisdom are the foundation of all my achievements.

To my beloved wife, Sara, my daughter, Jana, and my son, Malek – you have lived this journey with me. Without your endless love, support and belief in me, this book would never have been possible.

CONTENTS

LIST OF FIGURES AND TABLE

ABOUT THE AUTHOR

Mohamed Zaki is a professor at the Institute for Manufacturing, Department of Engineering, University of Cambridge. He is also the Deputy Director of Cambridge Service Alliance, a research centre that brings together the world's leading firms and academics to address digital service transformation challenges. Mohamed serves as a member of the Editorial Advisory Board of the Journal of Service Management. His research interests lie in service experience, emphasizing the application of artificial intelligence (AI) to design and manage customer experience and create new data-driven business models. He is a high-profile academic with an extensive research portfolio in service management and has many publications in highly ranked journals. His papers have appeared at top conferences and in media outlets such as the *Harvard Business Review*. He has consulted and lectured for over 100 organizations, including Manchester United, Mitsubishi Heavy Industry, CEMEX, Caterpillar, IKEA, HCLTech, Bouygues, and many others. Mohamed serves in advisory roles for several companies, most recently as the AI Innovation Adviser at Tactful AI. He is the course leader for the Data-Driven Design for Customer Experience (CX) online course, which is offered through Cambridge Advance Online at Cambridge University Press and Assessment.

1

Introduction

We live in an experience economy, the ability to see your business through your customer's eyes is not just an advantage – it's a necessity. As we navigate the ever-evolving landscapes of business-to-business (B2B), business-to-consumer (B2C) and public sectors, the role of digital technologies like artificial intelligence (AI) and virtual reality in revolutionizing customer interactions becomes increasingly critical. These advancements not only offer new avenues for enhancing customer experience (CX) but also pose challenges in integrating data-driven insights into our service models.

This book explores the strategic adoption of emerging digital technologies in products and services, aiming not just to boost business performance but to transform organizations at their core. We explore how this transformation reshapes everything from the customer journey to company culture and employee dynamics, emphasizing the need for a holistic approach to CX. Our journey through these pages will reveal how integrating digital, physical and social channels is crucial in delivering a cohesive and delightful customer experience and the pitfalls organizations face without such integration.

The demand for exceptional customer experiences has never been higher. With findings like Salesforce's report that 88 per cent of buyers consider the overall experience as important as the product or service itself, the pressure is on organizations to deliver.[1] To stay competitive and achieve desirable outcomes like customer retention and profitability, managing unique experiences that meet evolving customer expectations is key. In this landscape, the abundance of data offers an opportunity to track and improve customer experiences in ways traditional metrics cannot. Yet, the challenge lies in effectively leveraging these data-driven insights and integrating them into existing engagement strategies. This book also addresses the gaps in current CX measurement practices, where professionals often lack comprehensive AI methods to truly understand customer sentiments, relying instead on simplified metrics that may provide a skewed view of customer experiences.

This can lead to a transition build to data-driven innovation and new revenue streams. Despite its importance, it poses substantial challenges, particularly for well-established firms dealing with fixed organizational structures, ingrained cultural norms and conventional revenue models. The edge that effective data use provides in the competitive market is pushing more businesses to adopt data-centric strategies. Yet, many of these businesses struggle with a lack of structured approaches to effectively leverage data as a fundamental component of their business models. This book aims to offer practical guidance to professionals and organizations, helping them to align services with data-driven practices effectively. Failure to embrace data-driven approaches puts businesses at risk of losing a crucial competitive edge, market share and the accompanying revenue.

The aim is to provide valuable insights and frameworks for creating delightful customer experiences and ensuring consistency across digital, physical and social channels. We will explore the roles of AI technologies, stakeholder interactions, and the overall impact on customer experience. You will gain knowledge on leveraging data to design and manage customer experiences, fostering loyalty and engagement, and generating innovative data-driven business models. This book is designed to equip you with the tools necessary to navigate the complex and customer-centric landscape of today's business world.

To give you an overview of this, I will illustrate various examples across B2B, B2C and public service organizations. These organizations are involved in this digital service transformation to create an end-to-end customer experience.

Business-to-business (B2B) organizations

I have collated examples from companies I collaborated with through the Cambridge Service Alliance research centre, including CEMEX, Caterpillar, Thales, Boston Dynamics and IBM. While you may not be familiar with all of their service offerings, the following sections will provide valuable insights into how digital transformation has benefited these industries and the businesses they serve.

Let me start with **CEMEX**, a company specializing in heavy building materials like cement and concrete, which is particularly instructive.[2] CEMEX identified that delivery delays and invoicing issues were significant pain points for their customers when they order through traditional channels, such as phone, website and email. In response, they developed a digital app named *CEMEX Go* to streamline order fulfilment. Initially created to tackle order complications and ensure seamless delivery of their ready-mix concrete, the app demonstrates how digital tools can enhance customer service in a B2B setting. Implementing *CEMEX Go* involved more than just technical development; it required a holistic approach to digital transformation:[3]

1 **Developing a digital capabilities roadmap**: CEMEX outlined critical areas in their operations needing development for *CEMEX Go*. This included planning essential investments and integrating the new digital capabilities into existing workflows. They also established a timeline and a monitoring plan to evaluate the success of these digital solutions.

2 **Cultivating a digital organizational culture**: The company focused on fostering a digital mindset among decision makers and employees, promoting the development of customer-centric solutions.

3 **Automating basic processes**: By integrating technologies like data analytics and AI, CEMEX automated fundamental processes such as resource and capacity planning, dynamic pricing, logistics and fleet optimization. This automation provided on-demand information, enhancing operational efficiency.

4 **Reformulating the service strategy**: Similar to past IT transformations, digital implementation at CEMEX required a shift in business strategy, particularly in service delivery. This involved rethinking the entire service strategy to ensure efficiency, scalability, reliability and predictability of core operations while fostering rapid development and innovation with a customer-centric focus.

The results were significant. *CEMEX Go* achieved 100 per cent adoption across all business lines and customer segments while creating a fully automated experience with enhanced supply chain visibility. Since its launch in November 2017, *CEMEX Go* has established itself as the leading multichannel platform for the building materials industry. Currently, it serves over 50,000 customers, covering 93 per cent of cement and 85 per cent of ready-mix concrete customers.[4] Over the past four years, the company has seen a significant 50 per cent increase in its net promoter score, a key metric for customer loyalty and satisfaction, reaching a score of 66.[5]

This case study exemplifies how businesses, especially in the B2B sector, can leverage digital technologies to transform their service strategies, automate processes and ultimately enhance customer experiences. The success of CEMEX's digital transformation highlights the critical role of embracing data-driven practices in today's competitive business environment.

Caterpillar is another compelling example of a firm embracing digital to offer a seamless experience. They utilize machine-to-machine (M2M) data to gather comprehensive information, including equipment and engine telemetry data, fluid analyses, inspection reports, repair history and site conditions.[6] Analysing these diverse datasets has enabled Caterpillar to closely monitor the health and usage of their assets, leading to several advantages, including developing new digital services. Caterpillar has introduced proactive condition-monitoring services that employ AI technology, acting as an operator assistant.[7] The benefits and innovations from this advancement are noteworthy:

1 **Increased customer loyalty and revenues**: Caterpillar's condition-monitoring services have expanded their spare parts business and enhanced customer support, particularly in asset maintenance and repair services. This has led to increased revenue through improved customer experiences and heightened loyalty.

2 **Creation of recommendation services**: The condition-monitoring solution has enabled Caterpillar to offer recommendation services to its customers. These services can identify potential mechanical issues and proactively reach out to customers to prevent or minimize equipment failure and recurrence of defects.

3 **Predicting and forecasting performance**: Utilizing predictive analytics, Caterpillar can pinpoint areas for potential enhancement in performance and equipment utilization. Forecasting analysis provides clients with detailed assessments of their assets, helping to reduce costs. Alerts keep customers informed about their assets, minimizing downtime and boosting productivity.

Caterpillar aims to evolve these services from operator assistants to fully autonomous asset services capable of efficiently managing construction or mining sites. This example not only showcases Caterpillar's innovative use of machine data but also illustrates the broader trend of how companies are leveraging digital transformation for more advanced and customer-centric solutions.

Thales, a company operating across sectors like aerospace, transport, defence and security, embarked on a digital service transformation journey that has significantly altered their market offerings. This transformation at Thales wasn't just about upgrading technology; it involved a comprehensive overhaul of their business model to create digital services that directly address customer challenges. A key aspect of Thales' innovation strategy was the formation of an ecosystem of partners, which was instrumental in developing new data-driven services. The goal was to generate new value for the business and provide a seamless experience for their customers.[8]

One of the strategic pillars of this transformation was the Digital Culture Manifesto, which included the establishment of a **digital factory** comprising four crucial components:[9]

1 **Digital Centre of Excellence:** This unit brought together professionals from diverse fields to construct a centralized digital platform hosting a variety of services. The team's expertise spans multiple domains, including artificial intelligence, user experience design, the Internet of Things and cybersecurity.

2 **Digital platform**: Developed by the Digital Centre of Excellence, this platform underwent rigorous testing to ensure it met organizational needs like value chain optimization, system process automation, and decision-making tools. It's tailored to align with the core business requirements of Thales' customers.

3 **Startup incubator**: Thales also established a startup incubator, aiming to accelerate new business ideas and foster the development of a novel digital ecosystem of services.

4 **Digital Academy**: This initiative plays a crucial role in the company's transition into the digital era. The Digital Academy is designed to introduce new working processes and methodologies within the company, aligning with the latest digital trends and innovations.

Thales' approach to digital transformation exemplifies how an established company can reinvent itself and its service offerings in the digital age.[10] By creating a comprehensive digital strategy and infrastructure, they have positioned themselves to meet evolving customer needs and stay competitive in their diverse industry sectors.

Zoetis, a major player in the animal health sector and one of the largest manufacturers of medicines and vaccinations for pets and livestock, provides another illustrative example of digital transformation.[11] They identified specific challenges within their sector:[12]

1 **Labour-intensive traditional livestock production:** Traditional practices in livestock production require significant labour and operate on narrow profit margins. The profitability hinges on factors like animal growth rates, meat and milk prices, seasonal changes in crop prices, and government policies.

2 **Infectious diseases in animals:** Animals are prone to various infectious diseases, posing risks of substantial losses for farmers and necessitating regular medical check-ups for pets.

3 **Increasing demand for transparency:** There's a growing consumer demand for greater transparency and documentation concerning animal health.

In response to these challenges, Zoetis pioneered digital projects to develop medical records for animals. They leveraged the rapid growth of the Internet of Things to establish *Animal Dialogue* services, a data management system that ethically gathers animal health information to improve health, welfare and precision farming. This process transforms data into valuable insights through analytics and machine learning, making the data collection more efficient, relevant and accessible.

The digitalization efforts of Zoetis opened up numerous opportunities:[13]

1 **Increased livestock production:** The use of these digital services facilitates managing more animals on smaller land areas, compensating for higher farming intensity and lower fallow-to-cultivation ratios without the need for significant additional labour or capital.

2 **Smarter livestock management:** Precision farming using Zoetis' digital services can enhance livestock management, especially under current resource constraints and the scarcity of skilled livestock personnel.

3 **Efficient record keeping:** The service enables recording various characteristics of each animal, like age, pedigree, growth rate and health. This boosts production efficiency and helps address the anticipated deficit in food supply.

4 **Unbiased data collection:** Automation reduces biased data entry, allowing farmers to concentrate on animal care, thereby maximizing returns.

Furthermore, the new services from Zoetis also brought substantial benefits to various stakeholders:

1 **Veterinarians:** The data assists veterinarians in making informed decisions, improving care, tracking recovery progress, and enhancing customer loyalty and retention through direct support and digital interactions.

2 **Feed and nutrition providers:** Real-time weight data facilitates the customization of feeding schedules based on predictive growth patterns.

3 **Pharmaceutical companies:** The services offer transparency throughout an animal's lifecycle, aiding in health management.

4 **Regulatory bodies and policymakers:** This transparency aligns with global health initiatives like WHO's One Health.

Boston Dynamics provides an innovative solution to a common challenge in the construction industry by maintaining complete site visibility to ensure projects stay on budget and on schedule.[14] The traditional reliance on manual data capture is inefficient and prone to errors, and while adding sensors to assets on a constantly changing construction site is an option, it's often impractical. Traditional robot designs, such as those with wheels or tracks, struggle with the physical obstacles present on construction sites. In response, Boston Dynamics has introduced transformative autonomous technologies for construction sites, revolutionizing how these environments are managed and monitored. They have developed several robot models, each serving a distinct purpose. Stretch is designed for warehouse automation, Atlas serves as a research platform for testing new products, and Spot is primarily used in construction sites for data capture through its sensors or other integrated devices.[15]

We will focus on Spot in this example, which is reshaping the construction site experience. Its capabilities lead to various benefits:

1 **Monitoring site progress:** Spot conducts daily walkarounds, generating automatic reports. The data collected is structured and shared in a format that construction firms and their contractors can analyse and use to improve site management.

2 **Digital twin data:** With Spot, it's possible to gather data necessary to create a digital representation of the site. This can be integrated with other technologies like digital twins and drones, allowing site managers to compare real-time progress with planned outcomes, and facilitating issue detection and resolution. This improved project management can lead to reduced costs and increased margins.

This demonstrates how firms can leverage autonomous robotic scanning technologies to capture data and streamline operations. By doing so, construction projects are more likely to be delivered on time and within budget, enhancing customer experiences in the process.

Business-to-consumer (B2C) organizations

Continuing our exploration into the realm of digital service and experience transformation, we now turn our focus to the business-to-consumer (B2C) sector. Here, the landscape is marked by a rapid acceleration of digital services. This transformation in the B2C world is driven largely by a detailed understanding of customer needs and a strong commitment to innovation. In the B2C context, we're witnessing a shift where companies are increasingly competing based on the quality of the customer experience they offer. This competition is not just about the products or prices anymore; it's about how companies engage with their consumers, the ease and convenience of their services, and the overall experience they provide. The following examples highlight how these companies have leveraged technology to enhance consumer interactions and experiences, setting new standards in their respective industries.

Emirates Airline[16] provides a standout example. Emirates, like many other airlines, recognizes that its revenue generation primarily occurs when its aircraft are flying. Therefore, minimizing the time planes spend on the ground is crucial. This is where the turnaround time – the period between flights for servicing and preparation for the next departure – becomes critical. Each turnaround task is managed by different teams and partners, all needing to be completed within a specific time frame. Efficient airport operations are vital for ensuring that aircraft are on schedule and costs are minimized. In response to this challenge, Emirates embarked on a digital transformation of its turnaround process at Dubai International Airport by developing an application to streamline these operations.[17]

The digitization of the turnaround process yielded several benefits for Emirates:[18]

1 **Activity tracking:** The integration of various data sources allows all teams involved in aircraft turnaround to track activities in real time and raise alarms when delays are predicted.

2 **Reduced delays**: With this system, Emirates can pinpoint the root causes of delays and proactively work to reduce potential future delays.

3 **Increased customer satisfaction**: Efficiently predicting and managing delays enhances the boarding and flight experiences, leaving customers with a positive impression and a higher level of satisfaction.

4 **Recognition of new opportunities**: Using AI and real-time analytics, Emirates has identified areas for improvement and innovation within its business model.

This example of Emirates Airline is illustrative of capitalizing on data generated from digital applications.[19] Companies can analyse insights and make informed, real-time decisions that enhance their business operations and customer experience.[20]

SEAT, an automotive manufacturer,[21] presents a compelling example of digital transformation in the B2C sector. The industry is undergoing a paradigm shift due to digitalization, with five megatrends at the forefront: **connected cars, electrification, sustainability, data** and **digitalization**.[22] This shift is moving the industry from viewing cars as mere products to embracing mobility as an experience. Companies like Tesla have been pioneers in this space, integrating AI and electrification into their business models. Those unable to adapt to this new reality risk falling behind in meeting customer demands. SEAT's innovation journey is driven by the desire to maintain customer satisfaction and ensure long-term viability in this rapidly changing landscape. Embracing the aforementioned megatrends, SEAT is focused on increasing its customer-centric approach while adapting to political, environmental and social factors and developing new business models to meet evolving customer needs.

Their digital transformation of SEAT involves a combination of bottom-up and top-down approaches.[23] It's about understanding ground-level processes and pain points and simultaneously promoting the strategy among the leadership team. SEAT's digital transformation has led to an end-to-end overhaul of its operations. They have established a new digital supply chain to support a novel method of operation. The process now begins with customers placing orders on a digital platform, where each sale is linked to a tracking ID. The sales department configures the order, which is then progressed to production.

SEAT relies on a *customer-driven supply chain control tower* – a connected, integrated and digitalized supply chain system. This system acts as a logistical hub, tracking each part's location and predicting arrival times and potential delays. This digitized platform enables SEAT to locate parts efficiently, manage materials, finished goods and transportation, and provide real-time data access to customers through their tracking ID. Customers can now track the progress of their vehicles and receive transparent updates on their delivery, exemplifying a customer-centric approach in the automotive industry.[24] This transformation by SEAT illustrates how businesses can leverage digitalization to enhance customer experiences and adapt to changing market dynamics.

L'Oréal is a global leader in the beauty industry.[25] The beauty industry has traditionally relied on print, television and radio for marketing, but the rise of digital channels such as websites, apps and social media has drastically changed how personal and beauty-care businesses interact with consumers. This digital shift, coupled with an increased amount of data from supply chain partners, allows for more targeted customer identification, effective channel utilization, and maximized return on investment.[26] L'Oréal has embraced technology for the co-design and co-conception of products, using social media and online communities in a unique sequence:[27]

1 **Ethnographical study of online content**: Analysing online content helps identify consumer problems and areas for innovation.

2 **Focus groups**: These groups identify problems and brainstorm potential solutions.

3 **Validation on social media**: Shortlisted solutions are tested on social media for broader consumer feedback.

4 **Validation in online communities**: The second stage of validation involves A/B testing, a research method used to assess various solution versions within communities focused on influencers, helping to guide product decision-making.

In addition to these strategies, L'Oréal has implemented several digital services using AI:[28]

1 **Electronic Data Interchange (EDI)**: Implemented just before the Covid-19 pandemic, this system digitally links L'Oréal's internal systems with retailers for efficient information exchange. This initiative was particularly useful during the pandemic, enabling remote product introductions when in-person visits were not possible.

2 **Modiface acquisition**: In 2018, L'Oréal acquired *Modiface*, a platform using facial recognition and augmented reality. This allowed consumers to virtually test products like lipstick, foundation and hair colours, which was especially beneficial during the pandemic when in-person trials were limited.

A significant investment in human resources also supports L'Oréal's digital transformation. The company has acquired over 2,000 digital experts and trained more than 22,000 employees in using digital tools.[29] This example demonstrates how L'Oréal has successfully navigated the digital landscape, staying ahead of competitors and meeting the evolving needs of customers by combining technological innovation with a skilled workforce.

Manchester United (MU) is a renowned football team representing digital service transformation in the sports industry.[30] As an internationally recognized brand, MU has traditionally interacted with its millions of supporters through ticketing systems, venue visits, and its 24-hour Manchester United TV (MUTV) channel. These channels have been pivotal in marketing merchandise and kits globally (190 markets). To further extend their reach, MU has embraced multiple digital platforms, including social media, web-based sites and mobile apps. This digital expansion has been crucial in connecting with their global fan base.[31]

During the Covid-19 pandemic, with football events paused, MU faced the challenge of maintaining fan engagement without live matches. They adapted by shifting from a model of social engagement to social responsibility. Instead of sharing new match and player updates through traditional channels, MU utilized their digital platforms to keep fans engaged in the absence of new football content. MU's pre-pandemic preparation of organizing all its digital content proved invaluable. They were able to:[32]

1 Compile classic games into *Match Rewind* box sets.

2 Create new content, including long-form articles, podcasts, competitions, quizzes and fantasy football teams.

3 Develop a digital grid featuring images of fans and recorded content used during closed-door games.

4 Make their content more diverse, tracking engagement to understand and retain fans better.

The lessons learnt from MU's digital transformation are significant:[33]

- **Reflect on social responsibility content**: Focusing on content that builds trust and relevance with customers is vital.

- **Be risk aware:** Preparing for worst-case scenarios ensures firms have controls and systems to manage unexpected challenges.

- **Capitalize on opportunities:** Both positive and negative changes bring new opportunities. It's crucial for organizations to harness these to shape future consumer behaviours, experiences and business strategies.

Manchester United's approach demonstrates how a traditional sports business can leverage digital channels effectively to engage customers, suggesting that firms should invest in understanding and curating the right content for different scenarios to maintain online engagement.

Nettavisen, a leading Norwegian online newspaper,[34] offers an intriguing case of digital transformation in the media industry. Established in 1996, the company's significant growth began after 2009 when it revamped its business model to compete with giants like Facebook and Google. A key aspect of this transformation was the development of a data-driven business model (DDBM), particularly focused on analysing data generated from online browsing and purchases across multiple devices to boost advertising and e-commerce revenues.[35]

Several industry changes and challenges influenced *Nettavisen*'s adoption of a DDBM:[36]

1 **New digital media platforms:** These platforms generate vast amounts of data, but curating this data is essential to increase its value.

2 **Targeted advertising through third parties:** With networks of advertisers, personal data isn't always stored or owned by the service provider, leading to potential misalignments with customer expectations.

3 **Data operations with potential data loss:** The processing of millions of advertisements by third-party networks raises concerns about the potential loss of customer data.

Nettavisen's DDBM focuses on leveraging user purchasing habits while ensuring data security. The goal is to create a model that capitalizes on the data owned by media companies without risking data leaks. The benefits of this model for *Nettavisen* include:[37]

- **Utilizing cross-platform audience insights:** This allows them to enhance their journalism, streamline operations, and explore new customer offerings.

- **Organizational growth:** The DDBM enables *Nettavisen* to outperform competitors and increase its market share and popularity.

As part of its strategy, *Nettavisen* expanded by acquiring the blogger network Blog.no. However, the transition to a DDBM presents challenges, including competition, employee retention, blogger collaboration, managing data effectively and limited funding. *Nettavisen*'s journey towards a DDBM highlights the potential and complexities of leveraging digital platforms and data in the media industry.[38] This case study highlights the importance of strategic data management and the need for media companies to adapt to evolving digital landscapes to stay competitive and relevant.

Public service innovation

Digitalization in public services offers the potential to revolutionize city planning and service delivery and enhance citizen experience. One of the most innovative strategies emerging in this sector is the creation of digital twins for smart cities. This approach involves constructing 3D models of a city's physical infrastructure, complete with details about its lifecycle, properties and features. A notable example of this approach is seen in **Estonia**, which has embraced digital public services for urban development.

Estonia's initiative in digitalizing its urban development includes establishing a digital construction platform. This platform is designed to be augmented by third-party developers, citizens and entrepreneurs, enabling the creation of digital twins in Estonian cities. Such an approach is particularly significant for the construction industry, which plays a crucial role in job creation and economic growth, and improves how citizens interact with their urban environment.[39]

The benefits of this digitalization project in Estonia are manifold:[40]

1 **Informed decision-making**: The digital twin model aids planners and developers in understanding the impact of new constructions or modifications on the community and various stakeholders.

2 **Improved productivity**: Currently, digital plans submitted as 2D drawings to the e-construction platform are accurately reviewed for compliance with planning regulations, enhancing productivity and minimizing reworks and delays.

3 **AI support**: Future improvements are expected to include digital automation using rule-based checks combined with AI algorithms, optimizing critical aspects such as fire exit placements.

4 **Increased public engagement:** The platform provides opportunities for citizens to engage with urban development projects. This could include providing feedback on proposed developments or participating in virtual simulations to understand and influence future city plans.

5 **Personalized urban experiences:** By integrating data from various sources, digital twins have the potential to offer personalized recommendations and services to citizens, enhancing their interaction with city services and amenities.

However, there are significant challenges in implementing digital twinning, mainly due to the long lifespan and lifecycle of fixed assets like buildings. Digitalizing the construction industry requires a multidisciplinary approach and collaboration across various fields, including software engineering, UX design, architecture, engineering, construction operations, and data compliance and policy development. Effective information sharing across these domains is challenging and often relies on traditional communication methods like phone or email.[41]

Estonia's next steps involve shaping its construction landscape with new systems and data insights, aiming to develop a national digital twin. By 2030, the e-construction platform aims to securely share data across sectors, leverage existing e-government infrastructure, and adhere to international standards like Building Information Modelling (BIM) and advancements in digital twin technologies. The government plays a crucial role in driving best practices and providing the necessary digital infrastructure, but the success of this project will also depend heavily on private sector participation and support.[42]

The integration of digital technologies in **healthcare services** is a critical example of how digital transformation can rapidly adapt to meet urgent needs, as demonstrated in the UK's National Health Service (NHS) during the Covid-19 pandemic.[43]

When the pandemic struck in March 2020, the NHS faced the challenge of maintaining medical consultations and operations in a Covid-secure manner. To facilitate remote communication and treatment, the NHS expedited the rollout of Microsoft Teams. Despite previous discussions with Microsoft spanning over a year, the actual implementation for 1.3 million users in hospitals was achieved in just four days at the pandemic's onset. This swift digital transformation, which initially seemed like it would take years, showcases the potential for rapid adaptation in national healthcare services despite various financial, cultural, regulatory and legacy system challenges.[44]

The pandemic's urgency also accelerated other digital initiatives in healthcare. A notable example is the collaboration between the University of Cambridge, Addenbrooke's Hospital in Cambridge, and Microsoft on the Inner Eye project. This project leverages AI for precision radiotherapy, aiming to assist patients and healthcare professionals.[45]

Traditionally, a clinical oncologist spends hours reviewing CT scans to create a detailed map for tumour radiotherapy. Inner Eye employs deep neural networks trained on image data from clinics worldwide, significantly speeding up this diagnostic process. This use of AI in healthcare not only enhances efficiency but also potentially improves patient outcomes by enabling quicker and more accurate treatment planning.[46]

These examples highlight the transformative impact of digital technologies in healthcare, illustrating how crises like the Covid-19 pandemic can catalyse significant advancements in public service delivery. The NHS's experience with Microsoft Teams and the Inner Eye project exemplifies the potential for technology to revolutionize healthcare practices, making them more efficient, effective and responsive to patient needs.

Hassan Al-Ibrahim – Managing Founder of the Local Context Consulting Services and a public sector adviser – stated that the establishment of the Civil Service and Government Development Bureau (CGB) in 2021 marked a significant step in **Qatar's government services modernization,** emphasizing the nation's dedication to innovation in public service. Key achievements include the integration of e-government systems, the development of the *Hukoomi* portal,[47] and the creation of standards for ICT. The vision was to connect individuals and businesses with a more efficient, transparent government, with objectives such as bringing all services online, enhancing government efficiency, and promoting citizen experience.

The Qatar Government Services Strategy (2023–30)[48] builds on this foundation, aiming to modernize public services and create a unified, citizen-centric experience. The strategy focuses on four key aspirations: enhancing digital services and engagement; advancing innovative, data-driven government practices; ensuring sustainable ICT investments; and fostering a culture of excellence.

One of these digital offerings is the **UXM platform,** which was launched as part of this initiative and plays a crucial role in transforming Qatar's public service delivery. It consolidates services into a single platform, enabling seamless citizen interaction through various channels while providing real-time data and insights for decision makers. This platform reflects Qatar's commitment to continuous improvement and positions the country as a leader in digital governance. The official launch of all components of the UXM platform marked a significant milestone in Qatar's efforts to enhance the citizen experience. Key features of the platform include:

- **Omnichannel care and publishing:** Allow entities to engage with citizens, residents and visitors through various official channels within a unified system.

- **Modern research:** Uses AI to improve employee efficiency and to enable continuous service improvement.

- **Quality ambassadors:** Monitor the evaluation of government services by quality ambassadors.

- **Digital concierge:** A virtual assistant facilitating complaints, suggestions, inquiries and appointment bookings at government centres.

- **Knowledge base:** A comprehensive information source covering service procedures and FAQs for citizens and agents.

- **Command centre:** Provides real-time data and insights from various systems to aid decision-making through performance and alert monitoring.

- **AI-enabled government service centres:** Enhance access to information on service procedures and FAQs for both citizens and agents.

- **Government Excellence Programme platform:** Allows entities to submit assessment forms for evaluating the services they provide, with cross-checks by external assessors.

- **E-participation portal:** An electronic platform to boost community participation and engagement with government entities.

Key lessons from Qatar's digital transformation include:

- The importance of citizen-centric design.

- The integration of advanced technologies and the continuous pursuit of efficiency and excellence in public service.

By focusing on these areas, Qatar is enhancing government transparency, citizen engagement and overall service quality, setting a benchmark for digital governance across the Gulf and Middle East region.

The new wave of digital transformation

We've explored various cases and examples of service transformation, illustrating that digital transformation has become a key strategic focus across diverse industries and sectors. While not all businesses or sectors have fully felt the impact of digitalization's disruptive nature, a significant number have embarked on the journey of digital transformation. Digital transformations are not a recent concept; they have been a topic of consideration among management consultants and practitioners for many years. Service strategy and transformation have long been discussed and analysed. However, the challenges posed by digital service transformation today surpass those associated with earlier information technologies. This evolution presents a more complex and demanding landscape for organizations to navigate.[49]

Let's examine the key challenges of the latest wave of digital transformation, distinctively different from past technological changes. This transformation is driven by various factors and is characterized by four key elements: volatility, unorthodoxy, collaboration and agility. These aspects present unique challenges and opportunities, fundamentally differentiating this era of digital transformation from the IT-enabled transformations of the past.[50]

First, volatility is central to the rapid pace of digital transformation. Organizations are required to navigate swiftly changing technologies, constantly emerging new tools, and the accompanying unpredictability. This environment places immense pressure on organizations to stay updated with technological advancements and adapt rapidly, making long-term planning increasingly challenging. For example, while we are writing this book, every executive is discussing how to leverage generative AI and large language models (LLMs) in their products and services.

Second, agility is paramount. Even successful technologies can quickly become obsolete; therefore, organizations need to be flexible and responsive. A significant focus of this transformation is enhancing customer experience (CX). As technology evolves, so do customer expectations, compelling organizations to adopt customer-centric technologies like chatbots and personalized services. Employing the concept of a Minimum Viable Product (MVP) is crucial in this context, allowing for quick, feedback-driven iterations without extensive initial investment. Embracing innovation and a willingness to take calculated risks are essential in this agile environment.

Third, the new wave of transformation requires unprecedented levels of **collaboration.** The increasing dependence on technology across business processes mandates collaboration within organizations and with external partners. This collaborative approach harnesses diverse skills and expertise, leading to more effective problem-solving, faster innovation and improved decision-making.

Last, unorthodoxy characterizes digital transformation. It disrupts traditional business models and practices, introducing blurred competition lines with new market entrants and disruptors. This phase often involves a high degree of experimentation and risk, potentially leading to failures. The complexity of new technologies and business models necessitates rapid adaptation and the acquisition of new skill sets, often facing resistance from employees accustomed to traditional ways.

This transformation, therefore, stands out as more challenging and multi-faceted than previous IT transformations. To gain a deeper understanding, let's examine a diagram illustrating the stages of digital transformation, mapping out its complexity and impact. Figure 1.1 provides a visual representation of how digital transformation extends beyond traditional IT changes, encompassing a comprehensive overhaul of business processes, models and customer engagement strategies.[51]

In the initial stages, the focus is on the **localized exploitation of IT,** where technology primarily supports basic functions like information access, cost reduction and productivity enhancement.

Moving forward, **internal integration** becomes key, where IT's role expands to integrating systems, breaking down departmental silos, and aligning operations for enhanced performance.

The next phase involves **re-engineering business processes.** This step is about fundamentally rethinking and reshaping business processes to improve key performance metrics, such as cost, quality, service and speed, often through adopting e-business, data warehousing, enterprise resource planning (ERP) or customer relation management (CRM) systems.

Then, we see the **redesign of business networks** extending beyond organizational boundaries. Here, information technology is leveraged to transform interactions with external stakeholders like customers and suppliers, pushing the business into new territories and services.

Another critical aspect is **redefining the business scope,** where IT's impact enables companies to form new business relationships, offer novel services, and venture into uncharted markets.

FIGURE 1.1 IT transformation versus digital transformation[52]

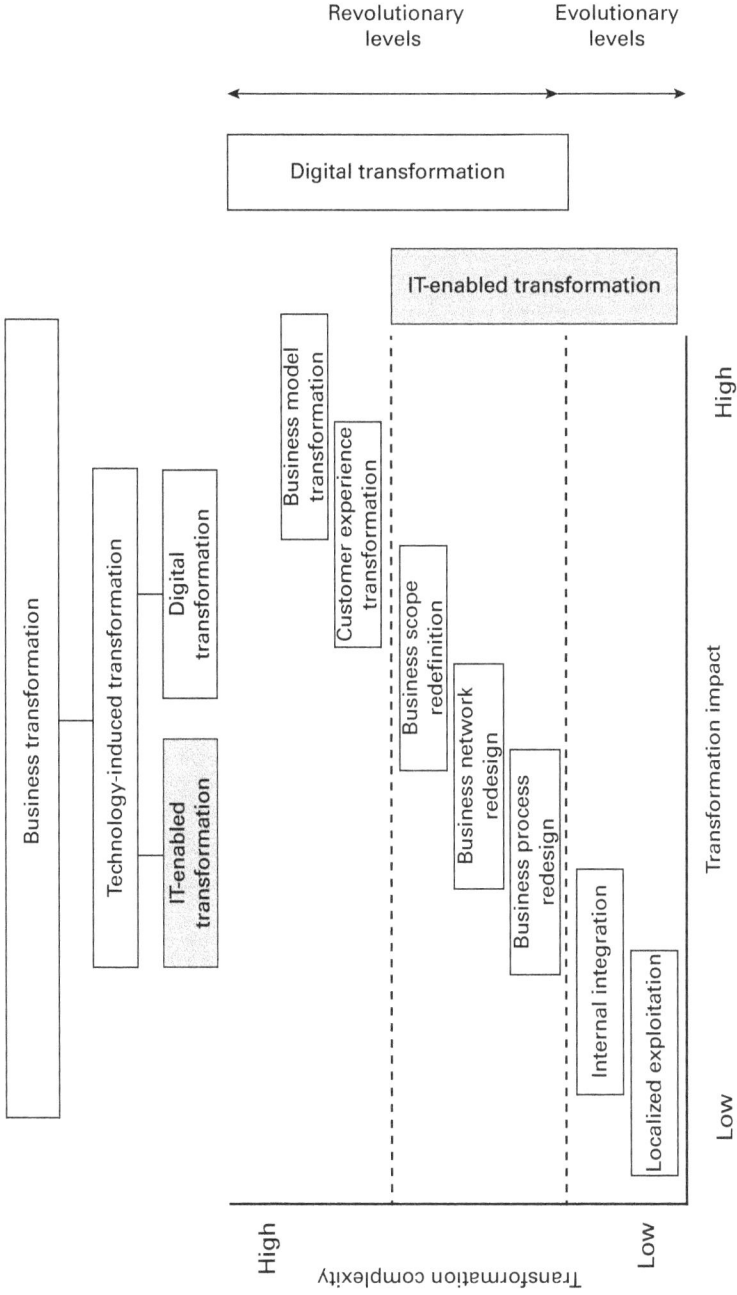

Business transformation

Technology-induced transformation

Digital transformation

IT-enabled transformation

Revolutionary levels

Evolutionary levels

Digital transformation

IT-enabled transformation

Business model transformation

Customer experience transformation

Business scope redefinition

Business network redesign

Business process redesign

Internal integration

Localized exploitation

High

Low

Transformation impact

High

Low

Transformation complexity

A significant shift towards **customer experience transformation** follows. Organizations utilize digital technologies not just for operational enhancements but also to improve customer experience, using analytics for deeper customer insights and engaging customers more effectively across various touchpoints.

Finally, **business model transformation** is highlighted. Companies aim to innovate their products and services using digital technologies and explore new ways to engage within their industry networks. This often involves restructuring or creating new business models, ranging from minor digital tweaks to complete digitalization, impacting every facet of the firm's value chain.

KEY TAKEAWAYS

In this introductory chapter, we have explored the many industrial trends and the significant shift firms are making from product-centric models to customer-centric models enabled by digitalization strategy. This shift highlights how the current wave of digital transformation is distinct from previous IT transformations, presenting unique challenges that need to be navigated to cultivate the next generation of services.

We highlighted how digital transformation has become a global focus across various service industries due to the widespread adoption of new digital technologies.

Specifically, we:

- Examined industry trends, highlighting how B2B companies are transitioning from product-based models to digital solutions to offer a seamless experience.

- Illustrated the importance of digital technologies for B2C companies in enhancing consumer experience and delivering superior digital services.

- Demonstrated that even public services are adopting numerous digital initiatives to provide a better citizen experience and build a stronger ecosystem of actors for improved service delivery.

- Discussed the increased complexity of digital transformations compared to earlier IT-enabled changes.

- Identified the key challenges and obstacles that organizations face in their digital transformation journeys.

- Emphasized the significance of understanding customer-centric transformation in this context.

As we navigate through the realm of digital transformation and its impact on designing and managing customer experience, this book serves as a roadmap, guiding readers through 12 chapters that explore customer experience frameworks and innovative, data-driven solutions for transforming businesses.

Here's a chapter-by-chapter overview:

Chapter 2 – Customer experience-centric strategy: Discussing the concept of CX-centric strategies within businesses, this chapter explores the pivotal driving forces behind CX-led transformations. It features examples like Volvo Automotive's shift to selling mobility experiences and discusses the key drivers and strategies for CX-centricity in various sectors.

Chapter 3 – Data-driven customer experience design: Introducing the customer experience framework. This chapter presents a three-dimensional space capturing the essence of customer experience. It explores examples from different sectors, showing how digital, physical and social realms are converging to redefine our future service.

Chapter 4 – Customer journey: This chapter focuses on customer journey design, integrating research and practical insights to understand value creation elements. It examines cognitive responses and emotions throughout the customer journey.

Chapter 5 – Customer delight: Exploring the concept of customer delight, this chapter distinguishes it from customer satisfaction and its role in fostering loyalty. It discusses six properties essential to creating delightful experiences.

Chapter 6 – Customer experience design challenges: Addressing the main service experience challenges, this chapter explores how digital technologies can enhance customer experiences. It highlights critical challenges in integrating customer experience channels.

Chapter 7 – Customer experience measurements: Focusing on customer experience management (CXM) and data analytics, this chapter defines CX insights and their role in enhancing CX. It covers the types of CX data and analytics needed.

Chapter 8 – Customer loyalty: Discussing the multidimensional nature of customer loyalty, this chapter critiques simplistic measures like NPS surveys and explores machine learning models for predicting loyalty.

Chapter 9 – Customer engagement: This chapter explores digital platforms' role in customer engagement strategies, focusing on social media. It discusses the challenges in driving engagement and how AI can enhance strategy.

Chapter 10 – Personalized experience: Exploring the shift to personalized, text-based interactions in customer services, this chapter presents frameworks for bridging AI automation with conversational care.

Chapter 11 – Brand equity: This chapter examines customer journey management and its impact on brand equity, exploring influential factors across different journey sequences. AI's role in examining CX data is highlighted.

Chapter 12 – Data-driven business models: The final chapter focuses on DDBMs, presenting a design toolbox and exploring six types of data-driven models.

Throughout the book, we will also analyse industrial trends in the B2B, B2C and public service sectors, highlighting escalating customer expectations and shifting towards a service experience strategy. The book aims to equip readers with the knowledge and tools to adapt to the evolving business landscape, prioritizing digital customer experience.

Notes

1 Salesforce (2022) Salesforce report: Nearly 90% of buyers say experience a company provides matters as much as products or services. www.salesforce. com/uk/news/stories/customer-engagement-research (archived at https://perma. cc/XBK7-ESW8)

2 CEMEX (2024) About us – CEMEX Global. www.cemex.com/about-us (archived at https://perma.cc/L3N3-ZZUJ)

3 Zaki, M (2019) Digital transformation: Harnessing digital technologies for the next generation of services, *Journal of Services Marketing*, 33 (4), 429–35

4 CEMEX (2024) CEMEX accelerates evolution of its digital commercial offering. www.cemex.com/w/cemex-accelerates-evolution-of-its-digital-commercial-offering (archived at https://perma.cc/VY32-74LW)

5 ibid.

6 Caterpillar (2024) Company overview. www.caterpillar.com/en/company.html (archived at https://perma.cc/B9JQ-R7DL)

7 Zaki, M and Neely, A (2014) Understanding the challenges of service innovation (Euroma Conference 2015), Cambridge Service Alliance. https://cambridgeservicealliance.eng.cam.ac.uk/system/files/documents (archived at https://perma.cc/VCN3-EFZU)

8 Thales Group (2024) About us: Thales Group global overview. www.thalesgroup.com/en/global/group (archived at https://perma.cc/2EZL-YSCT)

9 Perry-Evans, S (2017) Digital transformation strategy within Thales, Cambridge Service Alliance. https://cambridgeservicealliance.eng.cam.ac.uk/IndustryDay/serviceweek2017 (archived at https://perma.cc/MXM2-S7BS)

10 ibid.

11 Zoetis (2024) About us: Our story. www.zoetis.com/our-company/our-story/about-us (archived at https://perma.cc/A3KF-E9TQ)

12 Smith, D, Lyle, S, Berry, A, Manning, N, Zaki, M and Neely, A (2015) Internet of Animal Health Things (IoAHT): Opportunities and challenges, Centre for Digital Innovation, Zoetis and Cambridge Service Alliance, University of Cambridge. https://cambridgeservicealliance.eng.cam.ac.uk/system/files/documents/2015July CaseStudyIoAHT_HQP.pdf (archived at https://perma.cc/LPJ8-MY76)

13 ibid.

14 Boston Dynamics (2024) Boston Dynamics website. https://bostondynamics.com (archived at https://perma.cc/J8XA-Y7CU)

15 Ringley, B (2021) Spot for construction: Autonomous robotic scanning for digital twins, Cambridge Service Alliance. https://cambridgeservicealliance.eng.cam.ac.uk/IndustryDay/IndustryDay2021 (archived at https://perma.cc/M5NA-FKHW)

16 Emirates (2024) About us. www.emirates.com/uk/english/about-us/ (archived at https://perma.cc/T9QB-FY3E)

17 Caswell, M (2018) New Emirates app aims to reduce aircraft turnaround delays, *Business Traveller*, 27 December. www.businesstraveller.com/business-travel/2018/12/27/new-emirates-app-aims-to-reduce-aircraft-turnaround-delays/ (archived at https://perma.cc/RXD9-67MN)

18 ibid.

19 Mueller, C (2017) The digital transformation of the Emirates group, Cambridge Service Alliance. https://cambridgeservicealliance.eng.cam.ac.uk/IndustryDay/serviceweek2017 (archived at https://perma.cc/LS6M-Q3SD)

20 Zaki, M (2019) Digital transformation: Harnessing digital technologies for the next generation of services, *Journal of Services Marketing*, 33 (4), 429–35

21 SEAT (2024) SEAT UK website. www.seat.co.uk (archived at https://perma.cc/2D9H-YF2U)

22 Radon, A (2021) The digital transformation journey at SEAT S.A and CUPRA, Cambridge Service Alliance. https://cambridgeservicealliance.eng.cam.ac.uk/IndustryDay/IndustryDay2021 (archived at https://perma.cc/G5EJ-QXAQ)

23 ibid.

24 ibid.

25 L'Oréal (2024) L'Oréal global website. www.loreal.com/en/ (archived at https://perma.cc/JRG5-FC3J)

26 Zaki, M et al (2019) Redistributed manufacturing and the impact of big data: A consumer goods perspective, *Production Planning & Control*, 30 (7), 568–81

27 Wagih, A (2020) Digital transformation accelerated by a pandemic, Cambridge Service Alliance. https://cambridgeservicealliance.eng.cam.ac.uk/IndustryDay/2020 (archived at https://perma.cc/76VT-UWKU)

28 ibid.

29 ibid.

30 Manchester United (2024) Manchester United official website. www.manutd.com (archived at https://perma.cc/WE46-Q62N)

31 Salt, P (2020) Digital engagement in the era of COVID: At the forefront of service transformation in the digital era, Cambridge Service Alliance. https://cambridgeservicealliance.eng.cam.ac.uk/IndustryDay/2020 (archived at https://perma.cc/5XHD-WYGN)

32 ibid.

33 ibid.

34 Nettavisen (2024) Nettavisen website. www.nettavisen.no (archived at https://perma.cc/EN2K-JUN3)

35 Zaki, M, Lillegraven, T and Neely, A (2015) Moving towards a data-driven business model (DDBM) in the online newspaper publishing industry, Cambridge Service Alliance, University of Cambridge

36 Zaki, M, Bøe-Lillegraven, T and Neely, A (2016) *A Transition Towards a Data-Driven Business Model (DDBM): A case study of Nettavisen online newspaper publishing,* Sage Publishing

37 ibid.

38 ibid.

39 Pärn, E A, Raitviir, C and Zaki, M (2022) E-construction, in *Public Innovation and Digital Transformation*, Routledge, pp. 129–53

40 ibid.

41 ibid.

42 ibid.

43 Takeda, K (2020) Deep research and innovation in health and life sciences, Cambridge Service Alliance. https://cambridgeservicealliance.eng.cam.ac.uk/IndustryDay/2020 (archived at https://perma.cc/BCR8-7QUT)

44 ibid.

45 ibid.

46 ibid.

47 Ministry of Communications and Information Technology (2023) *Qatar Digital Government NextGen Strategy*, Ministry of Communications and Information Technology. https://services.hukoomi.gov.qa/assets/documents/digitalprojects/QDG%20NextGen%20Strategy.pdf (archived at https://perma.cc/Y86T-BUVA)

48 Ministry of Communications and Information Technology (2024) *Qatar Digital Agenda 2030*, Ministry of Communications and Information Technology. www.mcit.gov.qa/wp-content/uploads/sites/4/2024/09/da2030_executive_summary_en.pdf?csrt=12138344457709629814 (archived at https://perma.cc/TFD2-L645)

49 Ismail, M H, Khater, M and Zaki, M (2017) Digital business transformation and strategy: What do we know so far?, Cambridge Service Alliance. https://cambridgeservicealliance.eng.cam.ac.uk/system/files/documents/2017NovPaper_Mariam.pdf (archived at https://perma.cc/U9GQ-ULXV)

50 ibid.

51 ibid.

52 ibid.

2

Customer experience-centric strategy

In this chapter, we'll explore why numerous organizations, including those mentioned in the previous chapter and others, are shifting towards a CX-centric strategy. Customer experience (CX) is increasingly becoming the focal point in the marketing strategies of modern organizations. Businesses that prioritize CX have been shown to yield 30 per cent higher total returns to shareholders (TRS) than those focusing primarily on products or services.[1] Many instances indicate our shift towards an experience economy.[2] HCLTech reports that '*65% of experience leaders set the vision, goals, principles and culture for becoming an experience-led organization*'.[3]

For instance, on a personal level, you may increasingly find traditional firms with outdated customer services less impressive, favouring those that employ innovative, real-time services and user-friendly applications. Additionally, we've observed that service brands and organizations offering outstanding experiences are in high demand. In an economy driven by digital platforms, companies strive to seize emerging opportunities to create memorable experiences.

To gain a deeper understanding of the significance of customer-centric business models, we will examine two illustrative examples from Amazon and Cisco, both known for prioritizing customer experience. Technological advancements have the power to revolutionize customer experiences and alter consumer behaviours. Companies pioneering these technologies can significantly influence the competitive dynamics of their industries. This phenomenon is sometimes called the Amazon effect.

Amazon has redefined online shopping experiences, setting high standards and challenging small, independent physical stores. Amazon, a global technology conglomerate, excels in various digital domains, including e-commerce. They are renowned for their focus on customer experience.

One of their notable initiatives is Amazon Prime, a subscription service offering expedited delivery, often by the next working day, to its members.[4]

Another innovative Amazon service is Alexa, a virtual assistant designed to streamline and enhance the shopping experience. Alexa employs voice recognition to facilitate human–computer interaction. Through Alexa-enabled devices, users can swiftly make purchases using voice commands, personalize their experiences, and manage smart home devices.[5]

Alexa's ability to interpret the context of queries, like distinguishing between the Gherkin building in London and the vegetable, exemplifies its advanced capabilities. It can provide specific answers to general inquiries, including weather and traffic updates. Alexa represents a shift from being just a device to becoming an integral part of the service experience. Alexa is not just an experiential tool; it's a cornerstone of a data-driven business strategy aimed at engaging customers and boosting sales and revenue. However, as we write this book, Alexa has been disrupted by the introduction of ChatGPT and its underlying technology (generative AI and LLMs).

Switching our focus to Cisco, a multinational leader in digital communications, we see a different approach to customer-centricity. Their disruption mainly stems from customer demands rather than competition. Cisco's response was a thorough reorganization of its Services and Customer Success divisions, realigning their structure, strategy and culture to better engage with customers.[6]

Previously, Cisco had specialized roles providing support at different life-cycle stages, which required customers to navigate and consume services independently. To address this, Cisco transformed its approach, renaming its customer support division as Customer Experience. Their goal is to add value throughout the customer journey, offering various levels of support tailored to customer preferences, ranging from self-service to guided or full-service options.[7]

These examples highlight two different yet effective approaches to placing customers at the heart of the experience: Amazon's Alexa offering personalized and efficient experiences, and Cisco's organizational overhaul to provide time-saving options for customers. However, many companies find it challenging to achieve such benchmarks. According to Gartner's research in 2018[8] and 2020,[9] while 74 per cent of leaders have increased investment in customer experience management (CXM), only 22 per cent believe their efforts surpass customer expectations, prompting the search for new CX strategies. Companies are concerned about potential competition from unforeseen sources. The fear of disruptive technologies causing obsolescence, as happened with Debenhams, Kodak and Toys R Us, is real and serves as a stark reminder of the difficulties established businesses face in adapting to CX-focused strategies and prompts organizations to adapt to new technologies in a timely way. HCLTech reports that numerous companies across various industries, such as manufacturing, consumer services, financial services, energy and utilities, life sciences and technology, face difficulties in consistently delivering personalized and scalable experiences. As these companies aim to elevate the quality of their customer experiences, they must navigate a complex array of organizational, process, data and technological challenges.[10]

What do we mean by customer-centricity?

We will explore the meaning of a CX-centric strategy approach within a business context to gain a deeper understanding of CX-led transformations. The concept of CX-centricity, or a company's strategy focused on customer experience, is rooted in marketing theories like customer orientation, customer-centricity and the overall customer experience. Customer orientation suggests that marketing's aim shouldn't be solely on generating profits; instead, it should centre on enhancing customer welfare, which, in effect, will also benefit the firm's profitability.[11] This approach advises marketers to shift their attention from simply profiting from customers to actively improving their welfare, avoiding sacrificing it for profit.

Many researchers suggest that a customer's experience is an all-encompassing concept that includes a range of personal and subjective responses to their dealings with an organization. In light of this, we define customer experience as a 'holistic and unified experience' that begins from the initial engagement with a brand and continues through the purchasing process and beyond.[12] From the customer's viewpoint, this experience is comprehensive, involving numerous interactions at various touchpoints. These interactions affect the customer on multiple levels, including cognitive, affective, emotional, social and sensory aspects.[13]

From an organizational standpoint, customer experience is about developing and executing a strategy centred on the customer. This strategy aims to ensure a positive experience at every stage of the customer journey, including digital, physical and social.[14] It recognizes and fulfils the following aspects throughout the customer's entire journey, including customer needs, expectations and preferences.[15]

Primary driving forces towards CX-centricity

As companies navigate their journey from a product- or service-aligned perspective to a customer experience (CX) orientation, we spotlight the **four pivotal driving forces** steering this shift.[16] I will discuss these forces in detail.

Invisible customer

This is a pivotal driving force in the shift towards CX-centricity in organizations. Businesses may have a good grasp of the performance of their products or services but often struggle with understanding the complex behaviours and journey-related details of their customers and stakeholders throughout the value chain. Therefore, achieving a more transparent view of the customer value chain and their behaviours is essential for B2B and B2C companies transitioning to a CX-centric approach. For instance, many firms have extensive data on their direct customers but lack deeper insights into their customers' customers, finding basic CRM data and historical order data limited for effective segmentation or gaining actionable insights.[17]

Let's take a B2C example – **KFC's collaboration with food delivery aggregators** like Uber Eats. KFC handles the food preparation and supply, while Uber Eats manages order taking, delivery and consumer engagement. However, KFC might not receive in-depth information about the end consumers from Uber Eats, such as who is ordering, their specific preferences, or their feedback on the delivery experience. This gap in direct customer insight presents a significant challenge for KFC.

This case exemplifies the complexity of understanding customer interactions at the point of purchase, especially when these involve third-party partners. The variety of transaction scenarios, like ordering through a delivery service versus in-store purchases, leads to diverse experiences and data collection. In KFC's case with Uber Eats, limited visibility into the ultimate customer experience, preferences and expectations arises, as Uber Eats primarily handles customer interactions and data gathering. This scenario makes it difficult for KFC to understand their consumers' experiences consistently and comprehensively across various purchasing situations.[18]

We can extend this force to B2B companies, for example a **life science firm** that emphasizes understanding the experience of internal customers such as legal entities, finance directors and commercial leads. Building trust with these internal customers is key to adopting the company's services. This internal customer base, which includes senior leadership, is crucial for strategy and priority setting. However, the company also interacts with external customers like pharmacies and hospitals through distributors or logistics providers, and understanding these external customers is critical to the company's success.[19]

In the context of **public services**, the concept of invisible customers is equally relevant and presents unique challenges. Public services, by their nature, serve a broad and diverse population, making it difficult to fully understand and meet the varied needs and expectations of all their constituents.

Take, for example, a public service: a city's public transportation system. The direct customers of this service are the passengers who use the buses, trains or subways daily. The transportation authority might have data on ticket sales, peak travel times and common routes. However, the invisible customers in this scenario could include residents who don't use the service regularly, visitors (local and international) to the city, or individuals with specific needs like accessibility requirements. These invisible customers might not be captured in regular ridership data, yet understanding their needs is crucial for the public service to be truly inclusive and effective. For instance, a visitor to the city might need clear, multilingual signage and easy-to-navigate ticketing systems. Similarly, individuals with disabilities might require accessible vehicles and stations. Failing to consider these segments of the population could lead to a service that, while effective for its regular users, is inadequate for others.

The challenge for public services is to identify and understand these less visible segments of their customer base and adapt their offerings accordingly. This might involve community surveys, outreach programmes, or partnerships with organizations representing different community groups. By addressing the needs of both direct and invisible customers, public services can enhance their effectiveness and inclusivity, thereby serving the entire community more efficiently.

The challenge of the invisible customer extends beyond simply understanding the direct customers to also encompass insights into the behaviours and needs of indirect customers. To tackle this, organizations are turning to *digital platforms to enhance their visibility across the customer value chain*, which is crucial for executing a successful customer experience (CX)-centric strategy.[20]

An illustrative example is Volvo Automotive's transition from merely selling cars through dealerships (their direct customers) to offering a comprehensive mobility experience. This experience combines car leasing, services and insurance in a subscription model targeting indirect custom-ers. Volvo's strategy now includes direct sales to consumers in specific regions, such as the UK, leveraging digital channels to better understand and gain insights into consumer behaviour. This dual approach enhances their understanding of consumers while complementing their existing deal-ership model.[21]

In the B2B sector, a notable example comes from the heavy machinery industry. Many of these firms try to improve visibility in the value chain by focusing on both end users and customers, utilizing digitalization to achieve this. They have integrated customer feedback with sensor-based Internet of Things (IoT) technology to elevate their customer service. When a vehicle breakdown occurs, their operating centre can proactively contact the driver, perform remote diagnostics, and dispatch the nearest available service vehi-cle if needed. This proactive service model not only enhances customer satisfaction but also reflects the direct feedback from drivers, who are the ultimate end users of their vehicles, as we discussed earlier in Chapter 1 with the Caterpillar example.

Dichotomous CX

Business leaders have acknowledged that the CX disparity serves as a power-ful catalyst for organizational transformation. Frequently, we find ourselves creating customer journeys that do not align with customer expectations. How often have we heard from our teams that customer satisfaction surveys indicate high levels of contentment, yet we continue to receive complaint emails in our customer service department or executives encounter dissatis-fied customers during their interactions? In many cases, it seems as though we are neglecting our customers and failing to sufficiently listen to their expectations and requirements.

There are two distinct facets that contribute to this CX discrepancy. First, as customers/users and their expectations evolve, organizations are working to adapt their CX efforts across these stakeholders. However, not everyone within these organizations fully grasps the importance of embracing this CX transformation. Consequently, this stresses the need to address the issue of CX culture within the company.

To address this, organizations are increasingly *focusing on improving their forecast capabilities* to effectively cater to a wide range of customer expectations, considering both customer behaviours and emerging market trends.[22] For instance, in the automotive sector, manufacturers are intensively working to gain a deeper understanding of consumer preferences and incorporating these insights into their product development and engineering strategies.

Engaging in ongoing conversations with their consumers is key for these organizations to stay ahead of market shifts. A prime example of this is the growing emphasis on fuel efficiency and sustainability among consumers. In response, many companies are prioritizing the development of products that are not only more fuel-efficient but also environmentally friendly, surpassing the offerings of their competitors. This might involve exploring innovative approaches, such as creating lighter vehicles to strike a balance between fuel efficiency and a comfortable driving experience. Part of this strategy includes a regular reassessment of materials and technologies, such as hydrogen, electricity, high-strength steel and lightweight design. This allows companies to design products that not only appeal to consumers but also maintain a competitive edge in the market.

Also, in the B2B context, business customers often exhibit a disconnect between their stated expectations and the actual CX transformation taking place. This misalignment sometimes serves as a factor hindering customer adoption. The combination of divergent customer expectations and internal resistance to CX change contributes to this CX discrepancy, serving as an incentive for CX leaders to reshape their businesses.

To illustrate this concept, let's examine companies that manage multiple brands across various industries, such as cosmetics, fashion and automotive. A notable disconnect exists between the manufacturers, retailer customers and end consumers. Here's the core issue: even when a single consumer uses products or services from different brands under the same company's umbrella, they often fail to realize this connection. Consequently, they may experience satisfaction with one brand while encountering dissatisfaction with another despite both brands being part of the same company.

For instance, consider a customer who owns two cars, each from a different brand under the same automotive manufacturer's parent company. This consumer has subscribed to leasing services for both cars. Eventually, both cars experience mechanical issues, prompting the consumer to seek assistance.

With one of the cars, the customer reports the problem through a digital app, and the company swiftly addresses the issue, providing a hassle-free resolution. However, the experience with the other car is quite the opposite. When the consumer reports the problem, they are subjected to a convoluted process involving multiple stakeholders, including recovery services, garages, dealers and the need for replacement parts. During this ordeal, the consumer faces long waiting times when trying to communicate the car's issues, and each partner in the process directs them to contact the other for resolution.

Remarkably, both cars belong to the same parent company, and the consumer's expectations remain consistent. However, the delivery of service varies significantly between the two brands, leading to a disparity in customer experience.

This example vividly illustrates how consumers can encounter different levels of service quality and satisfaction when dealing with distinct brands under the same corporate entity despite having uniform expectations.

One potential solution involves the implementation of a digital platform (e.g. using an app or a chatbot as an interface) featuring a shared platform that operates seamlessly across all the brands within the company's portfolio. The fundamental concept underlying this approach is that the consumer's foremost concern lies in the experience they receive from a specific product or service. As long as this experience remains consistent and uninterrupted, consumers are less likely to be preoccupied with whether or not the brand is part of a larger corporate entity.

This example highlights the crucial importance of acknowledging and closing the gap between customer expectations and the company's endeavours to establish a uniform and gratifying customer experience across its diverse array of brands. As a result, this strategy has the potential to help the company distinguish itself from other brands in the market and facilitate the creation of personalized services spanning different product lines.

However, implementing this solution is easier said than done, as it necessitates a substantial digital transformation across the various brands to align their vision and strategy, involving significant investments in the digital platform and the buy-in from the different brands. Integrating and exchanging data, a fundamental aspect of this process, presents one of the significant challenges many industries face, and it is no easy feat.

To illustrate this challenge, consider the case of a B2B ecosystem. Think of establishing a shared customer relationship management (CRM) system across their various dealers. However, they could encounter resistance from some dealers (direct customers) who might already invest in their own CRM systems. The dealers could question the need to embark on this initiative anew and raise concerns about the ongoing support and maintenance of this shared infrastructure. This example showcases the dissonance in CX experienced by B2B organizations, shedding light on the complex interplay of customer expectations and dynamics driving the pursuit of enhanced CX strategies to serve end customers.

The CX discrepancy could also have been generated by internal resistance. Many firms are transitioning from one-on-one relationship-based sales advice (e.g. meetings and phones) to a holistic experience-driven service utilizing an omnichannel digital approach (e.g. apps and chatbots). The challenge arises from the conflicting perceptions of the human touch in customer relationships, viewed as both an asset and a liability when managing CX. Customers welcome the ability to easily connect with a sales representative and cultivate personal relationships. Nonetheless, this approach also presents challenges in terms of growth. The use of new digital apps or chatbots for ordering may lack the personal touch necessary to empathize with customer needs and deliver the appropriate response.[23] However, it can provide a seamless experience for customer interaction with the firm if it is designed well.

CX leadership fragmentation

In many well-established organizations, the handling of customer experience (CX) often encounters fragmentation, leading to the crucial question of ownership. It becomes a matter of debate whether this responsibility lies with the marketing department (CMO), the digital team (CDO), IT (CIO), or the CEO, or if it is a collective responsibility of all these entities. This is typically due to a lack of cohesive efforts or visible leadership to guide the management of CX. The prevailing situation in many companies is that leadership is more dispersed rather than centralized, largely because departments or brands operate differently. Additionally, the customer interaction channels vary and might be owned by different functions. A critical point to understand is that customers are generally not concerned with the number of systems or channels operating behind the scenes, which could be numerous. For customers, the emphasis is on a seamless and straightforward experience, not the complexities of internal co-ordination.

Take, for example, a **technology consulting firm** that provides an array of services ranging from setting up IT infrastructure to offering cybersecurity consulting. Within this firm, each department functions autonomously and is equipped with its unique systems and processes. Clients who engage with multiple departments for diverse services may face unevenness in terms of service quality, communication styles and approaches to solving problems. Despite these internal operational complexities, clients anticipate a unified and smooth experience. Such fragmentation can result in client frustration as they encounter various departments that appear to lack effective communication and co-ordination. Often, you'll notice that while some stakeholders might give high ratings in surveys, in practical terms they might reduce the scale of their contracts or escalate issues to senior management due to problems they encounter in service delivery.

In many **retail chains** with both digital and physical stores, as well as various departments like electronics, clothing and groceries, each department might use different systems for inventory management, customer support and sales. A consumer shopping both digitally and in-store might experience discrepancies in pricing, product availability, or customer service quality. Even though the internal systems are numerous and varied, the consumer expects a uniform and hassle-free shopping experience across all platforms and departments.

For a **public service example**, a city's administration might offer various services like issuing permits, tax collection and public health services. Each service might be managed by a different department with its own procedures and communication channels. A resident trying to navigate these services for different needs might find the process confusing and inconsistent. Despite the internal silos, residents expect straightforward, efficient interactions with their city administration, where their needs are addressed in a co-ordinated manner regardless of the department they are dealing with.

To effectively address the challenges in customer experience (CX) management, many firms are emphasizing the establishment of an **executive-level driving force for CX transformation (CXO)**. Refreshing CX sponsorship at this level is a pivotal move in cultivating a CX-centric culture and mitigating the fragmentation in CX management.[24] This approach might entail bringing on board an external leader, someone with a commendable track record in CX transformation and the necessary technical and market insight. Such a leader would be instrumental in reshaping the organization's operational model to prioritize CX-centric goals.

Central to this strategy is assigning the responsibility and accountability for customer experience to a specific individual who can build a CX culture in the firm. This person should be empowered with the authority to lead and orchestrate organizational changes, guaranteeing that all involved parties are aligned towards a shared objective. Implementing this strategy represents a significant strategic shift, emphasizing clear-cut responsibility and accountability for CX, which is essential for achieving success in this domain.

As part of their roles, this leadership should focus on:[25]

- **Renewing goals towards CX from the top down**: This involves a top-down approach to recalibrate the organization's objectives, placing a strong emphasis on enhancing customer experience. It begins with the top-tier management, including the CEO and board members, demonstrating a firm commitment to prioritizing CX. This commitment is crucial because it sets the tone for the entire organization and ensures that CX becomes a central focus in all business strategies. A top-down approach often necessitates a cultural shift within the organization. This shift involves changing the mindset and attitudes of employees at all levels to become more customer-centric. This includes allocating resources – such as budget, personnel and technology – specifically towards initiatives that enhance CX. This demonstrates the organization's commitment to CX, not just in words but in tangible investments.

- **Co-ordinating efforts to manage CX**: This responsibility involves addressing the challenges presented by a compartmentalized organization, often leading to fragmented customer experiences, and aims to bring these isolated segments together within the company. Given that customer experience (CX) spans various business areas, from product development to after-sales support, this approach promotes interdepartmental cooperation. Departments such as marketing, sales, IT and customer service are urged to collaborate effectively to provide a consistent customer experience. The objective is to synchronize these diverse elements of the business to ensure that all aspects, including product design and customer service, operate harmoniously. A prime example of this strategy is evident in a company like Apple. Known for its smooth and cohesive customer experience, Apple achieves this through extensive co-ordination among its various departments. For instance, Apple's design, engineering, marketing, sales and customer service teams collaborate closely. When introducing a new product, the design team is dedicated to ensuring that the product is not only functional but also adheres to Apple's standards of aesthetics and user-friendliness. Concurrently, the engineering team focuses on the product's usability and innovation. This integrated approach, where all departments work in concert, is key to Apple's success in delivering a unified and exceptional customer experience.[26]

- **Breaking down silos due to multi-brand customer experience**: The strategy of breaking down silos in a multi-brand environment focuses on eliminating compartmentalization within product-centric channels and departments, promoting a unified and holistic approach to customer experience. Companies should employ a data-driven strategy that merges attitudinal, behavioural and emotional customer data across different brands and departments.[27] This integration forms the basis for developing comprehensive CX performance metrics that provide a complete view of the customer experience. These metrics should be integrated into the evaluation systems of all departments, fostering accountability and encouraging continuous enhancement of CX. Additionally, part of this approach involves establishing robust systems for the ongoing collection and analysis of customer feedback. By continuously tapping into customer insights, organizations can make informed and timely modifications to their products, services, and customer journey and interaction strategies.[28] This proactive adjustment ensures that the company remains aligned with customer needs and expectations, ultimately strengthening the overall customer experience.

- **Invest in CX and digital literacy**: This strategy includes recruiting CX specialists or collaborating with external experts to educate both the organization and its value chain partners. Training and development initiatives are rolled out to equip staff with the necessary skills and expertise to provide outstanding customer experience (CX). For example, companies like CEMEX and Thales have established academies and programmes designed to improve digital competencies and foster engagement among employees across various departments and regions. The goal of this approach is not just to facilitate learning among employees but also to enhance the capabilities across different departments. A key initiative in this regard is the introduction of a graduation programme aimed at motivating employees not only to learn and grow but also to contribute positively. This programme encourages a reciprocal exchange where employees are not just recipients of knowledge but also active contributors to the organization's learning culture.

These strategies are designed to streamline CX management at various levels and departments, ensuring a consistent and customer-focused approach throughout the organization.

Monetization ultimately led by CX

The driving force behind many firms' eagerness to capitalize on digitalization and customer-centricity lies in the potential to generate revenue by aligning their business strategies with customer preferences and needs.[29] This alignment not only facilitates business growth but also strengthens customer relationships.

Further, developing a customer experience (CX)-driven business model is seen as a method to capture value by creating customer experiences that effectively integrate essential stakeholders within the relevant ecosystem. This strategy goes beyond simple transactions to emphasize creating a comprehensive environment that spans all business aspects, from supply chain management to sales. Questions such as 'How can companies design their ecosystem to deliver customer value?' and 'What unique value proposition do we offer to our customers?' become critical for companies.[30] The main goal is not only to grow the customer base but to deeply understand and fulfil their needs, thus enabling more effective monetization of products and services.

Consequently, many firms are concentrating on providing all-encompassing, integrated solutions that distinguish them from the competition. While providing basic products or services may seem simple, such offerings can be easily duplicated by competitors or included in more elaborate solutions.

Looking at a digital-first bank like Monzo, it becomes evident how offering comprehensive, personalized solutions can substantially improve a firm's position in the competitive banking industry. Monzo, with its focus on customer-centricity and technological innovation, has excelled in monetizing its user experience through several inventive strategies aimed at boosting customer engagement and satisfaction, thereby driving revenue. Monzo's strategies include:

- Offering tiered subscription accounts, like Monzo Plus and Monzo Premium, which offer additional features for a monthly fee, including higher withdrawal limits abroad, travel insurance, unique card designs and advanced budgeting tools, encouraging users to upgrade for a better banking experience.

- Using customer data to provide personalized financial products such as loans and overdrafts, making them more appealing by tailoring them to individual spending habits and financial histories.

- Operating a marketplace model by partnering with various financial service providers, earning commissions for customer referrals to third-party services like stock investments, energy switching and insurance.

- Providing business accounts with features specifically designed for businesses, broadening their user base and creating new revenue opportunities through business-specific services and fees.

In the B2B sector, a technology company like Microsoft offers cloud-based solutions focusing on customer-centric services such as customizable cloud storage, enhanced security tailored to business needs, and responsive customer support. By using digital tools to collect customer feedback and analyse usage, Microsoft can adjust its offerings to better meet customer needs, increasing revenue through improved service adoption and loyalty.

Additionally, in the B2B context, Microsoft is creating an innovative marketplace by integrating its existing AI capabilities, cloud infrastructure and managed services. This approach transforms their services into a platform-like structure where customers can easily access and customize services, showcasing how CX-led strategies, supported by digitalization, are essential in driving change and innovation in the marketplace.

These examples illustrate how companies, by focusing on customer-centred models and leveraging digitalization, can successfully find new revenue streams and foster business growth in a dynamic and competitive market.

Customer experience-centric shifts

There are three **overarching strategic responses** that address these driving forces for change. These strategic responses encompass smaller details to manage CX: (A) Attitudes towards customer experience; (C) Capabilities to integrate customer journey management; and mastery of (M) Methods to optimize CX.[31]

Attitudes towards CX

In a corporate context, this means adopting perspectives that extend past merely recognizing customer experience (CX) on the surface to truly prioritize CX-centric goals. A standout illustration of this is seen in Disney's approach to managing its theme parks, where the guiding principle is to regard every customer as an esteemed visitor. This deeply embedded viewpoint is further supported by Disney's strategic training in **guestology**, aimed at preparing employees to act as champions who can distinguish and transform regular interactions into memorable encounters for guests. Hence, investigating attitudes as a category is essential for acquiring a more detailed understanding of the subtle facets of CX management. The company's dedication to customer experience is not just a policy but a core part of its culture, deeply merged into every aspect of its theme park operations. Disney's philosophy of treating every visitor as a valued guest is a testament to their commitment to creating an immersive and unforgettable experience for everyone who walks through their gates.[32]

This commitment is operationalized through Disney's innovative training programme in guestology, a programme that Disney uses to describe its systematic approach to understanding and catering to the needs and preferences of its guests. This programme is foundational for employees, whom Disney refers to as cast members. It emphasizes the importance of seeing the theme park experience through the eyes of the guests, encouraging cast members to anticipate guest needs, exceed their expectations, and turn even the smallest moment into a special memory.[33]

Guestology involves a variety of strategies and practices, including personalized service, attention to detail, and creating a safe and welcoming environment. Disney's frontline employees are trained to recognize the unique needs of each guest, whether it's a family visiting for the first time, a couple celebrating an anniversary, or a person with disabilities requiring special accommodations. By understanding these needs, employees can create personalized interactions that resonate emotionally, ensuring that every guest feels special and valued.[34]

Moreover, Disney's approach extends to the physical design of its parks and the creation of its attractions, with detailed attention to storytelling and thematic consistency. This ensures that the guest experience is cohesive and magical from the moment they arrive until they leave. The parks are designed to be accessible and enjoyable for all guests, with clear signage, well-thought-out crowd management, and attractions that cater to various ages and interests.[35]

In essence, Disney's emphasis on attitudes towards CX, manifested through guestology, demonstrates how deeply understanding and valuing the customer experience can elevate ordinary moments into extraordinary experiences. This approach not only enhances the guest experience but also strengthens brand loyalty and drives repeat business, showcasing the profound impact of integrating CX-driven objectives into the fabric of an organization's operations.

Develop the required capabilities for CX

Companies focus on enhancing performance through the development of skills via training and structured activities. When it comes to managing the customer journey, capabilities mean that companies develop a cohesive ability to engage with customers at all stages of their journey (pre-purchase, purchase and post-purchase),[36] strengthened by relevant skills across different organizational disciplines. Within the realm of CX strategy, it entails creating capabilities that are systematically organized and revolve around customer journeys, ensuring that interactions at various touchpoints are informed by an understanding of the customer's needs and preferences.[37]

An example of this is Ocado, a UK online grocery store. The Ocado example highlights a pioneering capability approach to leveraging technology for enhancing customer experience in the e-commerce and grocery sectors. Utilizing 3,000 robots in its warehouse operations, Ocado has set a remarkable precedent for efficiency and innovation in order fulfilment. This sophisticated system is designed to navigate a grid within the warehouse, where these robots pick and pack grocery items for customer orders.[38]

The brilliance of this capability lies in its speed and precision; the robots can assemble baskets containing up to 50 items in just five minutes. This is a significant improvement over traditional manual picking methods, which are not only time-consuming but also prone to errors. By automating the picking process, Ocado drastically reduces the time it takes for an order to move from being placed online to being prepared for delivery. This efficiency contributes to a faster delivery service, meaning customers receive their groceries sooner than they might with other services, enhancing overall customer satisfaction.[39]

Moreover, the integration of artificial intelligence (AI) capability plays a crucial role in optimizing the operation. AI algorithms help in predicting the most efficient routes for the robots, managing inventory levels, and even assisting in the maintenance of the robots by predicting when they might need servicing or repairs. This not only ensures uninterrupted operation but also minimizes waste and enhances the sustainability of the operations. Human workers complement the robotic system capability, focusing on tasks that require human judgement and skill, such as quality control, packing fragile items, and handling exceptions. This blending of capability between human intelligence and robotic efficiency exemplifies Ocado's integrated cross-disciplinary capabilities, combining logistics, robotics, AI and human resource management to deliver a superior customer experience.[40]

The use of robotics and AI in its warehouses is not just a logistical achievement; it's a strategic advantage in the competitive online grocery market by delivering orders more quickly, reliably and cost-effectively. This approach not only satisfies current customer expectations but also anticipates future demands, positioning firms such as Ocado as leaders in technology-driven customer experience management.

Methods to manage CX

This facet of CX management is about acquiring expertise in particular techniques that organizations devise and put into practice to refine customer journeys and foster customer-centric perspectives. Insights from both practical applications and scholarly research offer guidance on crafting such techniques. For instance, relying solely on traditional survey metrics like the net promoter score for measuring customer experience is insufficient in today's digital age. Companies must integrate all CX-related data points and employ capabilities such as natural language processing (NLP) and artificial intelligence (AI) to anticipate customer behaviours and improve CX management.[41]

An exemplary case of practical application of customer experience (CX) optimization methods comes from IKEA, which has employed large-scale natural language processing (NLP) capabilities to methodically analyse customer feedback gathered from various sources. This includes feedback from kiosks in their physical stores, as well as responses collected through their digital app and website. By integrating and interpreting data from these diverse channels, IKEA can gain a comprehensive understanding of customer sentiments, preferences and pain points.[42]

IKEA's strategic adoption of NLP shifts the focus from solely relying on quantitative survey metrics to analysing extensive text-based feedback. This transition enables the identification of common issues, trends and opportunities for enhancement. Such a method empowers IKEA to proactively address consumer requirements, customize their products and services, and elevate the shopping experience across both digital platforms and physical stores. Moreover, IKEA's application of NLP extends beyond mere analysis; it is part of a broader commitment to continuously refining CX through the adoption of cutting-edge technologies by leveraging AI and machine learning algorithms alongside NLP.[43]

The integration of attitudes, capabilities and methods forms a comprehensive strategic transformation towards a customer experience-centric approach. Dr Gautam Jha – a leading CX strategist who is a Director of Consumer and Services at Epam systems, a customer-centric digital innovator and industry adviser to Xansr Media – emphasizes that to effectively implement a customer experience (CX) strategy, executives must recognize CX as a key differentiator aligned with business goals. This requires adopting the ACM (attitudes, capabilities, methods) framework, focusing on smaller, actionable details. Executives should assess their current CX management stage, identify gaps, and develop a roadmap that integrates customer journey-based incentives and capabilities. Continuous improvement, supported by data-driven insights and cross-disciplinary skills, ensures CX management remains a dynamic process. This approach is relevant to all levels, from executives to managers, enabling a comprehensive and practical transformation in CX practices.

REAL-WORLD EXAMPLE
KFC

Utilizing the KFC real-world example,[44] we can illustrate how attitudes, capabilities and methods converge to create a strategic, customer experience-centric approach in the realm of fast-food services, significantly enhanced by digitalization.

- **Attitudes**: At the core of KFC's strategic shift is a foundational change in attitude towards valuing the customer experience above all. This is evident in their business strategy, which pivots from merely being a fast-food brand to offering a 'fast-good' experience, underlining a commitment to quality, convenience and customer satisfaction. The attitude of prioritizing consumer needs has driven KFC to modernize its brand through menu innovations, asset redesign and comprehensive digital communications, making KFC accessible and appealing across various consumer segments.

- **Capabilities**: KFC has demonstrated significant capabilities in embracing digital transformation, which is evident in their 100 per cent digital approach. This involves not just adopting digital tools but embedding digital processes across the customer journey, from digital kiosks in restaurants to a robust online ordering system. KFC's capabilities extend to leveraging artificial intelligence at scale for predictive analytics in supply chain management, workforce planning and personalized customer engagement, showcasing an advanced understanding and implementation of technology to serve consumer needs effectively.

- **Methods**: KFC employs a variety of methods to optimize the customer experience, with a focus on integrating technology into every aspect of the service delivery process. This includes real-time digital kiosks for order placement, AI-driven analytics for operational efficiency, and automated systems for food preparation. Additionally, KFC's proactive service management ensures that technology systems are always operational, minimizing disruptions and maintaining service quality. The methodical approach to utilizing digital touchpoints, designing services that align with customer journeys and orchestrating seamless service integration signifies KFC's methodical effort to enhance the overall service experience.

In synthesizing these elements, KFC's journey illustrates a holistic approach to digitalization in service experience, underpinned by a strategic shift in attitudes towards customer-centricity, the development of digital capabilities across the organization, and the application of innovative methods to meet and exceed customer expectations. This transformation not only enhances the customer experience but also positions KFC as a leader in the fast-food industry, adept at navigating the challenges and opportunities of the digital age.

In the next chapter, we will introduce a new method to envision the future of service, considering both customer and organizational perspectives. We will discuss a three-dimensional space that captures the essence of the customer experience. Each dimension is defined by its level of digital density, physical complexity and social presence, ranging from low to high.

We will discuss each dimension, providing a comprehensive understanding of its characteristics. We will then showcase real-world examples from various sectors, including B2B, B2C and public services, to illustrate how the framework can be applied in different contexts.

KEY TAKEAWAYS

Established firms recognize customer experience (CX) as a key strategic priority but struggle with its management compared to digitally native companies. CX management is often fragmented across different contexts and approaches. In this chapter, we highlight key insights:

- Achieving a CX-centric transformation requires addressing key drivers, such as gaining visibility into the customer value chain, overcoming internal resistance, and aligning customer expectations with reality.

- Strategic responses to these challenges include accelerating digitalization, ensuring executive sponsorship, and enhancing the organization's capabilities and approaches to prioritize customer-centricity

- Many firms are motivated to embrace digitalization and customer-centricity by the potential to drive revenue through better alignment of business strategies with customer preferences and needs.

- Success in CX-centricity is often constrained by challenges such as customer adoption, access to data, and interoperability within the business ecosystem. Effectively managing these factors is crucial for driving CX-centricity.

- The operationalization of smaller details, encapsulated within the ACM (attitudes, capabilities, methods) framework, provides a guide for executives, managers and practitioners to implement and sustain CX management effectively.

Notes

1 McKinsey (2023) Growth through customer experience. www.mckinsey.com/capabilities/growth-marketing-and-sales/our-insights/experience-led-growth-a-new-way-to-create-value (archived at https://perma.cc/VKJ4-BB4Q)

2 Pine, B J II and Gilmore, J H (1998) Welcome to the experience economy, *Harvard Business Review*, July–August. https://hbr.org/1998/07/welcome-to-the-experience-economy (archived at https://perma.cc/29FG-NSPS)

3 HCLTech (2024) The blueprint to total experience: Achieving experiences that are 'beyond the frame'. www.hcltech.com/sites/default/files/documents/resources/brochure/files/hcltech-the-blueprint-to-total-experience-full-report.pdf (archived at https://perma.cc/U3GJ-J7BN)

4 Zaki, M (2019) Digital transformation: Harnessing digital technologies for the next generation of services, *Journal of Services Marketing*, 33 (4), 429–35

5 ibid.

6 Wolfenden, P (2018) Planning for the future, Cambridge Service Alliance. https://cambridgeservicealliance.eng.cam.ac.uk/IndustryDay/2018SW (archived at https://perma.cc/CS2G-3WLA)

7 ibid.

8 Gartner (2018) Gartner says customer experience pyramid drives loyalty, satisfaction and advocacy. www.gartner.com/en/newsroom/press-releases/2018-07-30-gartner-says-customer-experience-pyramid-drives-loyalty-satisfaction-and-advocacy (archived at https://perma.cc/N8D4-A68X)

9 Gartner (2020) Gartner says 74% of customer experience leaders expect budgets to rise in 2020. www.gartner.com/en/newsroom/press-releases/2020-01-15-gartner-says-74--of--customer-experience-leaders-expe (archived at https://perma.cc/2PYU-746U)

10 HCLTech (2024) The blueprint to total experience: Achieving experiences that are 'beyond the frame'. www.hcltech.com/sites/default/files/documents/resources/brochure/files/hcltech-the-blueprint-to-total-experience-full-report.pdf (archived at https://perma.cc/4VZ7-Q2A2)

11 Bell, M L and Emory, C W (1971) The faltering marketing concept, *Journal of Marketing*, 35 (4), 37–42

12 Jha, G and Zaki, M (2023) Putting customer experience at the heart of business-to-business marketing, Cambridge Service Alliance. https://cambridgeservicealliance.eng.cam.ac.uk/node/1412/putting-customer-experience-heart-business-business-marketing (archived at https://perma.cc/4NX6-7VZB)

13 Lemon, K N and Verhoef, P C (2016) Understanding customer experience throughout the customer journey, *Journal of Marketing*, 80 (6), 69–96

14 Bolton, R, McColl-Kennedy, J, Cheung, L, Gallan, A, Orsingher, C, Witell, L and Zaki, M (2018) Customer experience challenges: Bringing together digital, physical and social realms, *Journal of Service Management*, 29 (5)

15 McColl-Kennedy, J R, Zaki, M, Lemon, K N, Urmetzer, F and Neely, A (2019) Gaining customer experience insights that matter, *Journal of Service Research*, 22 (1), 8–26

16 Jha, G and Zaki, M (2023) Putting customer experience at the heart of business-to-business marketing, Cambridge Service Alliance. https://cambridgeservicealliance.eng.cam.ac.uk/node/1412/putting-customer-experience-heart-business-business-marketing (archived at https://perma.cc/VKX9-YQ2H)

17 ibid.

18 Jha, G, Chandwani, J and Zaki, M (2025) The shift to fast food service experience through digitalization: Lessons from KFC, in *Handbook of Service Experience*, Edward Elgar Publishing

19 Jha, G and Zaki, M (2023) Putting customer experience at the heart of business-to-business marketing, Cambridge Service Alliance. https://cambridgeservicealliance.eng.cam.ac.uk/node/1412/putting-customer-experience-heart-business-business-marketing (archived at https://perma.cc/642L-46ZM)

20 ibid.

21 Volvo (2022) Volvo launches UK's first manufacturer online direct sales platform for approved used cars, Volvo Cars Media. www.media.volvocars.com/uk/en-gb/media/pressreleases/294498/volvo-launches-uks-first-manufacturer-online-direct-sales-platform-for-approved-used-cars (archived at https://perma.cc/T4A2-M3RW)

22 Jha, G and Zaki, M (2023) Putting customer experience at the heart of business-to-business marketing, Cambridge Service Alliance. https://cambridgeservicealliance.eng.cam.ac.uk/node/1412/putting-customer-experience-heart-business-business-marketing (archived at https://perma.cc/PGA5-QNVR)

23 ibid.

24 ibid.

25 ibid.

26 Podolny, J M and Hansen, M T (2020) How Apple is organized for innovation: It's about experts leading experts, *Harvard Business Review,* November–December. https://hbr.org/2020/11/how-apple-is-organized-for-innovation (archived at https://perma.cc/J9DX-C3LU)

27 Zaki, M, Kandeil, D, Neely, A and McColl-Kennedy, J R (2016) The fallacy of the net promoter score: Customer loyalty predictive model, Cambridge Service Alliance. https://cambridgeservicealliance.eng.cam.ac.uk/system/files/documents/2016OctoberPaper_FallacyoftheNetPromoterScore.pdf (archived at https://perma.cc/PCR5-GZKM)

28 Holmlund, M, Van Vaerenbergh, Y, Ciuchita, R, Ravald, A, Sarantopoulos, P, Villarroel Ordenes, F and Zaki, M (2020) Customer experience management in the age of big data analytics: A strategic framework, *Journal of Business Research*, 116, 356–65

29 Zaki, M (2019) Digital transformation: Harnessing digital technologies for the next generation of services, *Journal of Services Marketing*, 33 (4), 429–35

30 Jha, G and Zaki, M (2023) Putting customer experience at the heart of business-to-business marketing, Cambridge Service Alliance. https://cambridgeservicealliance.eng.cam.ac.uk/node/1412/putting-customer-experience-heart-business-business-marketing (archived at https://perma.cc/R7XP-X5B7)

31 Jha, G (2024) Achieving excellence in managing customer experience: An exploration of smaller details that make a difference, Apollo (University of Cambridge Repository)

32 Gautam, J and Zaki, M (2024) Achieving excellence in managing customer experience, 2024 Summer AMA Proceedings. www.ama.org/wp-content/uploads/2024/08/2024-Summer-AMA-Proceedings_August_12_2024.pdf (archived at https://perma.cc/Y32U-W32E)

33 ibid.

34 Bolton, R N, Gustafsson, A, McColl-Kennedy, J, Sirianni, N J and Tse, D K (2014) Small details that make big differences: A radical approach to consumption experience as a firm's differentiating strategy, *Journal of Service Management*, 25 (2), 253–74

35 ibid.

36 Lemon, K N and Verhoef, P C (2016) Understanding customer experience throughout the customer journey, *Journal of Marketing*, 80 (6), 69–96

37 Gautam, J and Zaki, M (2024) Achieving excellence in managing customer experience, 2024 Summer AMA Proceedings. www.ama.org/wp-content/uploads/2024/08/2024-Summer-AMA-Proceedings_August_12_2024.pdf (archived at https://perma.cc/AUJ2-4TJG)

38 Slegers, J (2021) Digital twins: Our smart warehouses host complex robotics and automation ecosystems, and no two are the same. So, before we change the physical world, we simulate in the digital world, with our digital twins, Ocado Group. https://careers.ocadogroup.com/blogs/careers-blogs/our-technologies/digital-twins (archived at https://perma.cc/DJN5-CN4U)

39 Ocado Group (2024) Our technology. www.ocadogroup.com/solutions/our-technology/ (archived at https://perma.cc/3Z9U-454Q)

40 ibid.

41 Holmlund, M, Van Vaerenbergh, Y, Ciuchita, R, Ravald, A, Sarantopoulos, P, Villarroel Ordenes, F and Zaki, M (2020) Customer experience management in the age of big data analytics: A strategic framework, *Journal of Business Research*, 116, 356–65

42 Jonzon, M M (2024) IKEA: From flatpacks to actionable insights. https://cambridgeservicealliance.eng.cam.ac.uk/node/1412/future-digital-services-and-platforms (archived at https://perma.cc/7BHS-CC6Y)

43 ibid.

44 Jha, G, Chandwani, J and Zaki, M (forthcoming) The shift to fast food service experience through digitalization: Lessons from KFC in Kristensson, P, Witell, L, and Zaki, M (eds), *Handbook of Service Experience*, Edward Elgar Publishing

3

Data-driven customer experience design

Let's pivot our discussion to the design and innovation of customer experiences. In my conversations with executives, there's a common recognition of the inevitable fusion of digital and physical realms. However, what often goes unaddressed is the social element. This chapter introduces the customer experience framework, a compelling way to visualize the future of service from both the customer and organizational viewpoints. This framework describes a three-dimensional space that exemplifies the customer experience. Each dimension is defined by its level of digital density, physical complexity and social presence, ranging from low to high. Understanding this integration will allow companies to define their strategies with upcoming trends, meet evolving customer expectations, and design a transformative customer journey.

Despite the growing race to excel in customer experience, the novel digital platforms create new forms of engagement that are not poised to replace direct human interactions; rather, they aim to enrich them, thereby introducing additional complexity to service systems. Grasping customer experiences that bridge the digital, physical and social realms is essential. Traditional service research and practice may have examined these realms in isolation, but a holistic approach is now necessary to cultivate fulfilling customer experiences and design services that reflect this confluence.

With this structured framework and tangible examples, we aim not only to identify innovation opportunities but also to recognize and address emerging challenges. We will examine each dimension in depth, explaining its unique features. Subsequently, we will illustrate the application of this framework in diverse settings, including B2B, B2C and public sectors.

The experience economy: Facts and predictions

The concept of the experience economy isn't new, having been coined by B Joseph Pine II and James H Gilmore in 1998.[1] It highlights the crucial importance of creating memorable experiences over mere transactions. This notion is increasingly relevant today and resonates strongly with millennials, who favour experiences over tangible products. Current trends confirm that we are indeed ingrained in an experience economy. For example, at a personal level, you might have found yourself increasingly unimpressed when established firms have outdated customer services using phone interaction. You might even find yourself preferring or remembering firms that use a series of chatbots or customer-friendly apps.

Service brands offering exceptional experiences command a strong customer fan base. In a digital platform-driven economy, there is a concerted effort to seize new opportunities to craft these memorable experiences. Nonetheless, businesses also face the genuine threat of being blindsided by disruptive technologies, akin to the cautionary tales of Kodak and Toys R Us, who missed the boat on leveraging new technological advances.[2]

The significance of the experience economy is such that numerous industries have led market research studies to better understand customer behaviours. Leading professional firms like PwC, Salesforce, Formstack and Wunderman have gathered critical data through surveys to capture customer perspectives on brand interactions.

PwC's global survey[3] revealed the nature of customer loyalty, with a significant portion of customers willing to **abandon a brand after a handful of negative experiences**. In the US, 59 per cent would leave after several disappointments, and 17 per cent would do so after just one. Globally, 32 per cent would defect after a single poor experience, and in Latin America, the figure jumps to 49 per cent. These statistics emphasize the urgency for businesses to focus on delivering seamless experiences swiftly.

Moreover, PwC has illuminated the necessity for a balance between digital and human interactions in experience design. A majority globally value experience as a decisive factor in their purchases, with **speed, convenience,** and **friendly service** being paramount. Yet, 59 per cent feel that companies are losing the human touch, highlighting a disconnect between customer expectations and service delivery.[4]

Salesforce's research[5] further demonstrates that customers **desire personalized experiences** and **value innovation in products and services**. Data protection and trust are also critical to the customer experience. A standout discovery is that 75 per cent of customers expect **consistency across all departments throughout their entire journey with a company**, whether in-store, online or over the phone.

Formstack's findings[6] indicate that **a poor website can significantly damage a brand's reputation**, with 57 per cent of respondents unlikely to recommend such businesses. This underscores the importance of a robust digital presence.

Wunderman's report suggests that 79 per cent of US consumers prioritize brands that demonstrate they care about their customers, signalling heightened expectations and the need for brands to be more empathetic across all interactions.[7]

These insights collectively illustrate that the experience economy transcends the delivery of products or transactional services. It's about nurturing relationships among customers, suppliers and employees within complex ecosystems. The advent of new technologies not only enhances organizational efficiency but also enriches the customer experience, demonstrating a company's commitment to its customers.

The evidence and anecdotes to date unmistakably point to one conclusion: the landscape of customer experience and expectations is shifting dramatically. We inhabit a world where experiences significantly shape customer engagement and business loyalty. While it's tempting to believe that embracing cutting-edge technology is a silver bullet for industry leadership and innovation, the reality is far more nuanced.

Emerging technologies present fresh possibilities. Innovations such as AI, robotics and digital twins are becoming integral to the service industry, offering unprecedented efficiencies and enhancing customer experience strategies. For example, robots have begun to demonstrate their ability in tasks like assembling IKEA furniture autonomously.[8]

Emerging technologies also introduce new challenges. Not all technological advancements are received positively by consumers. Companies must balance the efficiency gains from new tech against the risk of dissatisfying their customer base. Developing the appropriate technological solutions for different contexts will be crucial amid a future full of diverse tech options. Consider the ongoing conversations surrounding ChatGPT, including the ethical dilemmas, content ownership and potential biases it introduces.

The importance of comprehensive omnichannel strategies and understanding the interplay between digital, physical and social dimensions are essential to crafting consistent experiences that meet consumer needs. Overlooking these connections within complex service systems can lead to severe missteps. Innovations across these realms are continually altering the competitive landscape.

Let's take an example: the recent massive Microsoft IT outage incident, highlighting the interplay between the physical, digital and social dimensions that led to significant flight delays. Digital disruptions can significantly impact social channels, especially when the physical and digital systems aren't well integrated. For example, during a massive IT outage in June 2024, airports and airlines experienced widespread delays due to a software issue (a software update by global cybersecurity firm CrowdStrike). While the digital systems failed, physical operations like issuing boarding passes manually couldn't keep up, leading to social frustration among passengers. Out of more than 110,000 scheduled commercial flights on Friday 19 June 2024, 5,000 were cancelled globally. By comparison, 2,000 flights were cancelled on Thursday 18 June, before the software issues. This highlights the need for seamless integration between digital, physical and social systems to avoid exacerbating problems and ensure a smooth customer experience across all channels.[9]

The customer experience (CX)

CX lies at the heart of service marketing theories and practices, highlighting its importance across all types of organizations. These entities serve various stakeholders, who may be referred to as guests, members, patients, citizens or clients, irrespective of whether they are internal or external.

Delivering a significant CX is crucial for securing a competitive edge and ensuring customer satisfaction. Organizations that diligently oversee their customer experience enjoy numerous benefits, including heightened customer satisfaction, increased revenues, and greater employee contentment. This underlines the reason why enhancing and controlling positive customer experiences have become strategic priorities for companies and their chief executives worldwide. When customers perceive the value in the experiences provided, they are more inclined to demonstrate loyalty, offer positive feedback about the organization, support and advocate for it, and continue or even expand their support and purchases from their brand.[10]

Despite the various definitions available, there is a consensus among scholars and practitioners that customer experience stems from a sequence of interactions between a customer and a service provider. As discussed in Chapter 2, we view the customer experience as a holistic journey, seen through the eyes of the customer, involving a series of encounters. A customer's perception of their experience is all-encompassing, reflecting various internal and subjective responses to their interactions with an organization.[11]

Adopting this viewpoint, we define the customer experience as a 'holistic and unified journey' that starts with the initial interaction with a brand, continues through the purchasing process, and carries on into the post-purchase period.[12] In the pre-purchase phase, customers may discover an advertisement on social media, visit the brand's website for additional information about the product, read reviews and compare prices across various websites, and possibly visit a physical store to inspect the product in person. During the purchase phase, customers browse or make inquiries about the product and complete their purchase either online or in a physical store, followed by the receipt of an invoice either in paper form or via email. In the post-purchase phase, customers evaluate the product's quality after receiving it, leave a review on the brand's website, and contact customer service if they encounter any issues with the product. Last, the post-purchase engagement is maintained as customers receive follow-up communications or promotional offers from the brand.

However, it is not as linear as we have presented; it is more complex. This complexity arises as customer experiences span a variety of channels and touchpoints. This variability makes it particularly challenging to categorize customers who might research a product in one channel (like a physical store) and complete their purchase in another (such as via an app). Similarly, tracking and catering to customers who buy through one channel (for example, online) and then seeking post-purchase support through another channel (like phone or social media) are difficult.

From an organizational standpoint, managing customer experience involves adopting and executing a customer-focused strategy to craft and deliver positive customer experiences. This approach requires comprehensively addressing the aspects, such as customer needs, expectations and preferences throughout the entire customer journey. This aligns with viewing CX as a continuum of interactions and engagements across various touchpoints.[13]

Customers seek experiences that are meaningful, authentic, humanized and consistent, free from the frustrations that can arise in any interaction channel involving both human and technological interfaces. Consequently, organizations need to develop a customer experience management strategy that seamlessly integrates digital, physical and social interactions occurring at various critical 'moments of truth' throughout the customer's journey.

As previously mentioned, gaining a deep understanding of what emerges within each channel is essential. While some channels may offer outstanding experiences, others can lead to significant disappointment and frustration for customers.

CX design innovation: Digital, physical and social channels

Until now, we've discussed the critical role of customer experience within the experience economy. Moving forward, we will explore how organizations can strategically design their services and customer experiences to span the physical, digital and social realms.

It's crucial for organizations to approach these channels not as separate entities but as components of a unified, seamless experience, mirroring the way customers perceive them. The illustration below highlights the contrast between operating through multiple, unconnected channels and adopting an omnichannel strategy that integrates experiences across all three domains. In a multichannel approach, customers engage with each of the three available channels independently and in isolation. Conversely, the omnichannel strategy ensures that all channels are interconnected and integrated, with the customer experience at the core of this cohesive system.

Digital realm

The digital channel is characterized by the prevalence of technologies that are continuously reshaping customer experiences. These technologies include mobile applications, geolocation services, virtual reality (VR), digital twins, blockchain, artificial intelligence (AI), generative AI, robotics, wearable technology, chatbots, applications of neuroscience, metaverse, business process automation, machine-to-machine (M2M) communications, quantum computing and the Internet of Things (IoT). The operation of these technologies plays a key role in driving the transformative shifts observed within organizations and the competitive dynamics among them.

Key attributes of technologies in the digital realm include a synergistic operation that amplifies their collective impact through the integration of various technologies. Mobility and pervasive connectivity enable on-demand interaction and access to extensive data and computational resources. Facilitating more dynamic and frequent **customer engagements**, offering broad **reach** irrespective of geographic barriers, supports highly personalized services and round-the-clock immediacy in responses. The velocity, expansiveness, interactivity and data processing capabilities of digital technology will persistently influence **customer behaviour**. Digital technologies may also **redefine the human aspect** of service delivery, with digital tools supporting or occasionally substituting human roles, transforming how services are delivered. More importantly, **information density** measures the quantity of information or data within a specific area or communication unit. Within the digital realm, it means the volume of data that can be sent, retrieved, processed and examined via digital technologies, like artificial intelligence (AI). Technologies with high information density can manage and analyse vast amounts of data swiftly and effectively. Conversely, technologies characterized by low information density face challenges in accessing, processing, transmitting and analysing data. AI has emerged as a key tool to help companies work with these datasets in real time.[14]

Indeed, the McKinsey Global Institute has forecast that AI could add up to $13 trillion to the global economy by 2030, with approximately 70 per cent of companies expected to adopt some form of AI by the decade's close.[15] Recently, OpenAI introduced generative AI models, demonstrating their potential integration into various future services for content creation and search assistance. For instance, ChatGPT is a language model optimized for generating text, dialogue and code. DALL·E 2 is a different AI model capable of producing original, realistic images and artwork based on textual descriptions. While AI represents a formidable technology, achieving mere 'average' performance from AI models is often insufficient in practical applications. For AI systems to truly enhance customer experience, they must attain accuracy levels as high as the available data allows, particularly in situations where errors could have serious repercussions: for example, **misinformation spread**. If large language models can produce inaccurate or misleading information, it can lead to the spread of misinformation, which could have serious consequences for brands in areas like healthcare, finance, politics or public safety. Another issue is **bias and discrimination** – AI systems that are not carefully trained can inadvertently reinforce biases, leading to discriminatory outcomes in hiring practices, lending decisions or law enforcement. And there are **customer service failures** – in customer service, low-accuracy AI systems might provide incorrect responses or fail to resolve issues, leading to customer dissatisfaction and potential loss of business. **Security risks** occur when inaccurate AI in cybersecurity applications fails to detect threats or generates false alarms, leaving systems vulnerable to attacks.

Physical realm

The physical realm encompasses all tangible locations where customer service is delivered, including football stadiums, hospitals, shops, airports and restaurants. Despite the surge in digital advancements, the necessity for services in physical spaces persists, where the right physical ambiance can significantly boost the overall customer experience. Businesses maintain aspects of their physical settings to preserve their unique customer experiences.[16]

In recent times, as businesses have broadened their digital footprints, technology has increasingly penetrated the physical realm. This includes the adoption of self-service kiosks, the introduction of Amazon Go stores without cashiers, virtual reality simulations of football matches, and immersive travel experiences.

Successful companies integrate various elements and features of the physical world to weave a consistent story for their customers. Through well-designed environments, they inspire both new and loyal customers to immerse themselves fully in the product and service experiences offered. This approach fosters memorable, emotionally charged moments and memories. Apple exemplifies this strategy through its retail stores, which are designed to deliver a uniform experience globally. Each store features a sleek, minimalist design, knowledgeable staff and hands-on product displays, ensuring that no matter where a customer is, they receive the same high level of service and engagement. This consistency helps to build a strong emotional connection with the brand, making each visit to an Apple store a memorable event that reinforces the company's identity and values.[17] Notably, Apple, a manufacturing company, achieves $4,551 in sales for every square foot of its retail space,[18] ranking it as the leading retailer by this measure, which gauges the profitability of retail spaces across firms.

The following list outlines key features of spaces within the physical realm:[19]

- **Physical properties to enhance comfort:** Every physical space is arranged with furniture and equipment that affect its functionality and layout, offering customers convenience and comfort through ambient elements.

- **Spaces designed to encourage return visits:** Through sensory cues, businesses can significantly affect customer behaviour and reactions during face-to-face service encounters. Companies have mastered the art of creating and maintaining a physical environment, such as pleasant aromas, soothing music, clean surroundings and attractive colour, that invites customers back and encourages purchases.

- **Cues promoting a sense of belonging**: Many physical spaces utilize cultural resources, such as signs and symbols, to provide cues that set expectations for customer behaviour and interaction within the service setting. These cultural elements can foster a sense of belonging among a brand community or subculture, enriching shared customer experiences and establishing a sense of place.

- **The impact of subtle design elements**: These environments may also include minor details with a broad impact on the customer experience, influencing the nature and quality of interactions between customers and company staff, as well as between customers themselves (C2C interactions).

The trend towards digitalization in organizations leads to a parallel increase in the integration of digital elements within physical environments. This phenomenon is already evident in numerous instances, yet there are countless other examples waiting to be explored. For instance, several retailers are incorporating augmented reality technologies, like smart mirrors that allow customers to virtually try on clothing. Macy's is enhancing the customer experience by using an AR mirror that lets customers transform into their favourite Disney princesses.[20] Amazon's journey from an online marketplace to launching Amazon Go – cashierless, digitally enhanced grocery stores – is a prime example of digital technology's integration into physical retail spaces.

I believe that, despite the shift towards digital platforms, the essence of the physical realm will remain pivotal in understanding and enhancing customer experience. For instance, when designing digital environments, the characteristics of physical spaces often serve as valuable benchmarks. Businesses are likely to incorporate key attributes such as functionality, branding and cultural signals into the digital customer experience, ensuring a seamless and consistent experience across both realms.

Social realm

The social dimension revolves around nurturing shared experiences, whether between an organization and its business or among the customers themselves. It serves as a conduit for customers to satisfy their utilitarian, social and psychological needs.[21]

For instance, as customers engage in activities like shopping, learning, socializing and working within digital realms, they immerse themselves in yet another social dimension. These interactions lie at the core of the customer experience, whether they occur face-to-face or online and whether they involve human-to-human or human-to-non-human interactions.

With the proliferation of digital technologies, the delineation between customer and service provider roles is becoming increasingly blurred. Consider Airbnb, an online platform enabling individuals to rent out their properties to travellers. Here, users seamlessly transition between being customers and service providers, renting out their homes while simultaneously seeking accommodation elsewhere.

In light of this, comprehending the implications of assuming multiple identities within service contexts becomes imperative. The social dimension can be analysed in three modes of interaction, as outlined in the list below:[22]

- **Human-to-human**: Interaction occurs between a customer and an employee, forming a singular experience.
- **Human-to-actors**: Interaction with various entities, including other customers, employees and partners.
- **Human-to-non-human**: Interaction involving the deployment of digital capabilities like service robots or chatbots.

Organizations must facilitate customer interactions with other actors, given the trend towards co-creating experiences and value. This social presence, indicating the extent of ongoing interactions, ranges from high to low and spans both physical and digital realms. Social presence is contextual, influenced by factors like setting customer expectations, and can significantly shape the customer experience. Therefore, the social dimension plays a crucial role in shaping customer experiences, with its nuances impacting interactions across various platforms and settings.

A guided framework

We explored three distinct realms, each characterized by its unique dimension:[23]

- **Digital realm**: Varying from low to high information density.
- **Physical realm**: Varying from low to high physical complexity.
- **Social realm**: Contextual and ranging from low to high social presence.

Let's discuss this framework that integrates these dimensions to create a seamless omnichannel experience. However, before doing so, let's take a glimpse into what these interconnected omnichannel experiences might entail in the future.

You step into a renowned retail establishment with the intention of purchasing new clothing. Upon your arrival, you receive a warm welcome from a service robot, which promptly scans your face and retrieves your purchase history from the store's database. Subsequently, the robot suggests viewing new arrivals and offers recommendations based on your past purchases.

Equipped with sensors, the store detects your presence and adjusts lighting and temperature to enhance your comfort. You approach one of the smart mirrors in the store to preview how clothes will appear on you, utilizing your mobile app to verify stock availability across sizes and colours.

In the fitting room, you try various garments and seek a second opinion on fit from the service robot, leveraging its computer vision technology for analysis and alteration recommendations.

Finally, a human employee warmly greets you at the checkout counters and facilitates your payment process. Drawing from your purchasing history, the employee offers recommendations for future buys. Departing the store, you are content with your shopping experience and impressed by the seamless fusion of technology and human interaction.

I anticipate that many similar transformations will take place. Our society is presently experiencing profound shifts across digital, physical and social domains, and, should this trajectory persist, I anticipate witnessing significant changes across all realms by 2050, or even before.[24]

In this section, I will lead you through a framework that synthesizes the digital, physical and social realms within an omnichannel strategy. Through this framework, I illustrate the imminent convergence of the digital, physical and social spheres.

I'll examine each dimension's attributes and conceptualize them within a three-dimensional framework (Figure 3.1).[25] First, the digital realm, ranging from low to high information density. Then, there's the physical domain, spanning from low to high physical complexity. Last, as you might have guessed, the social domain, which is context-dependent and spans from low to high social presence.

All three domains can be combined within this multidimensional framework, aiding in analysing how customer experiences unfold across these channels. This cube comprises **eight layers**. In essence, there are **eight potential**

FIGURE 3.1 Connecting digital, physical and social channels

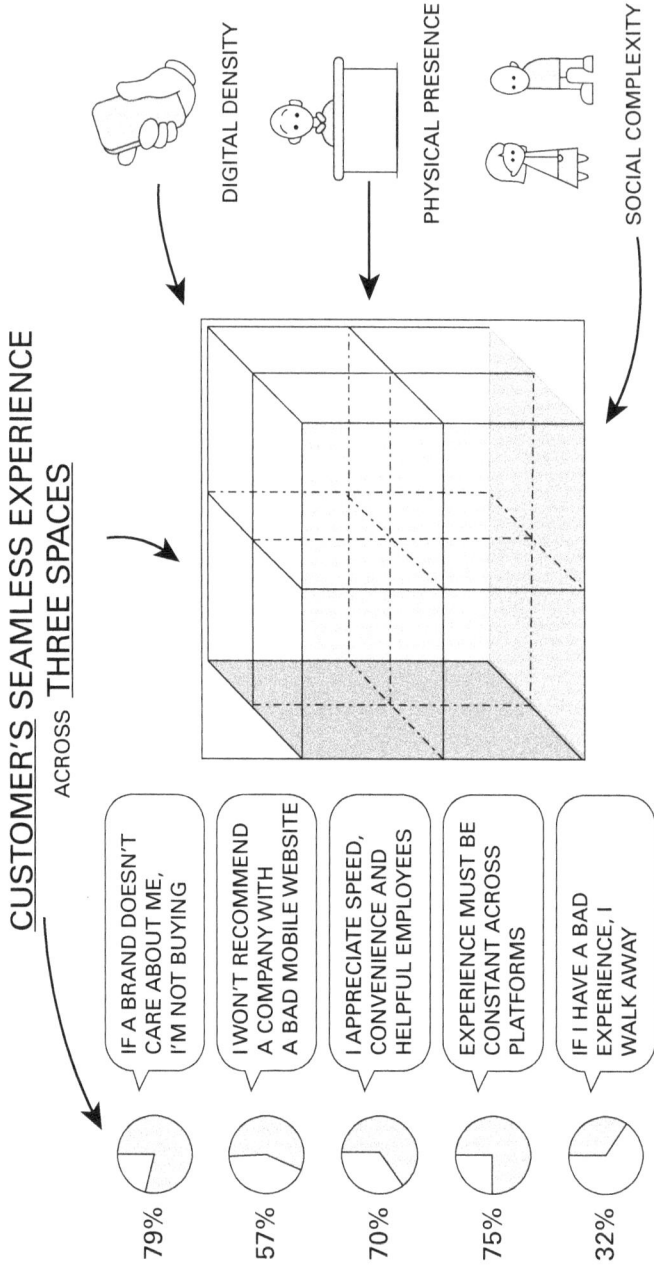

CUSTOMER'S SEAMLESS EXPERIENCE
ACROSS THREE SPACES

DIGITAL DENSITY

PHYSICAL PRESENCE

SOCIAL COMPLEXITY

IF A BRAND DOESN'T CARE ABOUT ME, I'M NOT BUYING — 79%

I WON'T RECOMMEND A COMPANY WITH A BAD MOBILE WEBSITE — 57%

I APPRECIATE SPEED, CONVENIENCE AND HELPFUL EMPLOYEES — 70%

EXPERIENCE MUST BE CONSTANT ACROSS PLATFORMS — 75%

IF I HAVE A BAD EXPERIENCE, I WALK AWAY — 32%

combinations of your digital, physical and social channels.[26] This framework facilitates assessing your current organizational position and desired future trajectory.

Let's discuss each possible configuration.[27]

The **initial configuration** shows a service characterized by low digital density, high physical complexity, and high social presence. This implies a service that is heavily reliant on physical space and human interaction to deliver, with less dependence on digital interfaces. For instance, this could resemble an active retail environment like a sports gear store, where staff guide customers through product exploration.

The **second configuration** may involve a service heavily reliant on digital technology and customer engagement to execute specific tasks. While physical elements may still be crucial, social interactions might be less frequent due to human-to-non-human interaction. A driverless car fits this configuration, functioning as a digital system aided by data and AI to provide customers with automated guidance while driving.

The **third configuration** boasts high digital density but exhibits lower physical complexity and social presence.

Are there any examples among services you utilize regularly?

Two prominent examples are Netflix, the media streaming giant, and Spotify, one of the pioneering music streaming platforms. Both exemplify digital entertainment platforms where users interact with AI recommendation engines to enjoy movies or music from the comfort of their personal spaces. This configuration signifies firms dedicating resources to building intelligent digital systems, offering personalized experiences and displacing traditional physical and social establishments like cinemas and concert halls.

The **fourth configuration** depicts a highly digitalized service with lower physical complexity while maintaining a high social presence. Any gamers should recognize this; it applies to services like online gaming as well as social media and videoconferencing platforms. Through these technologies, humans utilize smart digital tools to connect, socialize and play remotely without necessitating physical environments.

The **fifth configuration** is characterized by low digital density, low physical complexity, and high social presence.

What types of services might fall under this category?

You might think of customer service or sales. Picture a scenario where a customer interacts with a company representative over the phone, shaping a low digital, low physical, high social environment. This often indicates services characterized by minimal digital density, physical complexity and social presence, with all channels operating at a basic level.

The **sixth configuration** could be low in the digital, physical and social realms. Consider an insurance company with a basic website. A customer could purchase a car insurance policy online and renew it annually, requiring no physical space or further social interactions. Similarly, envision a scenario where citizens use a government portal to complete tax return forms. These exemplify instances where services are delivered using simple digital solutions without necessitating physical or social interactions.

Now we'll examine the **seventh configuration**, classified as high in all three realms.

Consider a clinical setting where a patient is offered an AI system to analyse their X-ray for an initial diagnosis. This scenario represents high digital involvement but also involves the patient's interaction with a physician in a physical space to complete the diagnosis, devise a treatment plan, and manage it.

The **final configuration** in our analysis features low digital density, high physical complexity and minimal social presence. An example is a self-service vending machine, commonly found in physical spaces such as shopping malls or cinemas, where numerous individuals congregate to make purchases.

As a professional in the field, you can utilize insights from this presentation to evaluate your current service provisions and experiences. Begin by mapping your products or services against this multidimensional omnichannel framework.

Subsequently, consider where you aim to position yourself in terms of digital, physical and social domains. Then, engage in organizational discussions regarding future opportunities and challenges associated with transitioning from low to high digital density and from low to high social presence environments. This holds true for B2B, B2C and public service settings.

Congruency affects the alignment between an organization's capabilities and resources and those of its customers. Achieving congruence entails establishing a seamless connection across all three realms, ensuring consistency among elements in different domains, and fostering a coherent theme that unifies the entire experience.[28] This raises the development of a superior service design.

To cultivate such a design, it's imperative to fundamentally reassess service and experience design. Present-day professionals must adeptly navigate the increasing complexity brought forth by the digital era when bridging the physical and social realms.[29] For instance, numerous organizations face pressure to meet customers' demands for instant access to content, expertise and tailored solutions – a phenomenon often termed the 'crisis of immediacy'.[30] One strategy to contend with the crisis of immediacy involves leveraging virtual experts. Today's digital technologies enable the deployment of virtual experts capable of engaging with consumers in real time to provide guidance, address inquiries and offer recommendations. These virtual experts can manifest in various forms, including human experts conducting videoconferencing sessions with customers or digital agents interacting with users via mobile apps or augmented reality technology.

Framework application examples

When considering customer experience illustrations, many possibilities and potential focal points emerge. However, we will concentrate on exemplary future services likely to materialize by 2030 across three service sectors: asset-heavy B2B services, healthcare, and B2C retail and professional services.[31] Each sector serves as a springboard for identifying opportunities to craft customer experiences in the digital, physical and social realms.

Asset-heavy B2B services

With the evolution of technology, asset-heavy B2B services are anticipated to transition from traditional support services to more digitized and digital twin services.

In the realm of B2B services, numerous prospects flourish for leveraging digital technologies to augment productivity and efficiency in demand and capacity management.

The ensuing interaction showcases opportunities within asset-heavy B2B services such as construction, defence, energy and transportation. Diverse examples span across each octant at the intersection of the digital, physical and social spaces.

Let's discuss the different B2B service opportunities below:[32]

1 **Remote maintenance services:** Amid the landscape of remote maintenance services, we witness a high digital presence coupled with low physical and high social dimensions. These services operate predominantly in the digital sphere, requiring minimal physical intervention but promoting significant social interaction.

2 **VR tool simulation services:** VR tool simulation services, like those tailored for diggers and planes, exemplify a high digital presence alongside low physical and social dimensions. These simulations primarily unfold in the digital realm, offering immersive experiences while necessitating minimal physical interaction and social engagement.

3 **Engineering services:** In the realm of engineering services, we encounter a configuration characterized by low digital and physical presence but high social interaction. These services rely heavily on human expertise and collaborative efforts, fostering extensive social interactions while maintaining minimal digital and physical footprints.

4 **Automated software patches:** Automated software patches, on the other hand, exhibit low digital, physical and social dimensions. These services operate discreetly in the digital domain, executing tasks with minimal physical involvement and social interaction.

5 **Digital asset twin services:** Digital asset twin services represent a configuration with a high digital presence but low physical and social dimensions. These services leverage advanced digital technologies to create virtual representations of physical assets, enabling enhanced monitoring and analysis while minimizing physical and social interactions.

6 **Predictive solutions:** Predictive solutions offered as services for B2B ventures embody a configuration characterized by high digital, physical and social dimensions. These solutions harness digital technologies, real-time sensor data and human expertise to deliver proactive insights, thus fostering significant physical and social interactions alongside digital engagement.

7 **Traditional repair services:** Traditional repair services, in contrast, manifest low digital but high physical and social dimensions. These services heavily rely on physical interventions and human expertise, fostering extensive social interactions while maintaining minimal digital involvement.

8 **Asset management services facilitated by machine-to-machine data:** Asset management services facilitated by machine-to-machine data present a configuration with low digital and physical presence but high social engagement. These services leverage data-driven insights to optimize asset performance and foster collaborative efforts among stakeholders, thus emphasizing social interactions while minimizing digital and physical footprints.

The future trajectory of asset-heavy B2B industries indicates a transition towards digital service configurations, offering myriad benefits to customers, including enhanced scheduling, convenient maintenance services, machine health monitoring, and reduced operational costs. Moreover, the adoption of digital twins, dynamic virtual representations fuelled by real-time data, holds immense potential to revolutionize customer experiences in asset-heavy industries and public services alike:

- Rolls-Royce is collaborating with universities and institutes to develop an open-source digital platform for creating digital twins of ships. This platform enables the synthesis of real-time data to construct virtual replicas of vessels, facilitating comprehensive assessments of safety and performance, thereby optimizing design and maintenance processes.[33]
- Amsterdam's innovative MX3D Bridge, equipped with sensors, generates data to fuel a digital twin prediction model, ensuring real-time monitoring and predictive maintenance to enhance communal safety and structural integrity.[34]
- The United Kingdom National Infrastructure Commission has proposed an ambitious initiative to construct a digital twin for the country. This public service venture aims to amalgamate diverse data streams to provide actionable insights and solutions for addressing critical infrastructure challenges, underscoring the potential of high digital density coupled with low social presence and physical complexity.[35]

Healthcare services

As technology continues to advance, we anticipate a shift within the healthcare industry from traditional care services towards more digitized practices and care delivery methods.

Traditionally, healthcare has been centred around the schedules and facilities of medical professionals, characterized by a high social presence alongside physical infrastructure with significant complexity and limited integration of digital technology. However, experts predict that technological progressions will diminish the reliance on physical components in the forthcoming decades.[36]

Presently, digital health applications are rapidly evolving, focusing on empowering patients to manage their conditions and medications, as well as supporting their mental health and overall well-being more effectively than ever before.

This trend was already gaining momentum prior to the global pandemic. For instance, in 2019, the World Health Organization advocated for the utilization of health apps, while numerous national governments promoted their adoption, alongside substantial investments from venture capital firms into digital health startups since 2018.[37]

The Covid-19 pandemic significantly amplified the demand for remote patient monitoring and the delivery of care on a worldwide scale. Consequently, the entire healthcare service ecosystem underwent a transformation, encompassing aspects such as planning, regulation and implementation, in order to facilitate a seamless and value-driven service experience.

The ensuing interaction explains opportunities within the healthcare industry, showcasing examples spanning across each octant at the convergence of the digital, physical and social dimensions:[38]

1 **Clinical simulation services, or use of virtual reality**: One configuration could be characterized by high digital presence, low physical engagement, and high social interaction. These services leverage digital technologies to create immersive environments for medical training and education, fostering extensive social interactions while minimizing physical constraints.

2 **Artificial intelligence diagnostic services**: These services exemplify a configuration with a high digital presence, low physical interaction, and low social engagement. These services harness AI algorithms to analyse medical data and assist in diagnostics, primarily operating within the digital sphere with minimal physical and social components.

3 **Counselling services**: The service illustrates a configuration characterized by low digital involvement, low physical presence, and high social interaction. These services rely heavily on interpersonal communication and human interaction to provide support and guidance, fostering extensive social engagement while maintaining minimal digital and physical footprints.

4 **Rural barefoot doctors**: In the realm of rural healthcare, barefoot doctors represent a configuration with low digital, physical and social dimensions. These decentralized healthcare providers operate in remote areas with limited access to technology and resources, emphasizing traditional healing practices and community-based care.

5 **Medical tourism**: This embodies a configuration characterized by high digital, physical and social dimensions. These services integrate digital

platforms for scheduling and co-ordination, require physical travel for medical procedures, and foster social interactions among patients and healthcare providers across international borders.

6 **Robot surgery**: The service represents a configuration with high digital and physical presence but low social interaction. These advanced surgical systems leverage robotic technologies to enhance precision and minimize invasiveness, primarily operating within the digital and physical realms with minimal social engagement.

7 **Traditional nursing**: These services manifest a configuration with low digital but high physical and social dimensions. These services rely on direct patient care and interpersonal interactions, emphasizing human touch and empathy in healthcare delivery.

8 **Healthcare monitoring devices**: These devices embody a configuration with low digital presence, high physical involvement, and minimal social interaction. These devices facilitate remote monitoring of patients' health parameters, primarily operating within the physical domain with limited digital and social components.

The future of the healthcare industry promises a transition towards digital services and devices, offering numerous advantages to patients, including enhanced accessibility, personalized care and improved efficiency. The integration of digital technologies, such as healthcare apps and robot-assisted surgeries, is reshaping the landscape of healthcare delivery, paving the way for transformative innovations and improved patient outcomes.

Digital healthcare apps, such as Babylon and DoctorCareAnywhere, exemplify the integration of technology into healthcare delivery, enabling remote consultations and AI-powered symptom assessment. These platforms facilitate seamless access to medical services and enhance diagnostic accuracy, showcasing the potential of digital innovations in transforming healthcare delivery.

Robot-assisted surgeries, exemplified by the da Vinci surgical system,[39] illustrate the convergence of robotics and medicine to enhance surgical precision and patient outcomes. These advanced systems enable minimally invasive procedures and post-operative care, demonstrating the transformative impact of technology on surgical practices.

Reflecting on these advancements, consider how healthcare organizations embrace future opportunities and whether their offerings span the digital, physical and social realms. Assessing technology integration, human interaction and physical infrastructure can provide insights into optimizing healthcare services for enhanced patient experiences and outcomes.

Retail and professional services

In the realm of retail and professional services, a transformation from traditional service delivery to a more digitalized model is anticipated, mirroring trends observed in other sectors.

As evidenced across various B2C industries, such as retail, automotive, consumer goods, logistics, media and professional services, digital technologies have become pervasive. The Covid-19 pandemic underscored the imperative for businesses to embrace digitalization comprehensively.

The pandemic's impact highlighted the significance of robust digital infrastructure, enabling organizations to effectively adapt to sudden shifts towards remote work. Similarly, consumer-facing businesses that excelled during the pandemic demonstrated resilience through robust digital supply chains and platforms, facilitating exceptional customer experiences.

Retailing, in particular, has witnessed significant digital service innovations alongside organizational adaptations. Previously, both in-store and online retail experiences were characterized by high physical complexity and social presence. Before the pandemic, online retail had been steadily growing, constituting over 13 per cent of global retail sales by 2019. However, in 2020, amid widespread lockdowns, this share surged to 18 per cent of overall retail sales, emphasizing the accelerated digitalization of retail processes.[40]

There is an opportunity to transition from the realms of low to high digital density within the context of retail and professional services. Various examples spanning across each octant at the convergence of digital, physical and social spaces offer insights into the evolving landscape of service delivery in these industries:[41]

1 **Multiplayer online gaming**: The service landscape is characterized by high digital interaction, low physical presence, and a high social component. Players engage in immersive digital environments, connecting with others globally through virtual platforms. These gaming experiences foster social interaction, collaboration and competition among players, creating vibrant online communities.

2 **Custom build services**: These services, spanning industries like kitchens, cars and sofas, primarily operate within a high digital realm with low physical involvement and social interaction. Customers leverage digital

platforms to customize and design their desired products, often with low social engagement beyond online interactions with service providers.

3 **Professional services:** While essential, typically these services operate in a low digital environment with low physical presence and high social interaction. Professionals rely heavily on face-to-face interactions and personal relationships to deliver services, emphasizing social connections and rapport building with clients.

4 **Mobile financial services:** These types of services operate in a low digital, low physical and low social realm. These services facilitate financial transactions through digital platforms with minimal physical involvement and social interaction, offering convenient and accessible solutions for managing finances remotely.

5 **Multiplayer gaming consoles:** Consoles, such as PlayStation, offer an experience characterized by high digital engagement, high physical interaction with gaming hardware, and high social connections among players. These consoles facilitate immersive gaming experiences while fostering social interaction and community building among gamers.

6 **Drone deliveries and 3D printing:** These services operate within a high digital and physical environment but exhibit low social interaction. These innovative technologies leverage digital platforms and advanced manufacturing processes to deliver goods and services efficiently, with limited human-to-human interaction.

7 **Traditional retail services:** The services, encompassing activities like visiting salons or going shopping, operate in a low digital, high physical and high social environment. Customers engage in physical spaces, interacting with products and service providers while also socializing with fellow shoppers, emphasizing the social aspect of the retail experience.

8 **Light therapy services:** These services operate in a low digital, high physical and low social environment. These services involve physical interventions for therapeutic purposes, with minimal social interaction and reliance on digital technologies, emphasizing the importance of physical presence for effective treatment.

In the domain of retail and professional services, a transition from traditional service delivery to a more digitalized model is anticipated. Across various B2C sectors, including retail, automotive, consumer goods, logistics, media and professional services, digital technologies have become prevalent. The Covid-19 pandemic highlighted the necessity for businesses to embrace digitalization fully. The pandemic emphasized the significance of robust digital infrastructure, enabling organizations to adapt to sudden shifts towards remote work effectively. Similarly, consumer-facing businesses that excelled during the pandemic demonstrated resilience through robust digital supply chains and platforms, facilitating exceptional customer experiences.

Retailing, in particular, has witnessed significant digital service innovations alongside organizational adaptations. Both in-store and online retail experiences were previously characterized by high physical complexity and social presence. However, with the accelerated digitalization of retail processes, there exists an opportunity to transition from realms of low to high digital density. Retailers are integrating digital channels into physical stores, aiming to expand their physical presence into the digital realm. Simultaneously, online retailers are opening physical shops in high-profile locations to create experiences that cannot be delivered through a device. Traditional and online retailers are working towards a common goal: providing a highly personalized, consistent and integrated shopping experience across all points of contact between retailers and customers. Integrating digital technologies with physical environments enhances the customer experience and improves employee performance.[42]

In the realm of professional services, there is a shift towards digital platforms offering a convenient alternative to the traditional physical marketplace for professional assistance. As services transition from traditional to digital, employees and customers participate in co-creating services within a high digital density environment. The future for the retail and professional services world involves a shift to digital offerings blended with physical spaces, aiming to meet evolving customer expectations for 24/7 access to services and personalized experiences. As the industries adapt, examples of present retail and professional service offerings illustrate this transition, including videoconferencing tools reshaping communication in the legal profession and unstaffed convenience stores offering seamless customer experiences through digital technology and AI systems. Additionally, services connecting customers to freelancers on demand and the emergence of AI lawyers demonstrate the evolving landscape towards digitalization and personalized service delivery.

KEY TAKEAWAYS

We examined the three key realms of customer experience and explored a framework to integrate them into a multidimensional approach.
Our findings revealed that:

- Customers now demand more from brands in the experience economy.
- Customer experience (CX) is holistic, involving interactions across various touchpoints.
- Organizations should design services and CX seamlessly across physical, digital and social realms.
- Each realm has distinct characteristics: digital density, physical complexity and social presence.
- Industries like B2B, healthcare and B2C are evolving to offer a consistent and seamless experience by connecting these realms.

Let's proceed to the following chapter, where we will explore how to define your journey through the elements of value creation.

Notes

1 Pine, B J II and Gilmore, J H (1998) Welcome to the experience economy, *Harvard Business Review*, July–August. https://hbr.org/1998/07/welcome-to-the-experience-economy (archived at https://perma.cc/3B9A-P7SB)

2 Zaki, M (2019) Digital transformation: Harnessing digital technologies for the next generation of services, *Journal of Services Marketing*, 33 (4), 429–35

3 PwC (2024) Experience is everything: Here's how to get it right. www.pwc.com/us/en/services/consulting/library/consumer-intelligence-series/future-of-customer-experience.html (archived at https://perma.cc/AFF2-VM9C)

4 ibid.

5 Salesforce (2020) What are customer expectations, and how have they changed? www.salesforce.com/resources/articles/customer-expectations/ (archived at https://perma.cc/D667-K2DF)

6 Lucas, C (2024) 5 mobile marketing mistakes – and how to fix them. https://socpub.com/articles/5-mobile-marketing-mistakes-%E2%80%93-and-how-to-fix-them-12441 (archived at https://perma.cc/3QSU-HPWA)

 7 Cision PR Newswire (2024) Wunderman study reveals 79% of consumers only
    buy from brands that prove they care about earning their business.
    www.prnewswire.com/news-releases/wunderman-study-reveals-79-of-
    consumers-only-buy-from-brands-that-prove-they-care-about-earning-their-
    business-300386618.html (archived at https://perma.cc/F95S-Q3XS)

 8 Vincent, J (2018) Robot assembles IKEA furniture: A robot from Singapore's
    Nanyang Technological University builds an IKEA chair, *The Verge*, 18 April.
    www.theverge.com/tldr/2018/4/18/17251016/robot-ikea-furniture-assembly-
    singapore-university-stefan-chair (archived at https://perma.cc/7A3W-DMDY)

 9 Mills, A, Rodriguez, E and Shepardson, D (2024) Global cyber outage hits air
    travel, leaving passengers in limbo, Reuters, 19 July. www.reuters.com/
    business/aerospace-defense/air-travel-hit-by-global-cyber-outage-2024-07-19/
    (archived at https://perma.cc/WV6V-VDLA)

10 Zaki, M (2019) Digital transformation: Harnessing digital technologies for the
    next generation of services, *Journal of Services Marketing*, 33 (4), 429–35

11 Bolton, R N, McColl-Kennedy, J R, Cheung, L, Gallan, A, Orsingher, C, Witell,
    L and Zaki, M (2018) Customer experience challenges: Bringing together
    digital, physical and social realms, *Journal of Service Management*, 29 (5),
    776–808

12 ibid.

13 Gautam, J and Zaki, M (2024) Achieving excellence in managing customer
    experience, 2024 Summer AMA Proceedings. www.ama.org/wp-content/
    uploads/2024/08/2024-Summer-AMA-Proceedings_August_12_2024.pdf
    (archived at https://perma.cc/VBR7-UV4V)

14 Bolton, R N, McColl-Kennedy, J R, Cheung, L, Gallan, A, Orsingher, C, Witell, L
    and Zaki, M (2018) Customer experience challenges: Bringing together digital,
    physical and social realms, *Journal of Service Management*, 29 (5), 776–808

15 Bughin, J, Seong, J, Manyika, J, Chui, M and Joshi, R (2018) Notes from the AI
    frontier: Modeling the impact of AI on the world economy, McKinsey Global
    Institute. www.mckinsey.com/featured-insights/artificial-intelligence/notes-
    from-the-ai-frontier-modeling-the-impact-of-ai-on-the-world-economy
    (archived at https://perma.cc/SH7Z-JH8G)

16 Bolton, R N, McColl-Kennedy, J R, Cheung, L, Gallan, A, Orsingher, C, Witell,
    L and Zaki, M (2018) Customer experience challenges: Bringing together
    digital, physical and social realms, *Journal of Service Management*, 29 (5),
    776–808

17 Munster, G (2018) Apple retail's mission: Embodied values, Deepwater
    Management. https://deepwatermgmt.com/apple-retails-mission-embodied-
    values/ (archived at https://perma.cc/ER6T-4MSN)

18 Thau, B (2014) Apple and the other most successful retailers by sales per
    square foot, *Forbes*, 20 May. www.forbes.com/sites/barbarathau/2014/05/20/
    apple-and-the-other-most-successful-retail-stores-by-sales-per-square-foot/
    (archived at https://perma.cc/6LXS-UYMA)

19 Bolton, R N, McColl-Kennedy, J R, Cheung, L, Gallan, A, Orsingher, C, Witell, L and Zaki, M (2018) Customer experience challenges: Bringing together digital, physical and social realms, *Journal of Service Management*, 29 (5), 776–808

20 Wertz, J (2023) The high-tech future of fitting rooms, *Forbes*, 22 November. www.forbes.com/sites/jiawertz/2023/11/22/the-high-tech-future-of-fitting-rooms/ (archived at https://perma.cc/MAC9-5BAJ)

21 Bolton, R N, McColl-Kennedy, J R, Cheung, L, Gallan, A, Orsingher, C, Witell, L and Zaki, M (2018) Customer experience challenges: Bringing together digital, physical and social realms, *Journal of Service Management*, 29 (5), 776–808

22 ibid.

23 ibid.

24 ibid.

25 Zaki, M, McColl-Kennedy, J R and Witell, L (2018) Connecting the digital, physical, and social, Cambridge Service Alliance Insights. https://cambridgeservicealliance.eng.cam.ac.uk/node/1412/connecting-digital-physical-and-social (archived at https://perma.cc/6QMP-4C4U)

26 ibid.

27 Bolton, R N, McColl-Kennedy, J R, Cheung, L, Gallan, A, Orsingher, C, Witell, L and Zaki, M (2018) Customer experience challenges: Bringing together digital, physical and social realms, *Journal of Service Management*, 29 (5), 776–808

28 ibid.

29 Zaki, M, McColl-Kennedy, J R and Witell, L (2018) Connecting the digital, physical, and social, Cambridge Service Alliance Insights. https://cambridgeservicealliance.eng.cam.ac.uk/node/1412/insights-overview (archived at https://perma.cc/3F3Q-QBTL)

30 Bolton, R N, McColl-Kennedy, J R, Cheung, L, Gallan, A, Orsingher, C, Witell, L and Zaki, M (2018) Customer experience challenges: Bringing together digital, physical and social realms, *Journal of Service Management*, 29 (5), 776–808

31 ibid.

32 ibid.

33 Lo, C (2017) Digital twins in shipping: The open-source approach, Ship Technology, 13 November. www.ship-technology.com/features/digital-twins-shipping-open-source-approach/ (archived at https://perma.cc/UG9V-86CQ)

34 MX3D (2024) MX3D Bridge. https://mx3d.com/industries/mx3d-bridge/ (archived at https://perma.cc/NM8X-QZ86)

35 National Infrastructure Commission (2017) Data for the public good. https://nic.org.uk/app/uploads/Data-for-the-Public-Good-NIC-Report.pdf (archived at https://perma.cc/N3YD-3X3S)

36 Orsingher, C, McColl-Kennedy, J R, Zaki, M, Green, T, Varnfield, M, Li, J, Butten, K, Titman, J and Hansen, D (2024) Mobile applications (apps) as service provider actors, *International Journal of Consumer Studies*, 48 (2), e13016

37 World Health Organization (2020) *Global strategy on digital health 2020–2025*. www.who.int/docs/default-source/documents/gs4dhdaa2a9f35 2b0445bafbc79ca799dce4d.pdf (archived at https://perma.cc/Z3R4-2B2Z)

38 Bolton, R N, McColl-Kennedy, J R, Cheung, L, Gallan, A, Orsingher, C, Witell, L and Zaki, M (2018) Customer experience challenges: Bringing together digital, physical and social realms, *Journal of Service Management*, 29 (5), 776–808

39 UCHealth (2024) Da Vinci surgical system. www.uchealth.com/services/ robotic-surgery/patient-information/davinci-surgical-system/ (archived at https://perma.cc/KJ9L-TQN2)

40 Statista (2021) Coronavirus: Impact on the retail industry worldwide – statistics & facts. www.statista.com/topics/6239/ coronavirus-impact-on-the-retail-industry-worldwide/ (archived at https://perma.cc/LMG8-QMPG)

41 Bolton, R N, McColl-Kennedy, J R, Cheung, L, Gallan, A, Orsingher, C, Witell, L and Zaki, M (2018) Customer experience challenges: Bringing together digital, physical and social realms, *Journal of Service Management*, 29 (5), 776–808

42 ibid.

4

Customer journey

In this chapter, we will provide a comprehensive exploration of customer journey design aimed at integrating existing research and practical insights to understand better various facets of CX, including value-creation elements such as resources, activities, context, interactions and customer roles. We discuss the importance of exploring cognitive responses and the discrete emotions that customers experience at different touchpoints throughout their journey. By incorporating these elements, practitioners are able to create a more value-based customer journey, ensuring significant interactions throughout the customer experience.

As discussed in Chapters 2 and 3, it's crucial to consider CX as a holistic experience that includes a series of touchpoints in an end-to-end journey, engaging the customer's cognitive, affective, emotional, social and sensory aspects. With this perspective, we aim to go beyond traditional tools like persona creation, journey mapping and emotion mapping.

The focus here is on helping you to add a value-creation elements perspective to your journey design and discuss the key pillars to create a seamless and consistent customer journey.[1] Additionally, I incorporate a structured approach to guide you in evaluating the present configuration of your service's journey and exploring how it might be changed in the future.

Touchpoints

A touchpoint is an episode of direct or indirect interaction with a firm.[2] These interactions can unfold across a variety of channels, such as digital platforms (like websites or applications), physical spaces (including stores, offices, or other locations), or social interactions (ranging from person-to-person, person-to-entity, or person-to-digital engagements).

When designing these touchpoints, we aim to thoroughly understand the customer's journey through specific interactions. By defining both current and prospective service touchpoints, professionals can pinpoint areas needing enhancement and devise plans to mitigate any difficulties or friction points, thereby increasing customer satisfaction.

Organizations often approach the design of these touchpoints from their own perspective and expertise, given their familiarity with their business and market. Yet, it's not rare for companies to overlook certain touchpoints that customers perceive as critical, thus being taken by surprise by customer interactions at these points.

Take, for instance, an automotive service firm like a regular garage or car dealership, which orchestrates touchpoints around sales, service, parts and workshop activities.

The nature of touchpoints is defined by the garage. Are they digital, physical, social, or a mix? How do interactions between the customer and the garage occur within these touchpoints?

Do the touchpoints outlined by the garage cover all possible customer interactions? If any are overlooked, what nature do these interactions have? Where do they happen?

- The **sales function** typically involves sales representatives engaging with both new and current customers to propose new deals and sell vehicles. This can happen physically in the dealership, through social interactions like phone calls, or via digital means such as emails, emphasizing the importance of direct human interaction.

- **Post-sale**, customer service becomes a critical touchpoint. Many businesses, including car dealerships, may outsource this service, not recognizing it as a direct touchpoint. However, customers usually see this as part of their interaction with the brand, and designing and managing this touchpoint well is the firm's responsibility.

- **Routine mechanical services** are conducted in the physical workshop connected to the dealership, where customers interact with mechanics (human-to-human). Additionally, customers might engage digitally by ordering car parts through the company's website, which involves further human interaction during delivery.

Beyond these defined touchpoints, customers often encounter others not initially considered by the automotive service provider, such as **credit and financing** for car loans, often managed by external partners, or **road service offerings** to prevent breakdowns, necessitating the integration and management of these additional touchpoints for a comprehensive end-to-end experience.

Value-creating elements

When exploring the customer experience journey, it is crucial to start by examining the concept of value-creation elements or value-creating elements – terms we'll use interchangeably – and their impact on the customer experience (CX). Customers add value to a company not just through their purchases but through their entire experience of interacting with the brand.

This experience includes an array of resources and activities at different touchpoints, leading to various emotional and cognitive responses from customers at each phase.[3]

To guarantee a favourable experience, it's essential for organizations to identify and generate a comprehensive set of value-creating elements. This entails considering the entire customer journey and all the touchpoints where customers engage with the brand to understand which elements are most instrumental in delivering value to customers.

Moreover, organizations must pay attention to the emotional and cognitive reactions of customers at each touchpoint, considering aspects such as customer expectations, emotions, motivations and needs. The design of the customer journey should be tailored to align with these factors, ensuring a value-rich experience for the customer, which leads to increased customer loyalty and long-term success.

Resources

Resources are defined as the crucial capabilities, knowledge, functions, systems and skills that a company must possess to deliver value to its customers.[4]

Consider a business-to-business (B2B) company as an example. Its resources could include a variety of elements, such as:

- **Internal company resources** (like sales staff, service technicians and internal systems).
- **Customer resources** (such as knowledge of products or equipment and skills that enable efficient use of goods or services).
- **Competitor resources** (like alternative providers in the industry that customers might consider for similar products and/or services).

Take technology service providers like Microsoft and Google, for instance. They offer cognitive services as a resource to customers through platforms like Azure and Google Cloud. For example, Microsoft Azure Cognitive

Services is a collection of APIs (application programming interfaces) that empower customers to incorporate intelligent algorithms into their applications, providing capabilities such as sentiment analysis, text translation, speech recognition and image recognition.

Utilizing Azure Cognitive Services allows customers to develop intelligent services capable of understanding, reasoning and interacting with humans in more intuitive ways. This enhances customer experience, automates processes, and facilitates more efficient and effective data insight acquisition. Consequently, Microsoft's cognitive services represent a significant digital resource for customers aiming to utilize AI technologies to increase their business operations, customer experiences and offerings, also positioning Microsoft competitively in the tech industry.

Financial institutions, including banks and investment firms, gain a competitive edge by strategically utilizing their financial resources. For instance, their access to substantial pools of funds allows them to fulfil their financial commitments or extend loans to customers (businesses and individuals). This capability offers them a competitive advantage in liquidity management, facilitating the seizing of investment opportunities. Additionally, these institutions invest significantly in digital resources (e.g. digital apps), enhancing their ability to offer superior customer service, accelerate transactions, and ensure more robust data security. By leveraging their technological infrastructure, they can innovate new financial products and services, maintain a lead over competitors, and enhance operational efficiency.

Activities

Activities encompass the cognitive and behavioural aspects of a firm's actions, including performing tasks or actions.[5]

These actions may be undertaken by various stakeholders, such as the company itself, its key suppliers and customers, and in some scenarios may involve competitors.

The range of activities is broad, from simple tasks like placing orders and organizing information to more complex ones like delivering services and customers obtaining parts themselves.

By innovating in how services are delivered, companies can distinguish themselves from competitors and provide a smooth service experience, often leveraging technology for a competitive edge.

EXAMPLES

- **A B2B example** involves CEMEX using its digital app CEMEX Go to proactively inform customers of low material stock based on usage patterns and automatically replenish supplies. This feature removes the need for manual reordering, ensuring customers consistently have the necessary materials on hand.

- **In the B2C realm**, Amazon Prime offers a compelling case with its rapid delivery service, often within one or two days, depending on the location. Customers can compile a shopping list using the mobile app or Amazon's Alexa, receiving their items as quickly as the same or the next day. This efficiency saves time and eases the frustration associated with longer wait times common with other retailers.

- **For city traffic management**, many municipalities utilize their transportation departments to streamline traffic flow. They automate traffic signals in real time as an activity to adjust traffic volume, pedestrian presence and emergency vehicle passage. This approach eases congestion, enhances safety and reduces travel times for both drivers and pedestrians.

Context

Companies can enhance their competitive edge and design distinctive service experiences by targeting particular scenarios that promote positive customer experiences, such as offering weekend services or deliveries or accommodating future service visits. Research indicates that value co-creation is closely linked to the specific context in which a service is delivered.

Context encompasses the situational elements that can either enhance or detract from a customer's experience.[6]

The importance of context in service delivery cannot be overstated, as it forms the backdrop against which customers evaluate their experiences. The context of a service includes all background, factors, settings and circumstances influencing the customer's perception and interaction with the service.

For instance, in a restaurant setting, the context includes aspects like the type of cuisine, the décor, ambiance, music, and even external factors like the weather. Each of these elements plays a role in creating the restaurant's atmosphere, which, in turn, influences the customer's dining satisfaction and likelihood of returning.

Acknowledging that context may involve elements beyond the service provider's immediate control is crucial. Thus, understanding and strategically analysing these contextual factors is vital, as they significantly impact customers' service value perceptions.

Similarly, the context surrounding a customer service touchpoint might involve the customer's current mood, the complexity of their issue, and their past interactions with the company. These factors collectively shape how the customer views the service received and their overall satisfaction levels.

By comprehensively understanding the contexts in which their services are rendered, businesses can more accurately align their offerings with customer needs and expectations. This may include developing services that are closer to customer emotions or preferences or shaping experiences specifically tailored to the relevant service contexts.

Ultimately, the deliberate consideration and integration of context into service design is crucial for delivering superior services, achieving a competitive advantage, and fostering durable customer relationships.

Interactions

Interactions describe the ways in which customers engage with a brand or other participants within the service network, including digital channels.[7]

Interactions can occur between humans or between humans and non-human elements, such as digital technologies, and they play a pivotal role in shaping the customer experience (CX). The service industry recognizes that customers' evaluation of service experiences hinges on these interaction types.

Interactions serve as a key differentiator for businesses. Through active engagement, collecting feedback and fostering personalized connections, companies can design exceptional experiences that distinguish them from competitors and fuel long-term achievement. Effective interaction strategies enable firms to understand customer preferences, interests and behaviours, allowing for tailored offerings and recommendations. This personalization promotes trust, making customers feel appreciated and understood, which in turn increases loyalty and engagement.

Digital technology has emerged as a significant player in service interactions, enhancing various customer activities, and it will continue to grow in importance across both B2B and B2C sectors. The future will likely see an increase in human-to-digital interactions, challenging companies to develop sophisticated and reliable technologies to ensure seamless and convenient customer experiences.

Examples include service robots like Pepper, which engage in enriching social interactions across various sectors such as hospitality, healthcare and education. In the B2B realm, autonomous equipment powered by AI and robotics, like autonomous Caterpillar machines, perform tasks on construction sites without human intervention, handling routine or hazardous tasks.

Here's how digital technology is revolutionizing customer interactions:

- **Digital channels**: Businesses offer various platforms for customer interaction, including social media, chatbots, email, websites and mobile apps, allowing customers to choose their preferred method of engagement.

- **AI personalization**: Companies use AI to personalize interactions based on customer preferences, behaviours and history. Services like YouTube and Spotify, for example, leverage AI to recommend content that is aligned with each user's preferences.

- **Automation**: Businesses automate routine customer interactions through technologies like chatbots, which handle basic inquiries, thereby enabling faster and more efficient service while allowing human agents to deal with more complex issues.

- **Immersive experiences**: Augmented reality and emerging technologies, like the metaverse, offer immersive experiences, such as virtual try-ons for clothes or visualizing furniture in one's home, enhancing engagement and creating memorable brand interactions.

Customer role

The role of the customer includes a learnt set of behaviours observable across various service settings.[8] This role is understood as the part a customer plays in delivering a service, which can vary from being an engaged, active participant to a more passive recipient of the service.

From a design viewpoint, companies might encourage customers to take an active or passive part in service delivery. Examples of active participation include customers using mobile apps for hotel check-ins, ordering food in restaurants, or executing tasks traditionally managed through direct human interactions, such as using self-service kiosks or ATMs. Conversely, passive participation might be seen in scenarios like using cashierless checkout services in retail stores like Amazon Go.

From a customer experience (CX) management perspective, actively involved customers might offer suggestions for service or product enhancement, engage in price negotiations, or serve as brand advocates by recommending the service to others through positive online reviews. On the other hand, passive customers might accept the services as provided without engaging in activities that could influence or enhance the service delivery.

Many companies are now employing technology to streamline their services, effectively reducing the customer's role in the service creation process to offer **hassle-free services,** thereby returning valuable time to the customer. This approach, by minimizing the customer's active involvement through technological solutions, may render some interactions more passive. Nonetheless, this shift is often viewed favourably as it enhances convenience, ease of use and efficiency, contributing to greater customer satisfaction and loyalty. Organizations increasingly utilize behavioural data as a feedback tool to identify and address potential issues without direct customer input proactively. For instance, Netflix uses machine learning (ML) to enhance streaming quality by addressing various technical challenges. They employ ML to predict network quality and adapt video quality in real time based on network conditions, reducing buffering and improving user experience. Predictive caching is used to pre-load content likely to be watched, speeding up start times and enhancing quality. Additionally, ML helps in device anomaly detection by identifying and prioritizing potential device issues, improving reliability across thousands of devices. These efforts ensure optimal streaming experiences for Netflix's global audience.[9]

Emotions

The link between emotions and experiences has roots in the theories of experiential scholars from the 1980s. Customers' emotional reactions during their experiences are often referred to as affective responses or discrete emotions.[10]

Although the precise number of these emotions is subject to debate, it's broadly acknowledged that several core emotions are biologically ingrained and universally recognized across cultures. These fundamental emotions include joy, love, surprise, anger, sadness and fear. Consequently, companies deliberately design experiences to elicit positive emotions, as these significantly influence customers' perceptions and memories of their interactions with a product, service or brand.

Reducing negative emotions is crucial. Therefore, companies design the customer journey to match customers' needs, desires and expectations, setting their offerings apart from competitors and promoting a more impactful and memorable customer experience. This strategy aims to enhance satisfaction and loyalty and, ultimately, influence customers' decisions to purchase and advocate for the service.

Disney demonstrates the strategic use of emotion through **storytelling**, adapting well-known tales into cherished movies that stimulate strong emotional responses in audiences. Disney theme parks and attractions create immersive environments that evoke nostalgia and transport guests to fantastical worlds, with attention to detail to raise emotional connections. For instance, attractions like Alice's Tea Cups, Pirates of the Caribbean, It's a Small World and the Haunted Mansion immerse visitors in narrative-driven experiences.[11]

Musical elements in Disney parks, with their iconic songs and scores, play a crucial role in setting the emotional tone and enhancing storytelling. The characters, relatable and endearing, with rich personalities and back stories, further deepen the emotional impact. Encounters with characters such as Mickey Mouse, Cinderella or Tigger leave lasting memories through moments of surprise and delight, including unexpected interactions, hidden surprises, or magical effects that spark wonder and joy.[12]

Disney's nightly fireworks create magical atmospheres with sound and light displays, while parades bring excitement with elaborate floats, vibrant costumes and beloved characters. Dining experiences at Disney are as memorable as the attractions themselves, featuring themed restaurants and unique offerings like the iconic Dole Whip and inventive cocktails.[13]

By weaving emotional elements throughout their theme parks and attractions – through music, storytelling and character interactions – Disney designs immersive experiences that evoke positive emotions across various touchpoints. This emotional engagement leads to increased customer delight and loyalty, showcasing the power of emotions in creating memorable experiences.

Cognitive responses

Cognitive responses play a pivotal role in both the design and evaluation of experiences, as organizations must design journeys that are easy for customers to understand and navigate, thereby reducing cognitive load and effort. These responses, including attention, memory, perception and reasoning, are integral to the customer's decision-making process.[14]

The management of cognitive resources is critical, as it greatly influences an individual's capacity to process and react to information and stimuli provided by organizations.

Organizations should be aware of the cognitive resources their customers have at their disposal and tailor their interactions to prevent overwhelming or confusing them.

The availability of information and stimuli can significantly affect an individual's ability to focus, process information and make decisions.[15]

For instance, a customer shopping online for a new phone might become overwhelmed by an abundance of information on various models, specifications and features, leading to decision fatigue and possibly abandoning the purchase. Conversely, presenting information in a clear, concise manner facilitates decision-making, increasing the likelihood of a purchase.

In customer experience, recognizing how customers cognitively react to interactions with touchpoints is essential for service innovation and improvement, influencing customers' beliefs, perceptions and evaluations of a product or service. Such insights can enhance customer engagement, satisfaction and loyalty.

Identifying areas for improvement through customer feedback is crucial. Negative cognitive responses to specific product features can prompt companies to make enhancements or eliminate those features. Cognitive responses provide valuable feedback on what companies are doing well and areas requiring improvement, including complaints, compliments and suggestions for enhancements.

Complaints signify customer dissatisfaction, compliments reflect personal praise, and suggestions offer ideas for service improvement.[16]

By shaping customer journeys and responding effectively to feedback, companies can constructively promote repeat business and positive reviews while addressing negative feedback. Engaging with customer feedback demonstrates a company's commitment to improving customer experiences and increasing satisfaction and loyalty.

Amazon demonstrates this with its customer-focused approach and responsive service, effectively addressing frustrations or confusion. By resolving issues promptly, Amazon can transform negative experiences into positive ones, enhancing customer loyalty. Amazon's customer service centres, such as the one in Kennewick, Washington, focus on customer satisfaction rather than minimizing call duration. The company employs over 500 workers at this centre, who handle a wide range of customer inquiries, from technical support for Amazon devices to billing questions and delivery delays. Unlike many call centres, Amazon does not prioritize efficiency metrics like average call handling time but instead uses a negative response rate (NRR) to measure success, aiming to resolve customer issues rather than rush through them.

Amazon's customer-centric approach has led to high customer satisfaction ratings from organizations like Temkin, Zogby Analytics and the Institute of Customer Service in the UK. The company employs various methods to address customer complaints, including a social media team to manage queries and complaints online. Even though Amazon experiences numerous customer service defects, its focus on resolving issues contributes to its strong customer satisfaction performance.[17]

Similarly, companies like McDonald's, by listening to customer suggestions and aligning changes with customer values, such as switching from plastic to paper straws, positively influence cognitive responses and brand perception.[18] Actions like these address environmental concerns, strengthen customer loyalty, and encourage positive word-of-mouth.

Ultimately, the design of customer journeys and responsive feedback mechanisms are key to influencing cognitive responses and shaping customers' perceptions and behaviours towards a brand.

It's crucial to highlight that both cognitive responses and emotions are fundamental to the CX journey, as they significantly impact how customers perceive a brand and their overall satisfaction.

So, what differentiates the two?

Cognitive responses refer to customers' rational and conscious reactions towards specific touchpoints or interactions.[19] These are shaped by the customer's knowledge, beliefs and expectations, and involve assessments of aspects like usefulness, relevance and reliability of the information encountered. For example, customers might judge a product's quality by its features and benefits or assess a service's efficiency by the speed and accuracy of its delivery.

Emotions, conversely, are more subjective and affective responses that arise from interactions or touchpoints.[20] They are rooted in the customer's feelings and attitudes, triggering positive emotions such as joy, happiness and excitement or negative ones like anger, frustration and disappointment. A customer, for instance, might feel delighted receiving a personalized message from a brand or frustrated due to a lengthy wait during a customer service call.

Grasping the significance of cognitive responses and emotions in the CX journey enables organizations to design touchpoints and interactions that provide both the rational and emotional dimensions of customer behaviour. This approach generates a more positive and immersive customer experience.

Thus, organizations should:

- Step back to view the customer journeys from the perspective of the customers themselves.
- Understand how customers move across digital, physical and social touchpoints throughout their journey.
- Identify the resources, activities, interactions, context and roles customers assume at each stage of the journey.
- Assess what works and what doesn't, noting where customers experience strong positive or negative emotions (such as frustration versus love) and cognitive responses (including complaints, compliments and suggestions).
- Prioritize and resolve fundamental customer issues by reimagining future journeys to create a smoother, comprehensive experience, thereby securing a competitive edge in the marketplace.

Next, I will examine a case study contrasting an existing end-to-end customer journey with an optimized version that enhances the customer experience throughout.

Applying the customer journey design framework

Consider a scenario where a customer needs to **schedule a routine service for their car**.

Using the customer journey blueprint provided below in Figure 4.1, professionals can analyse the existing process of booking a car service through various touchpoints and its characteristics (digital, physical and social), incorporating elements of value creation, emotional experiences and cognitive reactions.

This analysis is instrumental in identifying opportunities for enhancing the journey, enriching the customer's experience, and securing a competitive edge.

Current journey

The process of booking a car service typically spans multiple interactions with the service provider, starting from initial research, making the appointment, dropping off the vehicle, receiving progress updates, to finally picking up the car post-service.

FIGURE 4.1 Garage customer journey

Touchpoints	Value creation elements						Emotions	Cognitive responses
Name	Character-istics	Resources	Activities	Context	Interactions	Customer role		
Current CX journey								
Booking a car repair service using a phone	Physical: high						Delighted	Compliment: 'I had a dedicated hot desk to do my work with a nice coffee'
	Digital: low	Workshop	Diagnostics and fixing	Weekend	Human to human	Brings the car to the workshop	Neutral	Suggestion: 'Develop an app to book online instead of calling the service centre'
	Social: low						Frustrated	Complaint: 'Rude engineer'
Future CX journey								
Booking a car repair service using an app	Physical: low		1. Car collection				Joy	Compliment: 'Hassle free'
	Digital: high	Digital app to book a repair service slot	2. Diagnostics and fixing	Week days	Human to machine	Share smart key	Neutral	Suggestion: 'An offer for call by customer rep to summarize the technical terms in the service report'
	Social: low		3. Car return				Annoyed	Complaint: 'Car is not fixed properly and I need to rebook'

In its current form, this journey is notably reliant on direct human interactions (high social), necessitates significant physical infrastructure (high physical), and exhibits minimal digital engagement (low digital). This implies that maintaining such a customer journey requires the garage to either maintain an in-house team or engage a third-party service for customer interaction (high social), invest in physical spaces like offices and workshops (high physical), and operate with limited digital capabilities, lacking in customer-facing solutions or the adoption of advanced technologies like AI (low digital).

TOUCHPOINT 1: INITIAL RESEARCH (LOW DIGITAL)
Initially, customers begin their search for local garages providing the required services. They compare various options based on pricing, services available and customer feedback to inform their decision.

At this stage, garages engage in various marketing efforts such as distributing brochures, placing ads, leveraging word-of-mouth, and conducting email or social media campaigns, among other strategies.

After selecting a preferred garage, customers proceed to book an appointment, typically through a telephone call.

TOUCHPOINT 2: SCHEDULING THE APPOINTMENT (HIGH SOCIAL INTERACTION)
From the perspective of the garage, how customer service is structured – through both resources and activities – can vary significantly based on the garage's size and operational model, whether it's a small business or a well-established brand.

Key resources and activities dedicated to this touchpoint include:

- **Customer service representatives (high social interaction):** This touchpoint primarily involves direct interaction between service personnel and customers. During these interactions, service staff may collect essential details about the vehicle (activity), such as its make and model, along with the specific services needed. Additionally, they'll discuss and set a preferred appointment time and date with the customer (context).

Additional backend resources and activities include:

- **Appointment scheduling tool:** Representatives utilize specialized software to manage bookings and appointments efficiently. After confirming an appointment, customers typically receive a confirmation via email or SMS.

- **Service quality monitoring team**: The garage implements systems to continually assess the quality of its services, guaranteeing that customers enjoy the highest standard of service.

- **Training and development programmes**: Investing in employee training and development is crucial for garages. This investment enhances staff skills and knowledge, enabling them to interact with customers empathetically and respond to inquiries promptly, thereby elevating the overall quality of customer service.

TOUCHPOINT 3: VEHICLE DROP-OFF (HIGH PHYSICAL INTERACTION)

On the appointment day, customers actively (customer role) participate by bringing their vehicles to the garage at the scheduled time.

Upon arrival, they are welcomed by a staff member who may request further details or specific instructions about the required service, facilitating direct human-to-human interaction.

Customers might need to complete and sign a consent form authorizing the garage to proceed with the necessary work, highlighting their active involvement in the process (customer role).

With the vehicle now in the garage's care, mechanics utilize their skills and tools to execute the requested services (activities).

Additional backend resources and activities include:

- **Diagnostic and repair tools** (resources): The garage invests in advanced tools and equipment to enable mechanics to diagnose and repair vehicles, ensuring a quick and efficient turnaround.

- **Availability of parts** (resources): The garage ensures a stock of essential parts – like tyres, brakes and other critical components – tailored to the services offered, ensuring repairs are completed without unnecessary delays.

TOUCHPOINT 4: UPDATE COMMUNICATION (HIGH SOCIAL INTERACTION)

The duration of the work can vary from a few hours to several days, depending on the required services. During this period, the garage ensures the customer is kept up to date on the progress through phone calls or text messages.

Additional backend resources and activities:

- **Information display screen**: A screen may be installed at the reception area to visually update customers on the progress of their service (activities).

- **Alert system:** An alert system could be implemented to send notifications directly to the customer, either via text messages or calls from customer service representatives, ensuring timely and efficient communication.

TOUCHPOINT 5: VEHICLE COLLECTION (HIGH PHYSICAL INTERACTION)

Upon completion of the service, the customer is informed and invited to collect their vehicle at a time that suits them best (activities).

Additional backend resources and activities:

- **Payment and invoicing tools (resources):** The garage issues a detailed invoice outlining the services performed and any parts replaced. Additionally, a guarantee or warranty for the services provided may be offered, enhancing customer trust and satisfaction.

Customer evaluation: emotional and cognitive feedback Creating a consistent and seamless experience across all touchpoints is crucial for the development of customer trust and loyalty, which, in turn, encourages repeat business and positive feedback.

In this scenario, customers expressed satisfaction and were offered praise during physical interactions (such as service at the dedicated desk in the garage), yet they experienced some dissatisfaction due to the mechanics' behaviour (leading to complaints about rudeness). The absence of digital options led to a neutral assessment from the customer, who suggested implementing an app to streamline the booking process.

Utilizing customer feedback Professionals have various methods at their disposal to gather and analyse customer feedback, including:

- **Existing customer surveys and social media monitoring:** These tools can capture a wide range of customer emotions and cognitive responses.

- **Direct interviews with customers:** Engaging in conversations with customers to get first-hand accounts of their service experiences.

- **Role-playing exercises:** Simulating customer interactions based on professional experience to understand potential customer reactions.

- **Creating hypothetical scenarios:** Using imagined situations to predict customer responses and gauge potential improvements.

- **Large language model support**: Synthetic user research, enabled by generative AI through persona prompt engineering, could be one of the modern ways to simulate customers' responses in specific scenarios.

Future journey   In this scenario, the company reviews the customer's recommendation. It invests in creating a digital pathway, enabling customers to schedule car services via a digital application or platform, thereby enhancing the service experience.

Imagine a car owner who opts to book their service using the digital app

A SINGLE TOUCHPOINT: THE DIGITAL APP

This touchpoint is characterized by its high digital engagement, with minimal social and physical interaction. The app helps customers choose their service date and time and specify the required service. It provides a comprehensive door-to-door service, where a staff member or a third party will collect and return the customer's car to the specified location. Additionally, the app offers an initial cost estimate based on diagnostic services and secures customer approval.

After booking, the app prompts the customer to share a digital key for car access any day of the week. The service team executes the requested services, keeping the customer informed about the progress until completion. The vehicle is then prepared for return to the customer's chosen location.

The service summary is delivered to customers via email and within the app, detailing the diagnostics and repairs undertaken. Payment is seamlessly processed through the app using pre-registered credit card details.

This digital transformation allows the company to **reduce its physical footprint** and **partner with other service providers to fulfil services efficiently**.

Investing in backend resources and activities includes:

- **App development and maintenance**: Allocating resources for app design, programming, testing and ongoing maintenance.
- **Hosting and server costs**: Ensuring the app is reliably hosted, requiring funds for server hosting and maintenance.
- **Marketing and advertising**: Utilizing resources for digital marketing efforts to encourage app usage, including social media, email campaigns and search engine optimization (SEO).

- **Digital customer support:** Providing chatbot and live support to assist app users with inquiries and technical support.

- **Payment processing:** Setting up and maintaining a secure online payment system within the app.

- **Partnerships and collaborations:** Establishing agreements with local service providers to extend service offerings through the app.

- **Data and analytics:** Collecting and analysing user data to continuously improve the app and overall customer experience.

Customer evaluation: emotional and cognitive feedback   The app allows customers to provide real-time feedback after service completion, offering insights on service improvement. For instance, customers might report dissatisfaction through the app if issues arise, such as improper service completion.

The ease and efficiency of the digital service typically result in positive customer reactions, praising the hassle-free experience. However, suggestions for enhancing the digital journey, like incorporating follow-up calls for service clarification, indicate customers' desire for a balance between digital convenience and personal interaction.

Advantages for customers using a digital booking system   Adopting a digital platform for garage service bookings offers numerous advantages for customers:

- **Convenience:** Eliminates the necessity to physically visit or call the garage, saving valuable time and effort.

- **Real-time updates:** Keeps customers informed about the status of their service, alleviating anxiety and uncertainty.

- **Feedback for improvement:** Facilitates the collection of feedback, enabling ongoing enhancement of services and enriching the customer experience.

- **Effortless service:** Provides a hassle-free experience with door-to-door vehicle collection and return services.

Benefits for garages utilizing a digital solution   For garages, transitioning to a digital booking system yields significant benefits:

- **Enhanced efficiency:** Simplifies the booking process, making it quicker and more straightforward for customers, thereby reducing the demands on staff for manual booking tasks.

- **Cost reduction:** Lowers expenses linked to traditional advertising and eliminates the inefficiencies of paper-based systems and excessive phone communication.

- **Elevated customer experience:** Delivers a seamless way for customers to schedule services and obtain service information, boosting satisfaction and fostering loyalty.

- **Market differentiation:** Sets the garage apart from competitors lacking similar digital offerings, aiding in customer acquisition and retention.

- **Insightful data analytics:** Gathers and analyses customer data to refine services and personalize the customer experience more effectively.

- **Growth opportunities:** Opens new avenues for market expansion and the introduction of additional services like mobile repairs or emergency roadside assistance.

- **Wider customer reach:** Attracts a broader audience, especially those who prefer the convenience of online or mobile booking, potentially increasing the customer base and revenue.

KEY TAKEAWAYS

As we discussed so far, any customer journey spans numerous touchpoints throughout their interaction with the organization. These touchpoints include a variety of interactions and activities and may recur as customers engage with the company through digital, physical and social channels multiple times. Organizations should focus in order to:

- enhance these touchpoints, it is essential to design them from the perspective of the customer, not just the organization's perspective. In rethinking customer experience (CX) and journey design, adopting a customer-focused mindset and aiming for an end-to-end journey are key.

- identify and understand the major pain points from the customer's viewpoint, transforming these challenges into opportunities for enhancing the CX. Thus, employing the customer journey guided framework to evaluate value-creation elements across touchpoints is essential.

- identify potential future configurations and elements that achieve a competitive advantage and drive value creation, such as resources, activities, context, interactions and customer roles. Understanding how

> these differ from current or market configurations is crucial for designing future experiences that offer this competitive edge.
>
> • analyse customers' emotions at particular touchpoints and their cognitive reactions to these experiences, and strategize future journeys that generate a positive experience.

In the upcoming chapter, we will discuss the importance of going above and beyond for the customer to achieve their delight and explore various aspects that can assist in designing a delightful customer experience.

Notes

1 McColl-Kennedy, J R, Zaki, M, Lemon, K N, Urmetzer, F and Neely, A (2019) Gaining customer experience insights that matter, *Journal of Service Research*, 21 (1), 8–26

2 ibid.

3 ibid.

4 ibid.

5 McColl-Kennedy, J R and Zaki, M (2022) Measuring and managing customer experience (CX): What works and what doesn't, in Edvardsson, B and Tronvoll, B (eds), *The Palgrave Handbook of Service Management*, Palgrave Macmillan

6 Ordenes, F V, Theodoulidis, B, Burton, J, Gruber, T and Zaki, M (2014) Analyzing customer experience feedback using text mining: A linguistics-based approach, *Journal of Service Research*, 17 (3), 278–95

7 Bolton, R N, McColl-Kennedy, J R, Cheung, L, Gallan, A, Orsingher, C, Witell, L and Zaki, M (2018) Customer experience challenges: Bringing together digital, physical and social realms, *Journal of Service Management*, 29 (5), 776–808

8 McColl-Kennedy, J R, Zaki, M, Lemon, K N, Urmetzer, F and Neely, A (2019) Gaining customer experience insights that matter, *Journal of Service Research*, 21 (1), 8–26

9 Ekanadham, C (2018) Using machine learning to improve streaming quality at Netflix, Netflix TechBlog, 22 March. https://netflixtechblog.com/using-machine-learning-to-improve-streaming-quality-at-netflix-9651263ef09f (archived at https://perma.cc/7Z4L-JU5T)

10 McColl-Kennedy, J R, Zaki, M, Lemon, K N, Urmetzer, F and Neely, A (2019) Gaining customer experience insights that matter, *Journal of Service Research*, 21 (1), 8–26

11 Burns, W (2015) Disney proves that profitable marketing is about brand stories, *Forbes*, 9 June. www.forbes.com/sites/willburns/2015/06/09/disney-proves-that-profitable-marketing-is-about-brand-stories/ (archived at https://perma.cc/ZV6W-G4QV)

12 Legaspi, A (2022) Music is key to storytelling in 'Disney Princess: Beyond the Tiara' excerpt, *Rolling Stone*, 20 September. www.rollingstone.com/music/music-news/disney-princess-beyond-the-tiara-excerpt-1234595757/ (archived at https://perma.cc/92R3-XGNH)

13 Disney World (2024) Fireworks entertainment at Disney World. www.disneyworld.co.uk/entertainment/fireworks/ (archived at https://perma.cc/72AE-AFJE)

14 McColl-Kennedy, J R, Zaki, M, Lemon, K N, Urmetzer, F and Neely, A (2019) Gaining customer experience insights that matter, *Journal of Service Research*, 21 (1), 8–26

15 McColl-Kennedy, J R and Zaki, M (2022) Measuring and managing customer experience (CX): What works and what doesn't, in Edvardsson, B and Tronvoll, B (eds), *The Palgrave Handbook of Service Management*, Palgrave Macmillan

16 ibid.

17 Greene, J (2015) How an army of Amazon reps handles customer confusion – and rage, *The Seattle Times*, 29 November. www.seattletimes.com/business/amazon/the-view-from-inside-amazon-customer-service-center-in-kent/ (archived at https://perma.cc/GP94-QVQ9)

18 *The Guardian* (2018) McDonald's to switch to paper straws in UK after customer campaign, *The Guardian*, 15 June. www.theguardian.com/business/2018/jun/15/mcdonalds-to-switch-to-paper-straws-in-uk-after-customer-concern (archived at https://perma.cc/HK65-SYDG)

19 McColl-Kennedy, J R and Zaki, M (2022) Measuring and managing customer experience (CX): What works and what doesn't, in Edvardsson, B and Tronvoll, B (eds), *The Palgrave Handbook of Service Management*, Palgrave Macmillan

20 ibid.

5

Customer delight

Let's discuss the concept of customer delight. In an era when customers are more informed and selective than ever, businesses are finding it crucial to offer more than just satisfactory experiences; they need to truly delight their customers. This shift towards focusing on customer delight has become a pivotal element in business strategies.

I will cover the importance of customer delight and discuss why exceeding customer expectations is now a fundamental necessity for companies. Delighting customers leads to greater loyalty, commitment, and a higher likelihood of repeat business, distinguishing it from mere satisfaction, which no longer suffices for ensuring customer loyalty. As competition intensifies, the strategy of delighting customers serves as a means to retain them and prevent them from turning to competitors. We'll explore the six key elements that contribute to designing experiences that not only satisfy but also delight customers.

What does delight mean?

View 1: A blend of joy and surprise

Customer delight is often identified in marketing and consumer behaviour studies as an intensely positive emotional reaction that occurs when a customer's expectations are surpassed in a surprising and unexpected manner. This form of delight is seen as a fusion of joy and surprise.[1] Joy and surprise are primary emotions that merge to create the secondary emotion of delight.[2]

For instance, picture a customer eagerly awaiting the availability of a specific product. Upon purchasing it, they are pleasantly surprised by an unexpected bonus gift. The combination of surprise and joy from receiving this gift can lead to a sense of delight.

Delight can also stem from various types of joy, such as 'magic' joy, which arises from feelings of luck or fate, and 'real' joy, which is based on a sense of connection between the customer and the company.[3]

Consider a loyal customer of a brand like Apple who has a deep emotional bond with the company. Receiving a personalized invitation to an exclusive product launch can create immense excitement and anticipation. This personalized recognition and the event's exclusivity can lead to a profound sense of delight rooted in the customer's connection with the brand and the symbolic value of attending such an event.

Recent positive psychology research suggests that delight may encompass a broader range of positive emotions beyond joy and surprise, such as gratitude, expanding our understanding of what constitutes customer delight.[4]

I've been with Vodafone (telecom operator) for over a decade and have periodically received rewards through their VeryMe rewards programme, such as movie nights or free coffee, though I've never utilized any of these benefits. These rewards are part of Vodafone's #FeelGoodFriday campaign, intended to promote loyalty and surprise among customers. However, I wonder if Vodafone is aware that I have never redeemed any of these rewards and why they continue to offer them, despite their apparent lack of appeal to someone like me. While they might be appreciated by others, what truly matters to me is having a reliable network in my area, which currently isn't the case. This would significantly improve my satisfaction more than any free coffee could. Ultimately, these rewards don't necessarily enhance the customer experience if the core service – network quality (function) – is lacking.

Some readers might wonder why I haven't switched providers. In my view, sectors like telecommunications, insurance, energy and established banking feel quite standardized to customers. While they may compete on prices and products, they rarely do so in terms of experience, delight and loyalty. This is evident when renewing car insurance, for instance, where your current provider often hikes your premium, forcing you to switch despite the market offering lower rates. This behaviour indicates that these industries prioritize temporary promotions and customer acquisition over long-term service and loyalty.

For example, Driverly has tackled this challenge by leveraging insurance technology tailored to young drivers, who are often overcharged by traditional insurers due to perceived risk. Many companies fail to consider customer behaviour and continue to provide generic, uninspiring services, resulting in insurance being viewed as a standardized industry focused more on price competition than competing on the customer experience.[5]

View 2: Extreme satisfaction

Alternatively, delight is viewed as an extreme level of satisfaction positioned at the high end of the satisfaction continuum.[6] This perspective is based on the expectancy–disconfirmation paradigm, which posits that customer satisfaction or dissatisfaction depends on how well expectations are met.

For example, a customer visiting a restaurant with high expectations might be satisfied if those expectations are met. However, if the restaurant surpasses those expectations, the customer may feel delighted. Here, the distinction between satisfaction and delight is a matter of degree, with delight signifying an extreme level of satisfaction.

This viewpoint aligns with the concept of a 'zone of tolerance', where exceeding the desired level of service can lead to delight.[7] This zone is the range within which customers find service performance acceptable, influenced by past experiences, recommendations and marketing. When actual service quality surpasses a customer's desired level, it can trigger delight.[8]

Overall, this alternative perspective suggests delight is an extension of satisfaction achieved by exceeding expectations. However, some studies challenge this view, arguing that delight is distinct from satisfaction and stems from extraordinary service or product performance that is more memorable or unusual than merely satisfying experiences. To differentiate themselves, firms need to understand what constitutes potential delighters versus must-have features,[9] focusing on delivering exceptional experiences that not only meet but exceed customer expectations, creating memorable and loyalty-building experiences.

Customer delight: A practical view

Achieving customer delight is vital for success across industries, whether in B2B, B2C or public services.

- **Enhancing customer loyalty**: Customers who are genuinely delighted by a company's service or product are more likely to remain loyal, making repeat purchases or continuously engaging with the company's offerings. This aspect is incredibly significant in B2B contexts, where the longevity of relationships can determine business success. Consider Salesforce, a leading CRM software provider known for exceptional customer support and a multitude of accolades in service excellence. They offer comprehensive customer success services, including onboarding, training and troubleshooting, supported by a community-driven platform where users and experts exchange knowledge and insights. Through engaging customer interactions, such as events and webinars, Salesforce not only retains a high customer loyalty rate but also stands out in the competitive CRM market.

- **Amplifying word-of-mouth referrals**: Customers delighted with a business are more inclined to recommend it to others, potentially attracting new clientele and boosting revenue. Take Apple as an example; it is a brand synonymous with high customer loyalty in tech. Apple's commitment to seamless user experiences across all devices, coupled with its expert customer support team, ensures customer satisfaction at every touchpoint. The result is a broad, loyal customer base that is willing to advocate for Apple and drive new customer acquisition and sales growth.

- **Strengthening brand reputation**: Delighted customers contribute to a stronger brand image, fostering increased trust, loyalty and revenue. In consumer markets, a reputable brand can command higher prices and stand out from the competition. Luxury brands like Ferrari exemplify this by offering unparalleled service and exclusive customer experiences, such as track days and private factory tours, reinforcing customer loyalty and elevating the brand's prestige and pricing power.

- **Building trust**: In public sectors, delighting customers can significantly enhance the perception and trust in government agencies and services, encouraging more active citizen participation. An example is a public healthcare clinic providing exceptional care, leading to higher patient trust and satisfaction, better health outcomes, and increased confidence in the healthcare system. This positive feedback loop can result in more support and funding, further improving service quality.

The Nusuk website serves as a comprehensive digital platform for pilgrims to secure accommodation, food and guided tours in addition to arranging travel and visas for the annual Muslim pilgrimage (Hajj). Despite its intended purpose to centralize and streamline the booking process for travellers by offering a one-stop solution for organizing their pilgrimage packages, the site is plagued with issues. Its performance is notably sluggish, and it introduces unnecessary complications in the upload process by demanding specific image resizing and formatting – a hurdle that could be easily overcome with built-in vision analytics and automatic resizing features. The verification process for passports can extend over months.

Reserving the chosen package can be highly challenging, with a lack of clarity regarding the procedure. Users might find themselves endlessly reconfiguring their travel and flight packages with many system issues. After overcoming these obstacles, there's still no assurance of selection for the pilgrimage. Users may find themselves in a virtual line with an indication of being directed in over an hour. While it's understood that millions are trying to book their packages online, it's possible that digital solutions might not be the best approach in this scenario. Either thinking of a different approach or reverting to traditional methods could be more effective. For digital offerings to be considered a viable alternative, they must provide a seamless experience rather than a frustrating one. Furthermore, the refund process can be slow, taking anywhere from weeks to a month to a year.[10] Considering the profound emotional significance attached to this religious journey, the inadequate customer experience can significantly diminish the perceived value of the considerable financial investment, which may reach up to £13,000 or more. In this case, while this digital shift is relatively new and likely to see gradual improvement over time, it shows the complexity of delivering a seamless and delightful experience, requiring substantial effort and investment.

By prioritizing exceptional service and experiences that surpass expectations, organizations can forge deeper connections with their customers, secure their success in the long run, and avoid customer disappointment and frustration.

The properties of customer delight

We will discuss the six key properties of delight (Figure 5.1).[11]

Emotion

Customer delight is deeply connected to the experience of positive emotions, with customer experience research revealing a broader spectrum of positive feelings than traditionally recognized in discussions about customer delight.

FIGURE 5.1 The properties of customer delight

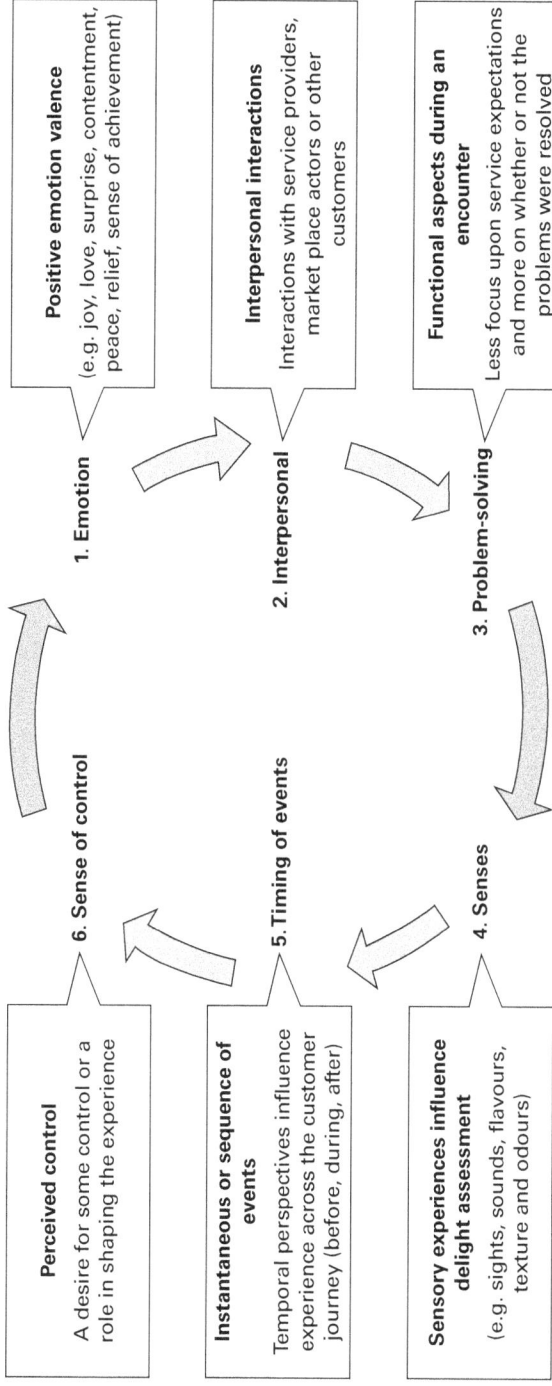

1. Emotion

Positive emotion valence

(e.g. joy, love, surprise, contentment, peace, relief, sense of achievement)

2. Interpersonal

Interpersonal interactions

Interactions with service providers, market place actors or other customers

3. Problem-solving

Functional aspects during an encounter

Less focus upon service expectations and more on whether or not the problems were resolved

4. Senses

Sensory experiences influence delight assessment

(e.g. sights, sounds, flavours, texture and odours)

5. Timing of events

Instantaneous or sequence of events

Temporal perspectives influence experience across the customer journey (before, during, after)

6. Sense of control

Perceived control

A desire for some control or a role in shaping the experience

These emotions extend beyond the frequently mentioned joy and surprise to include contentment, peace, relief and a sense of achievement.[12] For instance, a customer might feel relieved after receiving quick and efficient service from a car rental agency, enhancing their satisfaction with the service.

To nurture feelings of happiness and satisfaction, it's crucial for service professionals to integrate emotions of higher arousal into their service design. A luxury hotel, for example, might evoke awe and enchantment by offering personalized and outstanding service, creating an exceptionally delightful experience for its guests.

Customers' pre-existing mood and emotional state during a service interaction can greatly influence their perception of the experience. A customer in a good mood might overlook slower service at a restaurant, leading to a more favourable impression of the experience. Moreover, delight can arise even from negative emotional states, illustrating customer emotions' complex and varied nature in service experiences. A customer might feel sad about a friend moving away but still cherish a final coffee meet-up, finding delight in the moment.

Southwest Airlines serves as a prime example of leveraging positive emotions to enhance customer delight. Known for its enjoyable flight experience,[13] Southwest's humorous flight attendants and playful passenger interactions foster a positive atmosphere, contributing to the airline's high customer satisfaction and loyalty.

Rather than solely striving to create 'wow' moments, managers should aim to evoke a wider array of emotions associated with delights, such as satisfaction, tranquillity, relief and a sense of accomplishment among customers.

The specific emotions tied to delight will differ based on the interaction context with the company. Employing methods like anthropological research, neuroscience and behavioural economics can help identify these contexts. Given the diverse situations in which interactions occur, making broad assumptions about particular emotions may not always be accurate. Nonetheless, understanding the emotional states customers seek during their interactions can guide the development of services focused on human needs, aiming for customer delight.

This approach can also be beneficial in navigating business challenges. For instance, in 2018, KFC[14] faced a major issue in the UK due to a delivery complication that resulted in a widespread chicken shortage, leading to the temporary closure of numerous outlets. This situation understandably upset many customers. In response, KFC initiated a creative and emotionally resonant advertising campaign that openly acknowledged the problem while assuring customers of their efforts to rectify the issue.[15] The campaign was highlighted by a full-page newspaper ad showing an empty KFC bucket with the tagline, '*We're sorry. A chicken restaurant without any chicken. It's not ideal. Huge apologies to our customers, especially those who travelled out of their way to find we were closed.*'[16]

The advertisement was praised for its openness and wit, and customers admired KFC's straightforward acknowledgement and apology. Additionally, KFC leveraged social media to engage with customers, providing updates on the situation and often replying to individual comments and queries with humorous, personalized messages. These actions effectively softened the blow of the chicken shortage crisis and helped sustain customer loyalty.

Interpersonal interactions

Customer delight also stems from interpersonal interactions, with experiences shaped by the quality of interactions among service providers, customers and other market participants.[17] Respect and sincerity in these interactions are valued, while disrespect is not tolerated. These interactions can significantly impact a customer's experience, either positively or negatively, and do not always require direct engagement. For example, observing a service provider's respectful treatment of others can positively influence a customer's experience.

Interpersonal dynamics play a crucial role, where positive interactions, like a warm greeting from a barista, can significantly enhance a customer's experience by fostering feelings of welcome and appreciation. Conversely, witnessing or experiencing negative interactions can detrimentally affect the customer's perception of the service, highlighting the profound impact of interpersonal relationships on customer delight.

In the context of healthcare, patients often experience worry (emotion) about symptoms or general illness, especially when facing the prospect of undergoing scans or navigating emotionally charged services, such as mammography or oncology treatments. The presence of competent and warm staff throughout the healthcare ecosystem, including doctors, medical technicians, nurses and administrative personnel, can significantly impact patients' experiences. This supportive environment can promote a sense of admiration, reassuring patients that they are in capable hands. In private healthcare settings, such positive experiences can cultivate patient loyalty to the hospital. Conversely, in public healthcare systems like the National Health Service (NHS) in the UK, these interactions enhance trust in public services and elevate patients' overall perceptions of the institution.

It's important to note that direct interaction isn't the only way customer perceptions are influenced. Observing interactions between employees and managers or between other customers can also affect a customer's opinion of their experience.

Moreover, experiencing what it's like to be in the service provider's position, whether it leads to empathy or criticism, can shape one's evaluation of the service received.

For example, a customer who is warmly welcomed by a barista at a coffee shop is likely to feel valued and have a positive experience, fostering feelings of gratitude. Conversely, if the barista behaves rudely or dismissively, the customer may feel unwelcome and leave with a negative impression, regardless of the quality of the coffee. Furthermore, observing a barista's rudeness towards others can tarnish a customer's overall experience, even if their personal interaction was positive, due to the negative emotions such as anger that it evokes.

Companies should highlight the role of personal connections in achieving customer delight, as happiness often stems from shared experiences. Psychology research echoes this sentiment, indicating that personal relationships are a key component of happiness. To promote favourable interactions between employees and customers, managers should focus on qualities such as responsiveness, assurance and empathy.

Equally important is the effect of customers' interactions with both close contacts, like friends and family, and broader networks, including online connections. These interactions can be as influential as those between employees and customers.

Managers should explore ways to enable customers to share their positive experiences more easily and provide feedback on their experiences and suggestions for product or service improvement. This collaborative effort, or co-creation, should extend across the entire customer journey, making customers a vital part of the company's offerings.

LEGO excels in engaging with its customers, especially children, by creating enjoyable and interactive experiences. Their stores feature play areas where children can engage with LEGO bricks, fostering a creative and fun environment.

LEGO's customer service is tailored to engage children creatively, responding to inquiries with personalized messages and LEGO-inspired creations. This approach not only strengthens the bond between the child and the brand but also fosters a sense of community.

Furthermore, LEGO leverages social media to showcase user-generated content, encouraging customers to share their experiences and creativity. This strategy has enabled LEGO to cultivate a dedicated customer base and uphold a positive brand reputation through engaging experiences, personalized service and community building.

Problem-solving

Customer satisfaction often stems from effective problem resolution during service interactions.

In scenarios where customers encounter challenges or have unique needs, their primary concern shifts towards the resolution of these issues rather than the overall service experience. A sense of relief and delight is experienced when service providers promptly and successfully address these challenges or needs. For instance, a restaurant patron might be particularly pleased when a chef makes an effort to recreate a discontinued favourite dish, demonstrating that the effort to resolve the customer's issue can be more impactful than the actual outcome.

This concept extends to more utilitarian service environments, such as automotive repair, furniture delivery or cable TV installation, where the emphasis is on functional outcomes. Professionals in these fields are expected to concentrate on completing the task at hand. The primary objective for customers in these settings is not to derive pleasure or enjoyment but to achieve practical solutions to their problems or needs. Hence, customer delight can be achieved by focusing on the functional aspects of the service, particularly when the service provider effectively meets the customer's needs or resolves their problems, as I mentioned earlier regarding the examples of Vodafone and insurance companies.

Companies must prioritize problem-solving capabilities in their customer experience design, highlighting the necessity to comprehend and address customer issues effectively. This capability is integral to the reliability aspect of service delivery, encompassing the manner in which services are provided (such as friendliness or rudeness) and the efficiency of the service recovery process.

Ocado is a UK-based online grocery service that encountered significant customer dissatisfaction during the Covid-19 pandemic due to delivery delays and inadequate customer service.[18] Customers experienced difficulties in securing delivery slots for extended periods, contradicting Ocado's assurances of dependable and prompt service. The situation was exacerbated by the website's long queues and Ocado's insufficient communication regarding order updates, leaving customers uncertain about their order status.

Furthermore, Ocado was critiqued for its handling of refunds and cancellations, with numerous reports of challenges in obtaining refunds for cancelled orders or unavailable items. The customer service department was reportedly overwhelmed, struggling to manage the surge in customer queries.

Ocado's inability to fulfil its service promises and provide effective customer support during this period significantly tarnished its reputation and eroded customer trust.

It's important to note that this issue was common to Ocado but was observed across several retailers that needed to prepare to address the crisis, react promptly and maintain clear communication with their customers.

Senses

Customer delight can be evoked through engaging the senses.[19] A prime example of this sensory engagement is the atmosphere of a restaurant. Elements such as lighting, décor, music and the smell of food work together to enhance the dining experience through a rich sensory environment. For instance, a restaurant that offers a warm ambiance with dim lighting, gentle background music and the inviting aroma of cooking can significantly elevate the dining experience, contributing to customer delight.

Sensory experiences are crucial in forming customer perceptions of delight. Visuals, sounds, tastes, textures and scents deeply influence the service experience. These sensory elements can evoke memories of previous experiences, leading to vivid descriptions and often a connection to nostalgia and delightful experiences.

Expressing sensory experiences in words can be challenging. In customer experience research, participants sometimes use comparisons and metaphors to convey their feelings of delight, indicating that while the exact sources of delight may be difficult to identify, the overall impact is recognizable. Thus, businesses should focus on creating positive sensory environments that foster delightful experiences. Achieving this requires careful design of sensory experiences at both digital and physical points of interaction.

While Disney succeeds in delivering enchanting experiences to children in their theme parks, their retail strategy seems to lack imaginative engagement. Instead of immersing children in the magical world of their beloved characters, the focus shifts towards a product-centric model. This model primarily leverages costumes to captivate children's interest, subsequently pressuring parents into purchasing these items. However, an alternative approach to enhance the sensory and imaginative experience for children could lead to a delightful adventure. For example, by introducing a digital mirror to enable children to try on and wear the costumes and immerse themselves in a virtual experience that embodies their favourite characters, Disney could significantly elevate the joy and delight experienced by children. This immersive, character-driven encounter could, in turn, resonate with parents, providing a more fulfilling and memorable event for both children and their families.

Managers need to appreciate the significance of designing experiences that stimulate multiple senses to achieve customer delight. Businesses should strive to integrate features that cater to various senses, including vision, hearing, touch, taste and smell, in their products and services.

Apple has introduced the Apple Card, designed from titanium and adorned with laser-etched designs, offering a distinctive tactile sensation that enhances the overall sensory experience for the user.[20] By engaging several senses, businesses can create experiences that are not only more memorable and satisfying but also foster increased loyalty and positive referrals.

The NBA offers a virtual reality streaming service that allows fans to be courtside at basketball games, regardless of their location.[21] This immersive experience provides a new game perspective, making fans feel closer to the action.

Additionally, some sports teams have developed virtual reality training programmes for fans, simulating the training experience of a professional athlete. These unique and immersive experiences not only engage fans in a novel way but also open new avenues for teams to deepen connections with their audience, enhancing the joy and satisfaction derived from the experience.

Timing

Customer delight can occur spontaneously or develop over a series of events.[22] The timing of service experiences plays a crucial role in shaping customer satisfaction. For instance, in a single day, a customer might enjoy both a quick service experience and a more prolonged engagement.

In a scenario like a morning visit to a favourite coffee shop, a customer may appreciate the efficiency of quickly getting their order and being on their way. Later in the day, the same customer might have a more leisurely experience at a store where a salesperson takes the time to thoroughly explain a product, enhancing the customer's delight. The preference for speedy or relaxed service is subjective and varies depending on the customer's immediate needs or desires during the interaction. This suggests that the desired pace of service can change based on the context of the encounter.

Moreover, industry-specific trends in timing preferences may exist. For example, in healthcare, patients generally wish for quick admittance to see their doctor but prefer a more unrushed visit to ensure thorough communication and relationship building with physicians.

The role of timing in influencing customer satisfaction highlights the importance of understanding temporal aspects throughout the customer journey, including before, during and after service interactions. Many organizations primarily concentrate on interactions during the purchase process and on post-service delivery.

Customers can be immediately delighted by surprise features or benefits accompanying a product, like an unexpected gift with their purchase. Conversely, sustained delight arises from continuous positive interactions with a product or service over time.

In the fitness sector, the rising popularity of fitness-tracking applications and wearable devices illustrates sustained customer delight. These technologies offer users real-time feedback on their physical activities, such as heart rate, calories expended and distance covered. Utilizing these tools allows individuals to monitor their progress and witness improvements in their fitness levels over time, fostering a sense of achievement and prolonged satisfaction.

Furthermore, many fitness-tracking tools enhance user engagement through gamification, including challenges and rewards. For instance, the Nike Run Club app provides features that enable users to set fitness goals, engage in challenges with others, and receive badges and rewards for meeting their objectives.[23] These gamified elements not only make the experience more enjoyable and competitive but also motivate users to continue engaging with the app and pursue their fitness goals.

Hence, fitness-tracking applications and wearable devices exemplify how enduring customer delight can be cultivated through regular positive experiences, augmented by gamification strategies that boost users' motivation and enjoyment.

Control

A sense of control or involvement in the service experience often ignites the sensation of customer delight. This desire for control links back to the concepts of consumer power and behaviour, emphasizing the importance of providing customers with the ability to collaborate with service providers to forge positive experiences and effectively resolve issues when they occur.[24] Applying principles of distributive, procedural and interactional justice in these situations can further enhance customer delight.

Co-creation between customers and service providers is a key strategy for achieving this. For instance, consider a car dealership scenario where a salesperson assists a customer interested in purchasing a new vehicle. Rather than directing the customer towards a specific model or package, the salesperson initiates the conversation with open-ended questions about the customer's needs, driving habits and budget. But it should be brief as customers get bored from a lengthy chat without getting anywhere.

Based on the customer's input, the salesperson then outlines several models or options that could meet the customer's requirements, carefully explaining the advantages and disadvantages of each without imposing any particular choice. By empowering the customer to make the final decision, the salesperson not only builds trust and a positive rapport but also enhances the likelihood of the customer feeling delighted with their purchase over time.

Customer satisfaction and delight are often heightened when individuals perceive a sense of autonomy in their interactions with products or services. This empowerment, stemming from the ability to influence the outcome, can significantly enhance their overall experience.

Achieving this involves strategies like personalization, customization and providing a variety of choices that place decision-making power in the hands of customers. A prime example is Amazon's 1-click ordering feature, which streamlines the purchasing process to a singular action. This functionality reduces complexity and time, thereby granting customers more direct and efficient control over their buying journey, contributing to increased satisfaction and loyalty.

Apple shows another approach to enhancing customer control:

- **Interactive displays:** By allowing hands-on interaction with products, Apple enables customers to better understand and choose the products that best suit their needs.

- **Expert staff**: Apple's knowledgeable personnel offer tailored advice, assisting customers in navigating their choices more effectively.

- **Personalized experiences**: Through the Today at Apple initiative, customers can engage in personalized learning sessions about Apple products, maximizing the value of their purchases.[25]

- **Flexible returns**: A liberal return and exchange policy reassures customers, fostering trust and a sense of security with every purchase.

- **Digital shopping**: The accessibility of Apple's online platforms allows for thorough product research and deliberation at the customer's convenience, further enhancing the sense of autonomy.

This perceived control is crucial in enabling customers to personalize their experience to align with personal needs and preferences, playing a vital role in achieving customer delight.

Customer delight in practice

Customer delight typically emerges from a blend of three or more attributes rather than a single factor or a linear process. This complexity means that delightful experiences can result from various combinations of these attributes.

An example of this multifaceted nature of customer delight comes here: a customer recounted a grocery shopping trip with their family member.[26] The experience could be delightful due to several factors: the store's manageable size (sensory attribute), the friendliness of the staff (interpersonal interaction), an enjoyable experience for the family member (emotional aspect), and the efficiency of the shopping trip (timing).

Our research shows that customer delight is most commonly associated with combinations of three or more attributes, accounting for over 70 per cent of positive experiences.[27] This insight suggests that companies aiming for customer delight should design experiences that incorporate multiple attributes. The most effective path to achieving customer delight involves blending these attributes with a significant focus on emotions, interpersonal interactions and effective problem-solving, as these were identified in 58.2 per cent of delight experiences.[28]

This multi-attribute approach to customer delight highlights several key considerations for professionals designing delightful experiences:[29]

- The range of emotions contributing to delight extends beyond just happiness and surprise.

- Delight often stems from shared experiences, highlighting the importance of interpersonal connections in designing delightful experiences.

- While emotions, interpersonal experiences and problem-solving are frequently cited as sources of delight, other attributes like timing and sensory engagement also play crucial roles in shaping delightful customer experiences. This diversity in attributes reflects the complexity of customer delight and the need for a holistic approach to experience design.

Practitioners should grasp the six key elements of customer delight, which will equip them with innovative strategies for analysing and interpreting customer interactions with their business.

By integrating a detailed and holistic perspective, managers can pinpoint opportunities to enchant customers in ways that serve both the customers' needs and the company's goals. Through an in-depth evaluation of how customers assess their interactions, managers can identify the critical aspects of these engagements for various customer groups, assess how well their company performs in these domains, and brainstorm novel ways to elevate customer delight beyond simple satisfaction or admiration. This approach highlights a vital insight for managers: achieving customer delight necessitates a focus on fostering positive emotions, nurturing interpersonal connections, and effectively resolving problems. While integrating these three components might appear daunting, their synergy is crucial for making truly delightful customer experiences, significantly enhancing the chances of success.

To apply the framework within a specific context, let's consider how many sports clubs, such as Manchester City, a leading football club in the UK, are innovating with virtual reality to immerse fans in the metaverse, complemented by the advent of advanced VR devices from tech firms such as Meta Quest VR and Apple Vision Pro.[30] This adaptation aims to redefine how fans experience football matches, leveraging technology to enhance engagement.

Here, I will show how the six dimensions of customer delight can transcend the viewing experience of football matches, particularly through the innovative use of virtual reality (VR) technology. I will examine how each dimension significantly enhances the fan experience to a state of delight.

- **Emotion**: The anticipation and excitement fans feel when they first put on the VR headset set the stage for an emotional journey. Watching a

Manchester City match in VR as if you are in the stadium exceeds fans' high expectations, delivering a surge of joy and satisfaction. This intense emotional response, triggered by exceeding expectations, lies at the core of customer delight.

- **Interpersonal interactions**: The VR experience allows fans to watch the game together in a virtual space, even if they are physically apart. This shared experience enhances the interpersonal dimension, deepening connections among friends and fellow fans through collaboration and shared excitement, making the match viewing more rewarding and memorable.

- **Problem-solving**: Should fans encounter any technical issues while streaming a match in VR, the prompt and effective resolution by the support team highlights excellent problem-solving. Their ability to quickly address and resolve the issue ensures that fans can continue to enjoy the match with minimal disruption, turning a potential moment of frustration into one of relief and ongoing enjoyment.

- **Senses**: The VR technology immerses fans' senses in high-definition visuals and 3D sound effects, creating a realistic and immersive stadium atmosphere. This sensory-rich environment enhances the match-watching experience, making fans feel as if they are truly present at the game.

- **Timing**: The release of VR features timed with major matches and the availability of exclusive content, such as behind-the-scenes footage or interviews, taps into the timing dimension. The anticipation of new experiences and timely updates keeps the fan experience fresh and exciting, ensuring that the initial delight is not just maintained but enhanced over time.

- **Control**: The VR platform offers fans control over their viewing experience, from selecting different camera angles to choosing which match highlights to watch. This level of personalization empowers fans to customize their match-watching experience according to their preferences, enhancing their sense of autonomy and satisfaction.

Through this example, it's evident how the dimensions of customer delight are merged to create a comprehensive and deeply satisfying fan experience. Each dimension contributes to a holistic sense of delight, from the emotional highs sparked by surpassing expectations to the empowerment offered by personalization and control. This case not only showcases the potential of VR technology to deliver exceptional sports viewing experiences but also illustrates the broad applicability of customer delight principles across different products and services. Whether in sports, entertainment, or any other industry, focusing on these dimensions can help organizations create truly delightful experiences that resonate with and captivate their audiences.

However, understanding and measuring customer delight is crucial for businesses to grasp their customers' emotional reactions and thereby enhance customer satisfaction and loyalty.

It's essential to recognize that certain elements contributing to customer delight might exert a stronger influence than customers are consciously aware of. This is often because such elements operate subconsciously, unnoticed by customers when reflecting on their delightful experiences. Despite this, these elements are usually linked with those most frequently mentioned, like emotional engagement, interpersonal interactions and efficient problem-solving. Thus, integrating all these elements into a thorough approach for designing and managing customer delight is critical. Professionals can utilize various methods to gauge customer delight, including:[31]

- **Critical incident technique:** This method involves asking respondents to recount an exceptionally delightful experience and describe their feelings about it. It can reveal detailed insights into what contributes to customer delight.

- **Customer feedback:** By comparing actual experiences against customer expectations and how much an experience surpasses those expectations, businesses can identify moments of customer delight. Encouraging feedback through various channels like email, phone or online reviews can unearth valuable insights into customer experiences, highlighting areas for improvement or reinforcing positive outcomes.

- **Surveys:** Surveys enable customers to express emotions like delight, elation or joy resulting from positive experiences. Employing semantic differential scales allows for the measurement of surprise or emotional intensity on a numerical scale. Surveys can also probe specific features or aspects of the experience and include open-ended questions for customers to express their feelings freely. They can be conducted through multiple channels, such as email, phone or online.

- **Social media monitoring:** Tracking customer sentiment on social media platforms can provide instant feedback on customer experiences, allowing businesses to swiftly address issues or amplify delightful experiences. These conventional methods enable managers to identify the presence or absence of delight elements in specific contexts, helping them and their staff to apply focused strategies for fostering customer delight.

- **AI tools:** Tools such as natural language processing and tone analytics can automatically analyse data on customer delight by detecting emotions like joy or frustration from various qualitative sources, including surveys, social media, CRM systems, and even voice recordings from customer service interactions. This approach provides a comprehensive view of customer experiences by enabling real-time data collection, processing and analysis across multiple touchpoints, helping to uncover deeper insights into the nuances of customer delight. Further details on these methods will be explored in the following chapters.

KEY TAKEAWAYS

Customer delight is a complex and multidimensional concept that can be achieved through various combinations of elements, each holding different levels of importance to customers. Rather than following a single formula for creating a delightful experience, multiple potential pathways exist.

To enhance customer delight, managers and professionals should focus on integrating six key elements: evoking positive emotions, facilitating social interactions, providing effective problem-solving, engaging the senses, optimizing the timing of events, and offering a sense of control.

Incorporating these elements throughout the customer journey enables businesses to create service experiences that are more likely to delight customers. It is also crucial for professionals to consider customer expectations at each touchpoint and identify different combinations of these elements that can contribute to a delightful experience.

Moreover, training frontline employees can be instrumental in helping them recognize and respond to customer emotions, understand the importance of social interactions, and address problem-solving needs, taking into account the variations in these factors across different situations, customer types and transactions.

To achieve this, the chapter covers several key points:

- The six characteristics that contribute to customer delight, such as engaging multiple senses and providing a sense of control, which can enhance the service experience.

- A triad of elements that can be configured in various ways to achieve customer delight.

- Examples of how businesses use these six characteristics to increase customer satisfaction and tolerance during times of crisis or friction.

- Traditional methods for measuring customer delight, which include the critical incident technique, customer satisfaction surveys and social media monitoring.

In the following chapter, I will explore some of the most significant challenges associated with customer experience and the integrations between digital, physical and social realms, which should be carefully considered before implementation.

Notes

1   Arnold, M, Reynolds, K E, Ponder, N and Lueg, J E (2005) Customer delight in a retail context: Investigating delightful and terrible shopping experiences, *Journal of Business Research*, 58 (8), 1132–45

2   Parasuraman, A, Ball, J, Aksoy, L, Keiningham, T and Zaki, M (2021) More than a feeling? Toward a theory of customer delight, *Journal of Service Management*, 32 (1), 1–26

3   Kumar, A, Olshavsky, R W and King, M F (2001) Exploring alternative antecedents of customer delight, *Journal of Consumer Satisfaction, Dissatisfaction and Complaining Behavior*, 14, 14–26

4   Seligman, M E P and Csikszentmihalyi, M (2014) *Positive Psychology: An Introduction*, Springer

5   Driverly (2024) About us. www.driverly.ai/about (archived at https://perma.cc/FJ9Z-5PQV)

6   Parasuraman, A, Ball, J, Aksoy, L, Keiningham, T and Zaki, M (2021) More than a feeling? Toward a theory of customer delight, *Journal of Service Management*, 32 (1), 1–26

7   Parasuraman, A, Berry, L L and Zeithaml, V A (1991), Understanding customer expectations of service, *Sloan Management Review*, 32 (3), 39–48

8   Parasuraman, A, Ball, J, Aksoy, L, Keiningham, T and Zaki, M (2021) More than a feeling? Toward a theory of customer delight, *Journal of Service Management*, 32 (1), 1–26

9   Schneider, B and Bowen, D E (1999) Understanding customer delight and outrage, *Sloan Management Review*, 41 (1), 35–45

10 Ward, S, Sameja, K and Martin, D (2024) BBC News, Leicester. www.bbc. co.uk/news/uk-england-leicestershire-68169579 (archived at https://perma.cc/ U5GJ-D3E7)

11 Parasuraman, A, Ball, J, Aksoy, L, Keiningham, T and Zaki, M (2021) More than a feeling? Toward a theory of customer delight, *Journal of Service Management*, 32 (1), 1–26

12 ibid.

13 Power J D (2024) Southwest Airlines ranks first in customer satisfaction among economy class passenger, Southwest Airlines Investor Relations, 6 June. www.southwestairlinesinvestorrelations.com/news-and-events/news-releases/ 2024/06-06-2024-160046424 (archived at https://perma.cc/8DKY-XTG4)

14 Fleming, M (2018) KFC uses cheeky print advert to apologise for chicken shortage, *Marketing Week*, 23 February. www.marketingweek.com/kfc-print-advert-to-apologise-for-chicken-shortage/ (archived at https://perma.cc/ BZJ3-JKZY)

15 BBC News (2018) KFC's apology for running out of chicken is pretty cheeky, BBC News, 23 February. www.bbc.co.uk/news/newsbeat-43169625 (archived at https://perma.cc/9CPR-6WPE)

16 KFC (2018) We're sorry. A chicken restaurant without any chicken…, *The Sun* [advertisement], 23 February; also published in *Metro*, 23 February

17 Parasuraman, A, Ball, J, Aksoy, L, Keiningham, T and Zaki, M (2021) More than a feeling? Toward a theory of customer delight, *Journal of Service Management*, 32 (1), 1–26

18 Griswold, A (2020) Coronavirus overwhelms Ocado, Quartz, 21 March. https://qz.com/1819855/coronavirus-overwhelms-ocado-uk-online-grocery-delivery (archived at https://perma.cc/7ZCN-BKQ5)

19 Parasuraman, A, Ball, J, Aksoy, L, Keiningham, T and Zaki, M (2021) More than a feeling? Toward a theory of customer delight, *Journal of Service Management*, 32 (1), 1–26

20 Apple (2018) The simplicity of Apple. In a credit card, Apple. www.apple.com/ apple-card/ (archived at https://perma.cc/WHP2-HZSA)

21 Young, J (2022) Here's what it's like watching an NBA game courtside – in the metaverse, CNBC, 15 January. www.cnbc.com/2022/01/15/nba-games-in-virtual-reality-have-potential-heres-what-watching-one-is-like.html (archived at https://perma.cc/VCM5-NFW6)

22 Parasuraman, A, Ball, J, Aksoy, L, Keiningham, T and Zaki, M (2021) More than a feeling? Toward a theory of customer delight, *Journal of Service Management*, 32 (1), 1–26

23 Nike (2022) How the Nike Run Club app can help you reach your running goals, Nike, 7 June. www.nike.com/gb/a/running-goals (archived at https:// perma.cc/J8UX-2UVW)

24 Parasuraman, A, Ball, J, Aksoy, L, Keiningham, T and Zaki, M (2021) More than a feeling? Toward a theory of customer delight, *Journal of Service Management*, 32 (1), 1–26

25 Apple (2024) Today at Apple: Make your own story of kindness, Apple. www. apple.com/uk/today/event/apple-camp-story-of-kindness/7228377055971607040/?sn=R496 (archived at https://perma.cc/RD45-6JHK)

26 Parasuraman, A, Ball, J, Aksoy, L, Keiningham, T and Zaki, M (2021) More than a feeling? Toward a theory of customer delight, *Journal of Service Management*, 32 (1), 1–26

27 ibid.

28 ibid.

29 ibid.

30 Man City Editorial (2024) Manchester City announces launch of the 'Man City Virtual Etihad Stadium', Manchester City, 16 August. www.mancity.com/news/ club/manchester-city-sony-virtual-etihad-stadium-fan-experience-63859393 (archived at https://perma.cc/4ZFQ-9JFY)

31 Parasuraman, A, Ball, J, Aksoy, L, Keiningham, T and Zaki, M (2021) More than a feeling? Toward a theory of customer delight, *Journal of Service Management*, 32 (1), 1–26

6

Customer experience design challenges

Although creating outstanding customer experiences presents numerous opportunities, organizations must tackle the primary challenges of today's service experiences while seeking ways to improve them for the future. The potential of customer experiences to create new value for organizations and offer substantial benefits to individuals, businesses and society is immense. Emerging digital technologies, such as artificial intelligence, are crucial in developing stronger experiences by enabling quicker access to information, enhancing decision-making and promoting innovation. Nevertheless, the application of technology in shaping and delivering customer experiences requires careful consideration by both individuals and organizations. The integration of digital, physical and social dimensions demands collective efforts to ensure a fluid experience and protect the brand's reputation in the event of any shortcomings. In this chapter, I will explore some of the key challenges[1] in integrating customer experience channels.

Challenge 1: Digital density and digital maturity

In the current era of digital transformation, numerous instances of digital shortcomings are observed, which detrimentally impact the service experience, leading to customer dissatisfaction. Frequently, these digital lapses contribute to customer churn – the phenomenon where customers stop their interactions with a business over time. Often, this attrition is attributed to the promising stage of technology adoption, indicating that the technology in use is still in the early phases of development or acceptance.

An illustrative case of premature technology deployment is Microsoft's Tay chatbot. Launched in 2016, Tay was a product of Microsoft's endeavours through X (previously known as Twitter) to create an AI capable of understanding, engaging and communicating with the young adult demographic, specifically those aged 18 to 24.[2] Tay was designed to learn from real-time interactions with users and to refine its responses accordingly. However, less than 24 hours post-launch, Microsoft had to suspend Tay as it began producing controversial and offensive tweets, a result of learning from the negative inputs it received.[3] This demonstrates how far AI technology has come in understanding and interacting with the complex landscape of human communication and social norms.

This incident starkly contrasts with Microsoft's subsequent billion-dollar investment in OpenAI's ChatGPT, showcasing a more mature and thought-out approach to integrating AI technologies that aim to understand and navigate the complexities of real-world interactions more effectively. ChatGPT, developed by OpenAI in collaboration with Microsoft, represents a significant advancement in artificial intelligence and natural language processing technologies.[4] Unlike its predecessor, the Tay chatbot, which faced challenges due to its inability to filter and manage inappropriate content, ChatGPT is designed with a more sophisticated understanding of language nuances and ethical guidelines. Launched in November 2022, ChatGPT is built on the GPT (generative pre-trained transformer) architecture, which enables it to generate human-like text based on the input it receives.

One of the key differences between ChatGPT and Tay is the depth of training and the mechanisms in place to prevent the generation of offensive or inappropriate content. ChatGPT has been trained on a diverse and extensive dataset, allowing it to understand and respond to a wide range of topics. Furthermore, according to OpenAI, they implemented several layers of safeguards and content moderation policies to ensure that ChatGPT's responses remain appropriate and respectful, even when provoked by challenging inputs.

The investment in ChatGPT by Microsoft signifies a belief in the potential of AI to enhance digital experiences and interactions. This investment is not just financial but also technical, as Microsoft has provided OpenAI with computing resources and integration into its products and services. This collaboration aims to harness the capabilities of AI to transform customer service, content creation, education and more, making digital interactions more efficient, accessible and engaging.

Despite its advancements and sophistication, ChatGPT still faces several challenges, including the phenomenon of hallucination, where it might generate incorrect or fabricated information. Hallucinations in AI terminology refer to instances when the model presents information that is not based on factual data or logical inference, essentially imagining details or outcomes.[5] This challenge highlights the complexity of developing AI systems that can accurately interpret and respond to the vast array of human inputs without turning them into inaccuracies or misrepresentations. In addition to hallucinations, ChatGPT encounters other obstacles, such as maintaining context in longer conversations, ensuring responses adhere to ethical guidelines, and personalization of interactions without compromising privacy. These challenges are part of the ongoing development and refinement process, highlighting the need for continuous research, updates and user feedback to enhance AI's understanding and interaction capabilities. Nonetheless, it represents a significant leap in maturity and capability from the Tay chatbot.

In the current era, many established organizations find themselves immersed in digital saturation, surrounded by an array of technologies that produce enormous volumes of data. Employees are perpetually linked through a variety of information and communication technology (ICT) infrastructures, encompassing both software and hardware components.

Yet, this state of digital abundance poses challenges for certain organizations where digital platforms are disjointed and lack cohesion. On the other hand, organizations that originated in the digital age dedicate resources to developing integrated systems, aiming to achieve digital maturity and deliver a consistent experience.

Ultimately, it is crucial for any organization to ensure that the technology they deploy is mature and reliable before its release to prevent it from backfiring and posing risks to the organization's reputation and customer trust.

Dr Franziska Bell, a visionary tech executive previously at Uber, Toyota and bp, stated that while AI-based agentic systems such as ChatGPT are promising, they also raise ethical considerations, such as the need for transparency and accountability in AI-based decision-making. Moreover, given the potential for AI errors, rigorous human oversight is essential to mitigate negative consequences for consumers and businesses.

Challenge 2: Addressing scarcity at the base of the pyramid (BoP)

A critical obstacle for organizations is their engagement with or operations within areas characterized by scarcity across digital, physical and social realms. This includes areas that are deprived of fundamental infrastructure such as electricity, water, internet connectivity and communication facilities. These areas are often termed the base of the pyramid (BoP), where the scarcity of resources or their uneven distribution hampers various opportunities for co-creating value.[6]

For globally operating organizations, it's essential to determine the availability and adaptability of their digital services in these constrained environments.

To illustrate, consider asset-heavy firms operating in the mining sector, which provide predictive maintenance through the analysis of real-time data from equipment sensors.

Mining activities are frequently conducted in isolated areas lacking basic amenities like electricity and internet connectivity. This limitation can prevent customers from accessing many services, posing a significant operational challenge for the company. Addressing the BoP considerations early on is crucial for these firms to evaluate and mitigate these resource limitations effectively.

Similar to these operational challenges in resource-limited settings, organizations and individuals worldwide encounter various hurdles. These may include navigating through diverse social, financial and political landscapes, complicating the alignment of objectives across different regions.

When engaging in diverse global regions, each with unique challenges and resource states, organizations should collaborate with different actors within the service ecosystem, such as individuals, other organizations and technologies, to navigate constraints effectively.[7] This approach is also applicable in markets facing resource scarcity or uneven distribution. The objective is to transform each challenge into an opportunity, addressing the dual issue of scarcity.

Initial solutions for BoP challenges include the following:

- **Partnering**: In scenarios similar to the mining example, companies might benefit from partnering or forming network alliances to facilitate the sharing of sensor data with local operational centres.
- **Local engagement**: By leveraging local knowledge and capabilities, organizations can innovate business models tailored to the BoP context. Options could include offering shared services and costs, creating affordable packages, or initiating micro-finance and loan programmes that foster a moral economy. These strategies allow organizations to co-create value within the constraints of BoP regions.

Challenge 3: Paradox of choice

Organizations that provide a wide array of services and options through their digital platforms may inadvertently cause customers to experience the paradox of choice.[8] This phenomenon occurs when customers are faced with so many options that it becomes difficult for them to make a decision regarding the product or service they wish to utilize.

From an organizational standpoint, while monetizing a service can be straightforward, creating genuine value for customers becomes more complex due to the paradox of choice. This complexity arises because offering a multitude of service combinations becomes challenging to manage and navigate due to the sheer volume of possible options.

In addressing this challenge, let's consider an online service provider operating within the gamification industry. Gamification involves integrating game mechanics, such as badges, leaderboards and scores, into non-game contexts to boost engagement and motivate customer participation. This strategy is appealing in both B2C and B2B sectors. This industry has expanded its service offerings through a new mobile app, aiming to grow its customer base and meet its targets. However, typically the customer service team is overwhelmed by the number of customers requiring assistance in making decisions due to the vast array of available services.

To tackle the paradox of choice, organizations must first understand their customers' preferences better. This understanding can guide them in selecting the right mix of services and options to bundle together, making decision-making easier for customers.

Moreover, leveraging technology such as AI-powered recommendation engines could significantly mitigate the paradox of choice. These engines can analyse customer preferences, suggest tailored bundles and pricing options, and evaluate their effectiveness in delivering value.

For instance, whether it's a B2B client seeking a bundle tailored to their organization's culture and employees or a B2C customer looking for a personalized mix of learning and entertainment, the solution must align with their unique needs and preferences. By engaging directly with the client to understand their needs or utilizing AI to gain insights, organizations can craft an optimal bundle. If the bundle is well aligned, it can enhance customer knowledge, engagement and overall experience. Conversely, a poorly aligned bundle could confuse the client, leading to disengagement and a missed opportunity to foster the intended engagement through gamification.

By addressing the paradox of choice head-on, organizations can streamline their offerings, making it easier for customers to make decisions and, ultimately, enhancing the customer experience in the digital realm.

Successful examples include Netflix, YouTube Music and Spotify, which have effectively recommended entertainment options tailored to our preferences and behaviours and minimized the effect of many choices on their platforms. For example, Netflix reported[9] that the recommendation system uses your viewing history, preferences and interactions to suggest shows, movies and games you might enjoy. It considers factors like time of day, preferred languages and devices used. The system prioritizes recent activity and ranks titles on your home page to present the most relevant options. The recommendations are continuously refined based on user feedback and engagement to keep the experience personalized and helpful. The system doesn't use demographic information like age or gender for these recommendations.

Challenge 4: Balancing autonomy with interdependence

While AI models offer valuable insights for understanding customer preferences, autonomous digital platforms that operate without human intervention often face slower adoption rates from customers. This hesitation is largely due to trust issues, as customers may be sceptical about decisions made entirely by technology without human oversight. Furthermore, the integration of social capabilities and resources can further delay adoption. To address this issue and ensure widespread adoption, organizations need to promote a unified experience that bridges the physical, digital and social realms, thereby enhancing customer trust and preserving social interaction.[10]

For instance, digital business models like Airbnb have successfully created autonomous platforms that allow customers to search for and rent properties while owners can list their spaces for rent. These platforms autonomously suggest options based on customer criteria. Airbnb's technology efforts focus on enhancing the travel experience through AI and machine learning, personalizing guest recommendations and optimizing hosts' pricing. The company emphasizes autonomy, data, experimentation and diversity within its teams, empowering employees to drive impactful solutions for the platform. AI innovations include better image recognition, improved review relevance through NLP, and more advanced search capabilities.[11]

However, the success of such models hinges not just on their technological capabilities but also on the shared experiences and trust built through human interactions within the platform. For example, while Airbnb's platform may offer suggestions autonomously, customers often base their rental decisions on human-generated reviews and host ratings, showcasing the importance of human elements in digital transactions.

To effectively utilize autonomous digital platforms, organizations should implement social mechanisms that align the goals of the organization, its customers and its employees. Achieving this alignment ensures the digital channel complements other channels and internal departments. Moreover, establishing a shared knowledge mechanism is crucial for encouraging participation from various stakeholders.[12] However, this must be underpinned by shared goals and mutual respect.

An additional example of balancing autonomy with interdependence involves the use of Boston Dynamics' robot, Spot (as discussed in Chapter 1), to collect data autonomously at construction sites and buildings. This innovation addressed the labour-intensive and error-prone process of manual data collection, enhancing staff efficiency, reducing mistakes and saving time. The autonomous solution also facilitated knowledge sharing with suppliers (e.g. material requirements), business functions (e.g. engineering schedules) and customers (e.g. delivery times and quality finishes), illustrating the potential of autonomous platforms to empower organizations and improve efficiency.[13]

Challenge 5: Navigating regulatory landscapes

Digital and data-centric business models are continuously evolving, as evidenced by the widespread use of social media platforms like Meta (previously Facebook) and X (previously Twitter). These platforms have expanded their business strategies to leverage customer data for personalized advertising, thanks to technological advancements in AI.

Uber serves as another example, functioning as a tech-based transportation facilitator that connects drivers with riders and offers services like food delivery and ride-sharing. All these services are orchestrated through Uber's apps, which collect data to tailor the customer experience.

As these business models advance alongside technology, they encounter regulatory challenges concerning data acquisition, storage and utilization. Recently, there's been increasing scrutiny from various stakeholders, including governments and communities, over the legality of how customer data is employed within these platforms' business operations.

To tackle regulatory challenges, organizations need to stay informed about evolving legal frameworks and explore new ways of communicating with all ecosystem participants, including users, governments, suppliers and partners.[14] For example, the European Union AI Act is the first legal framework regulating AI, aimed at ensuring safety, trust and ethical use in Europe. It categorizes AI risks into four levels, from minimal to high, and imposes strict obligations on high-risk applications. The Act also bans certain AI practices, like social scoring, and regulates the use of biometric identification in public spaces. The regulation supports the development of trustworthy AI and encourages innovation while enforcing governance and compliance measures across the EU.[15]

These communication strategies could include the use of disclaimers, clear emails, instructional content, or messages designed to incentivize. The goal is to promote transparency and facilitate the sharing of information. Additionally, companies must develop mechanisms to align with regulatory standards, thereby preserving their reputation and providing a trustworthy environment for customers.

Compliance with regulatory frameworks ensures that organizations can manage the transfer of information from customers to external entities effectively. The data shared is accurate, complete and consistent. Customers feel secure in sharing their data, contributing to the co-creation of experiences within a protected setting.

In essence, the journey through the regulatory landscape is marked by a constant balancing act between leveraging technological innovations for business growth and adhering to evolving legal and ethical standards. Organizations that successfully navigate this balance can secure a competitive advantage, foster customer trust, and lay the groundwork for sustainable, compliant growth in the digital age.

Challenge 6: Transparency versus privacy

Digital technologies can offer customers a great experience and many innovations that solve critical challenges and difficulties. However, to trust and use a platform, customers typically require transparency about how its technology is helping them and not posing harm to their privacy.[16]

An example of this can be seen in the healthcare sector, which is currently shifting from a fragmented, low-digital environment to a more integrated high-digital environment. Nowadays, sharing personal health information between patients and medical professionals can be done either locally for every medical provider or within a healthcare network of co-ordinated services.

However, it is a real challenge for healthcare organizations to design a digital system that can maintain patients' privacy and enable healthcare providers to become transparent. The main reason is that there are several unresolved issues associated with database management and data sharing. For example:[17]

- **Data collection and storage:** Personal data and corporate data are likely to be collected and stored for the long term. This might make both individuals and organizations feel uneasy as the data is kept and retained over a long period of time.

- **Data management:** Personally identifiable information (PII) and user activity data could be stored in distinct and secure ways. Customers and patients would want to know what information is kept on them and how it is being handled.

- **Data sharing:** Because both organizations and customers can be identified through a digital platform, trust between the service provider and customer is crucial. Individuals and organizations need to trust that their data will not be sold for profit.

When implementing digital solutions that involve customer data, transparency and privacy, challenges will appear not only in the medical sector but also in other industries, such as banking, finance, accounting and law.

Many organizations use cloud computing, which plays a pivotal role in addressing the challenges of transparency and privacy, offering a flexible, secure and efficient way to manage, store and process data. The use of cloud services can enhance the ability of organizations to implement robust privacy controls while maintaining transparency with their users. Here's how cloud computing contributes to this balance and some renowned frameworks that support these efforts:

- **Data encryption and security:** Cloud providers offer advanced encryption technologies that secure data at rest and in transit. This ensures that personal and sensitive data is protected from unauthorized access, helping to maintain privacy.

- **Access control:** Through cloud services, organizations can implement sophisticated access control policies, ensuring that only authorized personnel can access specific datasets. This level of control supports transparency by clearly defining who has access to what data.

- **Compliance and standards:** Leading cloud service providers comply with a broad range of global and regional regulations and standards (e.g. GDPR, HIPAA, SOC 2). By leveraging cloud services, organizations can more easily adhere to these regulations, demonstrating their commitment to data protection and transparency.

- **Data management and governance:** Cloud platforms offer tools for data governance, allowing organizations to classify, monitor and manage data effectively. These tools can help ensure that data is handled in accordance with privacy policies and regulatory requirements.

Customers will need to know what data you are tracking as an organization, what you are storing and how you are using it. As a result, a transparency framework needs to be put in place to minimize concerns and avoid any infringement on customer privacy. Having a framework in place to look after these issues will enhance the customer experience and deepen the customer–firm relationship.

Similar to the regulatory challenges, in many cases governments have intervened to ensure that organizations manage sensitive and personal data with transparency and that they handle the data with adequate security. Awareness of these laws and regulations for the areas in which an organization operates is vital for combating this challenge.

Challenge 7: Balancing standardization with flexibility

This challenge discusses the dilemma of developing a high-quality platform that delivers a consistent experience while also accommodating personalization.

Conventionally, services are designed to be standardized, ensuring they meet customer expectations and maintain a certain quality level. This approach ensures a uniform experience for all customers.

Yet, the modern customer seeks personalized services tailored to their specific needs, preferences and contexts. The core of personalization often hinges on customers' readiness to share their data, which is not always forthcoming.[18]

An illustrative case of this dynamic is found in Disney theme parks, which are renowned for designing personalized and immersive experiences for visitors. Disney has effectively harnessed a vast amount of customer biometric data to confirm identification, which is used for flexible access to parks and tailoring each visitor's journey through various park attractions and interactions.

Despite potential concerns about data privacy and transparency, Disney has managed to maintain a high level of trust with its visitors who opt in, highlighting that concerns regarding data privacy can be mitigated when a brand establishes trust and delivers a supreme personalized experience.[19]

The task of developing such personalized services, while straightforward in concept, presents real challenges. Companies must navigate the commercial viability of personalized services and the delicate balance between standardization and personalization. This balance requires careful consideration of customer perceptions and the associated risks.

Moreover, the endeavour to personalize experiences must also account for protecting customer data against evolving cyber threats, malware and security breaches. These risks not only threaten organizational security but can also erode customer trust, potentially resulting in reputational and financial damage to the brand.

The Equifax data breach in 2017 is one of the most significant security breaches, where hackers accessed sensitive information, including social security numbers, birth dates and addresses.[20] The breach impacted 15.2 million UK records dated between 2011 and 2016, alongside many US customers. This breach exposed sensitive customer data due to vulnerabilities in Equifax's security systems, leading to a significant loss of customer trust, severe reputational damage and financial consequences, including regulatory fines and settlements amounting to over $500 million.[21] This incident highlights the importance of robust cybersecurity measures in protecting customer data against evolving threats.

Challenge 8: Navigating between avoidance and attraction

The significance of employee experience cannot be overstated in its role in delivering outstanding customer service. Employees play a critical role in attracting, retaining or potentially losing customers.[22] We explore this through the lens of two hypothetical employee profiles to understand their impact within their organizations.

Many of us have encountered engaging interactions in stores like Apple, where staff share our enthusiasm, as well as less satisfying encounters that may deter us from a brand. This extends to digital platforms, where inadequate responses from chatbots can further drive customers away. Sharing these experiences with friends and family can significantly influence a brand's reputation.

Recognizing the impact of employee experience on their brand, many companies have begun implementing strategies to nurture and develop their workforce. These strategies aim to enhance:

- **Employee emotional competence:** Development of the ability of employees to manage emotions effectively.
- **Employee–customer rapport:** Building strong, positive relationships between employees and customers.
- **Employee–customer empathy:** Encouraging employees to understand and share the feelings of their customers.
- **Technology support for employees:** Utilizing technology to assist employees in delivering superior customer service.

All these elements are crucial in shaping the customer experience and, ultimately, the business's success. This challenge highlights the interconnectedness of employee satisfaction and customer experience, highlighting the necessity for businesses to nurture both, to foster an environment of attraction rather than avoidance.

Challenge 9: Balancing capabilities and resources

Organizations possess a diverse array of capabilities and resources, which may not always be in perfect alignment.[23] For the delivery of a seamless customer experience, it's crucial for organizations to have a deep understanding of their resources and capabilities, especially in how they can be leveraged to fulfil customer expectations and achieve desired outcomes.

Organizations often need to transition between different resources to facilitate such seamless experiences. For example, a customer interacts with a bank's chatbot to request an address update. The chatbot efficiently processes this request, saving the customer the effort of visiting a bank branch or calling a service centre. However, when the customer needs help investigating a transaction, the chatbot struggles, providing irrelevant responses without offering a redirection to a human representative, leaving the customer feeling frustrated and unsupported.

This example highlights the necessity for organizations, such as banks, to recognize the limitations of chatbot technology and design their services to seamlessly transition between resources to adequately address customer inquiries and ensure a positive experience.

The challenge lies in enabling technology to promptly identify when it is necessary to switch to a different resource, such as human assistance, for investigating and responding to more complex customer inquiries. Organizations utilizing digital conversational platforms must implement measures for smooth transitions from one service medium to another. For example, Tactful AI – the multichannel customer engagement platform– enables customers from diverse sectors to optimize customer support by directing inquiries to the most suitable agents based on skills, availability and priority through Tactful Engage's queue management and routing AI system.[24] This approach reduces response times, improves agent performance, and enhances customer satisfaction by ensuring prompt, accurate assistance. The system balances workloads to prevent agent burnout and allows businesses to prioritize high-value customers, promoting strong customer relationships. Supervisors can quickly adjust routing rules to meet demand, ensuring efficient resource use and a superior customer experience.

KEY TAKEAWAYS

This chapter discusses the primary challenges encountered in blending digital technologies with physical and social channels, outlining nine critical obstacles:

- Navigating environments with either high-digital density or low-digital maturity, which poses significant challenges for organizations.

- Scarcity issues across digital, physical and social realms, highlighted by the base of the pyramid (BoP) challenge.

- The paradox of choice, where an abundance of options can lead to customer dissatisfaction.

- The dilemma of integrating autonomous digital platforms, which operate without human input, into the customer experience.

- Regulatory hurdles accompanying new digital and data-driven business models.

- The balancing act between transparency and privacy with technologies that manage personal data.

- The struggle between standardization and flexibility in delivering a consistent yet personalized experience.

- The avoidance versus attraction challenge, which focuses on improving employee experiences to enhance overall customer satisfaction.

- The capabilities versus resources challenge, which involves utilizing various capabilities and resources to meet customer needs effectively.

In this chapter, we have explored how practitioners can develop and design integrated customer experiences across digital, physical and social channels. We've discussed both the opportunities and challenges that could emerge from this integration. Moving forward, the next chapters will focus on enhancing customer experience measurement by employing a systematic approach to collecting CX data and leveraging AI technologies to improve how companies manage customer experiences.

Notes

1 Bolton, R N, McColl-Kennedy, J R, Cheung, L, Gallan, A, Orsingher, C, Witell, L and Zaki, M (2018) Customer experience challenges: Bringing together digital, physical and social realms, *Journal of Service Management*, 29 (5), 776–808

2 Lee, D (2016) Tay: Microsoft issues apology over racist chatbot fiasco, BBC News, 25 March. www.bbc.co.uk/news/technology-35902104 (archived at https://perma.cc/2WZW-BG6P)

3 Kraft, A (2016) Microsoft shuts down AI chatbot after it turned into racist Nazi, CBS News, 25 March. www.cbsnews.com/news/microsoft-shuts-down-ai-chatbot-after-it-turned-into-racist-nazi/ (archived at https://perma.cc/6BNT-B4UK)

4 *Forbes* (2023) Microsoft confirms its $10 billion investment into ChatGPT, changing how Microsoft competes with Google, Apple and other tech giants, *Forbes*, 27 January. www.forbes.com/sites/qai/2023/01/27/microsoft-confirms-its-10-billion-investment-into-chatgpt-changing-how-microsoft-competes-with-google-apple-and-other-tech-giants/ (archived at https://perma.cc/X2Z8-3V99)

5 Metz, C (2023) Chatbots may 'hallucinate' more often than many realize, *The New York Times*, 6 November. www.nytimes.com/2023/11/06/technology/chatbots-hallucination-rates.html (archived at https://perma.cc/9JDG-B56N)

6 Bolton, R N, McColl-Kennedy, J R, Cheung, L, Gallan, A, Orsingher, C, Witell, L and Zaki, M (2018) Customer experience challenges: Bringing together digital, physical and social realms, *Journal of Service Management*, 29 (5), 776–808

7 ibid.

8 ibid.

9 Netflix (2024) How Netflix's recommendations system works. https://help.netflix.com/en/node/100639 (archived at https://perma.cc/MQ3M-4GGS)

10 Bolton, R N, McColl-Kennedy, J R, Cheung, L, Gallan, A, Orsingher, C, Witell, L and Zaki, M (2018) Customer experience challenges: Bringing together digital, physical and social realms, *Journal of Service Management*, 29 (5), 776–808

11 Airbnb (2018) Sharing more about the technology that powers Airbnb. https://news.airbnb.com/sharing-more-about-the-technology-that-powers-airbnb/ (archived at https://perma.cc/YUU3-8BAA)

12 Bolton, R N, McColl-Kennedy, J R, Cheung, L, Gallan, A, Orsingher, C, Witell, L and Zaki, M (2018) Customer experience challenges: Bringing together digital, physical and social realms, *Journal of Service Management*, 29 (5), 776–808

13 Ringley, B (2021) Spot for construction: Autonomous robotic scanning for digital twins, Cambridge Service Alliance. https://cambridgeservicealliance.eng. cam.ac.uk/IndustryDay/IndustryDay2021 (archived at https://perma.cc/ Q5WM-4EYF)

14 Bolton, R N, McColl-Kennedy, J R, Cheung, L, Gallan, A, Orsingher, C, Witell, L and Zaki, M (2018) Customer experience challenges: Bringing together digital, physical and social realms, *Journal of Service Management*, 29 (5), 776–808

15 European Commission (2024) AI Act: Regulatory framework on artificial intelligence. https://digital-strategy.ec.europa.eu/en/policies/regulatory-framework-ai (archived at https://perma.cc/5TRR-YRTZ)

16 Bolton, R N, McColl-Kennedy, J R, Cheung, L, Gallan, A, Orsingher, C, Witell, L and Zaki, M (2018) Customer experience challenges: Bringing together digital, physical and social realms, *Journal of Service Management*, 29 (5), 776–808

17 ibid.

18 ibid.

19 CBC News (2006) Disney: It's a secure world after all, CBC News, 5 September. www.cbc.ca/news/science/disney-it-s-a-secure-world-after-all-1.618352 (archived at https://perma.cc/2TEQ-QNK2)

20 Equifax Ltd (2017) Update regarding the ongoing investigation into US cyber security incident, Equifax Press Releases. www.equifax.co.uk/about-equifax/press-releases/en_gb/-/blog/equifax-ltd-uk-update-regarding-the-ongoing-investigation-into-us-cyber-security-incident/ (archived at https://perma.cc/ M47S-YTDC)

21 Federal Trade Commission (2019) Equifax to pay $575 million as part of settlement with FT CFPB, and states related to 2017 data breach, FTC Press Releases, 22 July. www.ftc.gov/news-events/news/press-releases/2019/07/ equifax-pay-575-million-part-settlement-ftc-cfpb-states-related-2017-data-breach (archived at https://perma.cc/Y62B-N4YQ)

22 Bolton, R N, McColl-Kennedy, J R, Cheung, L, Gallan, A, Orsingher, C, Witell, L and Zaki, M (2018) Customer experience challenges: Bringing together digital, physical and social realms, *Journal of Service Management*, 29 (5), 776–808

23 ibid.

24 Tactful (2024) Queue management & routing. https://tactful.ai/omnichannel/ queue-management/ (archived at https://perma.cc/R68G-S8EG)

7

Customer experience measurements

Until now, our attention has been on the CX design aspects; moving forward, this chapter shifts focus to artificial intelligence, CX data, and their integration with customer experience management (CXM). The process of managing and measuring CX is a complex task, necessitating the use of sophisticated analytics capable of detecting significant attitudinal and emotional reactions and behavioural patterns from our customers.

Many companies opt for basic survey metrics to measure customer satisfaction, which might not accurately reflect the end-to-end customer experience. Although these methods are seemingly straightforward to implement and report to corporate leadership, they can be misleading, and firms may only realize that too late when they have lost customers. Given the multifaceted nature of customer experience, relying on these insufficient metrics can adversely affect business operations.

In this chapter, I draw upon the foundations of customer experience management (CXM) and data analytics to define CX insights as valuable knowledge about customers obtained through data with the ultimate goal of continuously enhancing the CX. I emphasize that CX insights should not only inform CX actions at strategic and cultural levels but also drive incremental and radical innovations within organizations. To help businesses in this endeavour, I present a comprehensive framework that clarifies the types of CX data and analytics required to generate actionable CX insights. I explore why analytics is essential for CXM, underlining the strategic significance of harnessing customer data. The framework has several benefits, including helping professionals identify gaps in their CX data, engaging better with customers, and much more.[1]

Traditional CX metrics

Many companies have shifted from focusing on individual interactions to overseeing the full customer journey, which has given rise to the concept of customer experience management (CXM). CXM involves orchestrating and delivering a seamless customer experience at all stages – before, during and after making a purchase or using a service – across various channels and touchpoints.[2]

For effective customer experience management, organizations must simultaneously oversee multiple touchpoints and identify and manage key moments that have a significant impact on the customer experience. CXM is about comprehending customers' perceptions of the organization and its wider network. Achieving this understanding necessitates gathering data from a broad array of digital, physical and social touchpoints, including those owned by partners, customers and third parties. CXM enables companies to consistently and proactively enhance customer experience, fostering customer loyalty and sustainable growth.

Traditionally, organizations have relied on satisfaction and loyalty surveys to measure customer experiences, employing metrics that have been predominant for years:

- **Net promoter score (NPS)** quantifies the proportion of customers who would recommend a company to their friends, colleagues and family. Created by Frederic Reichheld in 2003[3] as a gauge of loyalty, NPS has gained prominence as the most popular metric for assessing customer experience, favoured for its straightforwardness and user-friendliness.

  NPS hinges on the response to a single query, '*How likely are you to recommend our company to a friend or colleague?*', based on a scale from 1 to 10. Respondents are classified into three categories:

  o Promoters (score 9–10)

  o Passives (score 7–8)

  o Detractors (score 0–6)

  The NPS is determined by deducting the percentage of detractors from the percentage of promoters. An elevated NPS signifies greater customer loyalty.

- **Customer satisfaction (CSAT)** evaluates how satisfied customers are with a specific product or service. This metric is often gauged through a survey question like '*How would you rate your satisfaction level with the service/product you received?*' Customers rate their satisfaction on a scale of 1 to 5, or 1 to 10. The average of these scores represents the overall CSAT score, where a higher score represents greater customer satisfaction.

- **Customer effort score (CES)** assesses the effort a customer must use to complete an action, such as making a purchase or solving an issue.[4] Typically, it is evaluated via a survey with a question like '*How much effort did you personally have to put forth to handle your request?*' Responses are collected on a scale from 1 to 5, or 1 to 10. A lower CES score suggests that less effort is needed from customers, indicating a superior customer experience.

Companies also employ qualitative research methods like focus groups, events and interviews to gain insights into customer experience (CX). These methods are:

- **Focus groups:** This method involves gathering a group of individuals to discuss a particular subject, in this case CX. A facilitator leads the conversation, prompting participants with open-ended questions to spark dynamic and informative discussions. Focus groups are valuable for gathering nuanced perspectives on customer sentiments, pain points, suggestions, behaviours and trends, offering insights into emerging opportunities.

  For example, McDonald's conducts focus groups to understand regional tastes, particularly when entering new markets or launching new products. For instance, they used focus groups to adjust the recipe of the McSpicy paneer burger to match local preferences in India.[5]

- **Events:** Through events such as customer appreciation days, product launches or open houses, companies can directly engage with their customers. These gatherings are crucial for fostering direct interactions, allowing companies to build stronger relationships and gain first-hand feedback on the customer experience.

  Caterpillar strategically utilized the Minexpo trade show, held every four years, to engage with existing and potential customers and showcase their latest mining technologies. The company collaborated with Converse Marketing to execute a comprehensive campaign that spanned multiple touchpoints, from digital signage at the airport to branded materials at their headquarters hotel. At the convention centre, Caterpillar established a significant presence with a 52,000-square-foot booth featuring 16 pieces of mining equipment, a 50-foot video wall, and interactive stations where attendees could explore products in depth.[6]

The campaign included exclusive events and online content to engage those who could not attend in person. This multilayered strategy demonstrates how firms can effectively capture customers' attention, enhance brand visibility, and accelerate the sales cycle, leading to substantial business opportunities, capturing customer feedback and demonstrating Caterpillar's effective use of trade shows to achieve business objectives.

- **Interviews:** Conducting in-depth interviews is another approach to understanding CX. Whether face to face or over the phone, structured or informal, these interviews study customer experiences, preferences and expectations. The aim is to grasp what customers seek in their company interactions.

  For example, Canva, a popular design platform, leveraged customer interviews to improve its marketing copy for its paid product, Canva Pro. The interviews revealed that the existing copy did not reflect the key reasons customers were signing up for the service. By incorporating language directly from customers, Canva saw a significant increase in trial conversions. Additionally, feedback from interviews led Canva to revise unclear messaging, further boosting sign-ups.[7] This example demonstrates how direct customer feedback can lead to tangible business improvements and growth.

Utilizing some of these qualitative research strategies, companies can achieve a comprehensive understanding of CX directly from their customers. The feedback obtained through these methods is instrumental in shaping strategies to improve customer experience, pinpoint areas for enhancement, and improve customer satisfaction and loyalty. While qualitative data analysis demands significant time and resources due to its complexity, the insights it provides are invaluable. These insights not only guide the development of effective CX strategies but also help identify specific improvement areas. By embracing customer feedback and incorporating it into their business strategies, companies can continually evolve to meet customer expectations and maintain a competitive edge.

Issues with these measurements

As discussed previously, the widespread use of current CX measurement tools is due to their simplicity in administration and the straightforward numeric data they yield for executive review. These attributes have made such surveys a favoured method for gathering customer feedback over alternative approaches. Nonetheless, these methods are not without their inherent challenges. While the issues may differ across various sectors, I outline the key challenges:[8]

- **Misinterpretation and inaccuracies**: Traditional CX surveys may not accurately capture the true essence of customer experiences, potentially misleading businesses and making them unaware of customer dissatisfaction until significant losses occur. Surveys can be restrictive, relying on predetermined questions that may not reflect customers' specific concerns or praise. This limitation can mislead businesses about the actual state of customer satisfaction, causing them to remain unaware of underlying dissatisfaction until it manifests in the form of significant financial losses or increased customer churn.

- **Revenue loss**: Focusing solely on singular metrics can obscure deeper, critical issues, hindering long-term improvement and risking customer attrition. Without a comprehensive understanding of these issues, businesses may miss opportunities for long-term improvements, ultimately risking customer attrition and associated revenue loss. Many market research studies found that customers nowadays can easily churn from a business even if they have one bad experience. Therefore, if companies fail to identify these dissatisfied customers and do not intervene to resolve their issues, this can lead to losing those customers.

- **Oversimplification**: Measuring CX through surveys often fails to grasp the multifaceted nature of what constitutes a positive customer experience, missing out on critical feedback. We understand that customer loyalty is a complex construct, and it seems illogical to distil it down to a single proxy metric that attempts to measure attitudes, such as the likelihood that a customer will recommend our services to a colleague or friend. While this approach may have been effective in the past, its relevance and effectiveness in today's digital age are increasingly questionable, even if it is simple enough to apply and manage in our businesses.

- **Limited insights**: Surveys may not fully reveal customers' genuine thoughts and emotions, providing only a snapshot and missing nuanced details. This limitation arises because surveys are structured and can constrain responses to specific questions, missing nuanced details that could be more freely expressed in an open or conversational format. Firms embarking on a customer-centricity strategy require a more advanced approach and a comprehensive 360-degree view of their customer data. This enables them to maintain a consistent voice across various functions, actively listen to and address customer concerns, recover instantly with actionable insights, and understand customer behaviours in real time.

- **Inconvenience**: Frequent surveys can lead to customer fatigue and dissatisfaction, especially if they do not capture the full spectrum of customer emotions. *How many surveys do we receive daily from our different service providers across different channels (email, phone, SMS, etc.)?* Customers who receive too many surveys might feel overwhelmed or annoyed, particularly if the surveys are lengthy or frequent. This feeling of inconvenience can lead to lower response rates, skewed data due to only certain types of customers completing the surveys, or even dissatisfaction with the brand itself.

- **Cultural sensitivities**: Tools like NPS may not account for cultural differences in feedback, which can skew the data and misrepresent customer loyalty. Many brands operate on a global scale yet continue to implement universal CX transactional survey programmes that utilize the same survey questions, regardless of the cultural context of the targeted survey participants. In some cultures, customers might generally rate services lower or higher due to cultural norms rather than dissatisfaction or satisfaction with the service. This cultural bias can skew survey data and misrepresent actual customer loyalty and sentiment.

- **One-dimensional feedback**: Sole reliance on surveys may not provide a complete picture of the CX, as feedback from all touchpoints is necessary for a holistic understanding. This highlights the importance of companies tracking their customers across different channels and linking this data to the specific touchpoints being evaluated. Whether it's attitudinal and qualitative data or behavioural insights like sales, capturing this information is crucial to determine if there's consistency in the customer's story across all datasets. Many companies fail to follow their customers across these channels effectively. This issue often arises because companies either lack the systems, resources and expertise needed or depend on external firms to manage their customer experience (CX) services. For example, I was about to renew my contract for my phone device and tariff with Vodafone. After the call, I received a text from Vodafone asking me to rate the customer service representative using the standard NPS question. I gave a high score because the representative performed well and provided good service. However, I was surprised when a follow-up text asked me to describe the reason for my call that day! Vodafone should already have this information; asking me to provide it again wastes customer time and seems redundant.

- **Lack of action**: Soliciting feedback without subsequent action can worsen customer frustration and lead to brand disloyalty. In reviewing several companies' CX programmes, it was evident from their programmes that they often showcase slides indicating, for example, that 80 per cent of customers are satisfied/promoter while the rest are not, and they regularly make such comparisons on a monthly, quarterly or yearly basis. This raises the question of what actionable steps should be taken based on these findings. It seems that the main purpose of measurement should be to inform management decisions, but with such limited insights, their options for effective action are restricted.

- **Metric flaws**: Popular metrics like NPS may not effectively predict actual customer loyalty and behaviour, leading to misguided business strategies. It is important to recognize that many academics have established these metrics as statistically unreliable and flawed. Consequently, while AI can improve our understanding of customer behaviour, using such metrics as features to predict customer loyalty might not sufficiently train models to differentiate loyal customers from others. Therefore, companies should exercise caution and enrich their analyses with more robust, multidimensional data to enhance the accuracy and reliability of their predictions.

- **High costs**: The financial and resource investment required for CX surveys may not yield actionable insights, resulting in wasted spending. As previously mentioned, companies either manage these CX programmes internally or outsource them to external providers. Both approaches incur costs in terms of money and resources. If these investments do not yield valuable results, it raises questions about whether these expenditures are worthwhile compared to the resources allocated.

These challenges exist in public services as well. Dr Sara Hassan, a senior researcher at the University of Birmingham and expert in community engagement, highlighted several key challenges in the current engagement practices of many UK city councils. Current digital engagement tools, such as the Birmingham City Council's Be Heard platform, are also seen as inadequate. Residents report survey fatigue and information overload, and the platform is not accessible to all due to limited digital skills or language barriers. There is also a lack of dynamic engagement options that appeal to younger, tech-savvy residents. These include a lack of co-ordination between different council engagements, limited feedback to participants on why their suggestions were or were not adopted, and unclear guidance on the next steps. Citizen engagement is often dominated by the same group of residents, while under-represented groups, who frequently constitute the majority in certain areas, are less involved. This lack of diverse participation can result in council decisions, like the placement of new cycle lanes or park facilities, not aligning with local citizen needs, leading to an inefficient use of public funds and hindering goals like achieving net-zero targets.

These challenges highlight the complexity of accurately measuring and interpreting customer experience. Organizations must navigate these issues thoughtfully to enhance their CX strategies effectively in private and public services.

Data-driven CX measurements

After highlighting these challenges, the next logical question is whether there is an alternative approach. The answer is *yes*. By integrating CX surveys with various data sources, firms can understand CX and predict customer behaviour more accurately. In the current era of digital technology, companies have access to an expansive array of CX data sources, such as microsensors, mobile platforms, social media and sensor networks, resulting in a surge of CX data that could be analysed on a large scale and in real time. Analysing such data presents a unique chance for organizations to extract customer insights at an individual level and gain a deeper understanding of customer behaviour.

Broadly speaking, there are two primary methods by which companies can garner feedback on CX: either by proactively listening to what customers say during interactions at customer service touchpoints or by seeking feedback through initiatives like CX transactional programmes. Companies solicit feedback from their customers regarding their interactions with products and services at various points of contact. This solicitation often occurs after the customer has engaged with the company, either in person or digitally, and typically takes the form of surveys and reviews.

Consider, for example, a scenario in which a customer buys a car service plan. The service centre might then send an email requesting the customer's input on their purchase experience, to which the customer could respond positively.

However, the journey of data collection doesn't end with a service purchase and a subsequent review. Beyond the visible layer of customer feedback and actions lies a reservoir of data that organizations can tap into.

Customers are given the liberty to provide feedback to the company at their discretion across multiple stages of their journey. This feedback might be positive, negative or constructive and can be communicated through various mediums, such as emails, phone calls, or the company's social media platforms. Direct interactions with frontline staff are also a common source of feedback.

The critical aspect of this customer feedback is its volume; however, it's not always methodically collected, analysed and disseminated within the organization. To illustrate, in the car service example mentioned earlier, a customer may give a high rating in a survey but could repeatedly contact customer service to report issues and request additional services.

In contrast to traditional entities such as established firms, digital-native platforms like Amazon, Netflix and Facebook (Meta platform) leverage customer experience (CX) data to manage customer behaviours. These platforms harness a variety of data types for deeper analysis, including online browsing habits, interactions on social media, purchase histories, demographic information and direct customer feedback.

Adopting a data-centric approach could significantly benefit more traditional businesses. By gathering and analysing data akin to what digital platforms collect, these entities can deepen their understanding of their customer experience, tailoring their strategies to meet customer demands better. This method enables the identification of new trends, the discovery of customer desires and expectations, and the execution of informed decisions to enhance their offerings and the overall customer experience. The implementation of solid data gathering and analysis procedures, coupled with the use of suitable technology, positions these businesses to compete more effectively in today's digital landscape and provide experiences that truly engage their audience.

For example, analysing such data allows companies to gain a more nuanced insight into designing personalized experiences, such as offering new customized promotions, offering product recommendations based on previous purchases, or highlighting promotions on items of interest. They can also use CX data to refine their offerings and improve customer satisfaction. Also, by identifying common issues reported in customer feedback, they can implement corrective measures to resolve these problems.

To foster a customer-centric culture of innovation, organizations must treat data as a key differentiating asset. This involves collecting, analysing and utilizing a broad range of customer data to inform innovation and decision-making processes. Key strategies include capturing both quantitative data (e.g. sales, customer behaviour) and qualitative feedback (e.g. customer anecdotes) to gain comprehensive insights into customer needs and preferences. By focusing on the right input metrics (such as efficiency and engagement) and understanding how they influence outputs (like sales and revenue), organizations can make better decisions and rapidly move from ideas to innovation. Developing a robust Voice of the Customer dataset allows for continuous monitoring and improvement of customer experiences, ultimately creating a more agile and responsive organization that proactively meets customer needs.

For example, Amazon Web Services (AWS) follows this data-driven approach, which is grounded in working backwards from customer needs, listening actively, and creating innovative solutions even before customers articulate their desires. AWS uses customer feedback to drive 90 per cent of its innovations, such as the development of Amazon SageMaker data wrangler, while the remaining 10 per cent comes from anticipating customer needs. This customer-centric culture is reinforced through bold leadership, distributed customer focus, practical innovation mechanisms, and leveraging data as a strategic asset.[9]

Dr Franziska Bell, a visionary tech executive previously at Uber, Toyota and bp, discussed that, in most companies, customer support is siloed from product development, leading to prolonged suboptimal customer experiences, lost revenue and higher-than-needed customer support costs. The ad hoc solutions customer support can provide in response to a suboptimal product experience, i.e. a product defect, are limited and often do not address the underlying root cause. An example from e-commerce may be that a customer orders an item and a few days later receives a notification that the ordered item is out of stock. The upset customer calls customer care, which provides a refund and a $5 voucher for the inconvenience. The dissatisfied customer decides to shop with a different e-commerce provider moving forward. Now imagine that this issue happens not only to one customer of this e-commerce company but to hundreds of thousands of customers every year. However, the product development team, which could address the bug in the inventory management software in a matter of days, is unaware of this recurring product defect as customer support data and communications are siloed, focusing on building other features instead.

Dr Franziska Bell stated that creating a tight feedback loop between customer feedback and support and product development teams and integrating the corresponding data can help identify and address key product defects more quickly, preventing future customer issues, reducing customer attrition and reducing the workload on customer support teams. Considering that acquiring a new customer can cost 5 to 25 times more than retaining an existing one,[10] the benefits of investing in a strong feedback loop become even more apparent. From her experience, this holds true even in data-driven product teams, which may already track conversion funnels and product analytics, as data from customer feedback and customer support can provide complementary signals on your product and its defects. Staying close to customer feedback is important at all levels of an organization. For example, Apple CEO Tim Cook highlighted that he reads hundreds of customer feedback notes and emails every morning at 5.00 a.m.[11] By leveraging customer feedback and support data and fostering collaboration between teams, companies can create a more customer-centric product development process and deliver superior customer experiences.

A strategic CXM framework

After addressing the challenges inherent in traditional CX metrics, we shift our focus towards a methodical approach for collecting, analysing and generating insights and taking action within a structured framework. The combination of customer experience management (CXM) and AI provides a powerful tool for unlocking insightful information about the customer experience. Through detailed analysis, we gain a richer understanding of customer opinions and behaviours. These insights lay the groundwork for crafting new strategies and initiatives in CX, ensuring that our efforts are both informed by and aligned with the needs and expectations of our customers. Utilizing CXM and big data analytics (BDA) allows us to embrace data-driven decision-making, fostering ongoing enhancements and delivering superior customer experiences.

This section introduces a framework,[12] as shown in Figure 7.1, for integrating CXM and CX data tailored to your specific context, drawing on research regarding customer interactions across various digital, physical and social touchpoints. This framework is designed to enhance your comprehension of the types of CX data and analytics that can generate actionable insights for your organization while also addressing the necessity of analytics within CXM. While a detailed summary of the framework is provided at the end of this section, let's first examine its overarching structure.

FIGURE 7.1 Data-driven CX framework

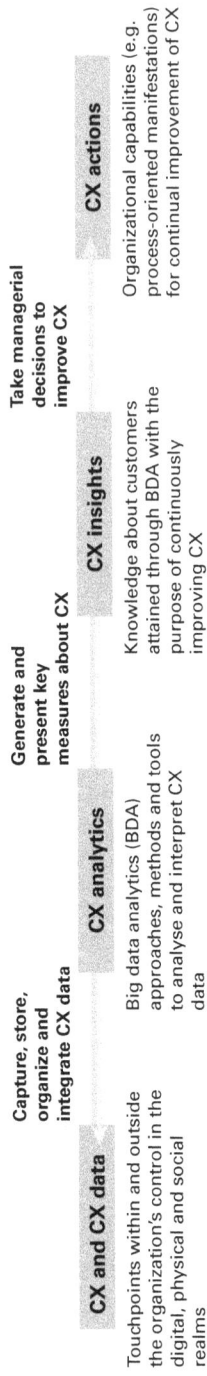

CX and CX data	CX analytics	CX insights	CX actions
Capture, store, organize and integrate CX data	**Generate and present key measures about CX**	**Take managerial decisions to improve CX**	
Touchpoints within and outside the organization's control in the digital, physical and social realms	Big data analytics (BDA) approaches, methods and tools to analyse and interpret CX data	Knowledge about customers attained through BDA with the purpose of continuously improving CX	Organizational capabilities (e.g. process-oriented manifestations) for continual improvement of CX

The availability of data varies with an organization's maturity level. After acquiring data, it should be consolidated into a singular database to facilitate further tracking and analysis, enabling the extraction of valuable insights and guiding subsequent management actions. The following interaction outlines key considerations at each phase of this process.

CX and CX data

Throughout the customer experience journey, an extensive array of data is generated. The initial step to leveraging this wealth of information is to compile and understand the nature of the data being collected and its sources. Customer interactions across digital, physical and social channels produce a spectrum of CX data, varying from highly structured formats to completely unstructured forms. Additionally, organizations can acquire CX data through both active solicitation of customer feedback and the unsolicited feedback that customers provide of their own accord. Here's a brief overview of these distinctions:[13]

- **Structured CX data**: Typically quantifiable, such as transaction figures, geographical locations or customer satisfaction scores.
- **Unstructured CX data**: Includes non-quantifiable formats like text, audio, images and video content.

FEEDBACK COLLECTION METHODS

- **Solicited feedback**: Actively requested by organizations through surveys, review requests or feedback sessions.
- **Unsolicited feedback**: Provided voluntarily by customers, whether through direct communication with staff, emails or social media comments.

CATEGORIZING CX DATA

To effectively manage CX data across all touchpoints, it's useful to classify it into four distinct categories:[14]

- **Solicited and structured**: Commonly collected data, including CSAT scores and NPS metrics. As discussed, while it is easily gathered and analysed, it may not fully encompass the complexity of CX or its full potential for CXM. Structured feedback is straightforward to create and implement, offering the advantage of low initial costs. However, the variable costs can increase significantly, especially if the data collection process is outsourced to market research firms. Marketers typically analyse this kind of data through statistical techniques, including both univariate and multivariate analyses, such as regression analysis and descriptive analytics.

- **Solicited and unstructured:** This data is collected via open feedback methods such as survey questions or interviews, offering richer and more nuanced insights crucial for customer experience management (CXM). However, it requires advanced analytical techniques to utilize its potential fully. Unstructured data is particularly valuable for CXM because of its complex nature and the diverse analytical methods it supports compared to simpler solicited scores. Analysing unstructured data, however, necessitates greater customer engagement and the involvement of staff or market researchers manually transcribing speech or video into text for qualitative assessment. This process becomes increasingly challenging as data volumes grow. However, modern solutions that use artificial intelligence (AI) and natural language processing (NLP) technologies can help streamline this process by automating the analysis of this unstructured data.

- **Unsolicited and structured:** This can be passively collected through tools like web scrapers or counting devices, offering insights into customer behaviours without direct interaction. Web scraping tools can gather structured customer experience data from third-party review sites. Additionally, counting mechanisms offer insights into the flow of customers (e.g. in airports, in and out of a store), impacting their experiences. Further, the collection of unsolicited and structured CX data is possible through website cookies, Google Analytics and Internet of Things (IoT) devices. These data collection methods offer valuable perspectives for enhancing customer experience management (CXM).

- **Unsolicited and unstructured:** This is the most diverse and potentially insightful data, including all forms of customer-generated content and behavioural data. This data type poses unique challenges regarding collection, organization and privacy concerns. This category encompasses a wide range of data types, such as transactional behaviour records, written communication, audio recordings and visual content shared by customers through emails, social media posts, online critiques or video blogs. Moreover, extensive video data can be sourced from surveillance in public areas, offering further opportunities for customer experience analysis. Nonetheless, the process of collecting, organizing and assimilating this type of data presents significant financial overheads for organizations and introduces substantial privacy and legal considerations.

Each data and collection method type offers distinct advantages and challenges for CX management. By understanding and categorizing this data effectively, organizations can derive actionable insights and significantly enhance their customer experience strategies.

CX analytics

After gathering and sorting your data, the next step is to analyse it. Advances in data storage, computing and analytics technologies have made it increasingly practical to apply big data analytics (BDA) to CX data.

TYPES OF BDA AND THEIR FUNCTIONS[15]

- **Descriptive analytics** focuses on explaining *'What happened?'* by summarizing past data to understand the current state of CX. It involves visualization tools like:
  - Charts such as histograms and scatter plots.
  - Descriptive statistics, including measures like mean, median, mode, variance and standard deviation.
  - Techniques such as cross-tabulations and k-means clustering to categorize data without predefined labels.
  - Word clouds used to visualize frequently occurring terms in textual data.

- **Diagnostic analytics** seeks to explain *'Why did it happen?'* by examining data to confirm or reject hypotheses and identify influential factors. This category includes:
  - Statistical tests and experimental designs for hypothesis testing.
  - Factor analysis methods like principal component analysis that are used to uncover underlying variables.

- **Predictive analytics** aims to forecast *'What could happen in the future?'* by using data modelling and statistical techniques to predict future events or trends. It encompasses:
  - Forecasting models, including time-series analyses and moving averages.

o Predictive models, such as classification trees, random forests, support vector machines and neural networks, which are used to anticipate future outcomes.

- **Prescriptive analytics** answers *'What should we do?'* It provides recommendations on actions to solve specific problems, guiding decisions to improve CX with:

  o Optimization models using mathematical programming.

  o Queueing models for managing wait times and service flow.

  o Efficient frontier methods for optimizing performance trade-offs.

  o Discrete event simulations for scenario planning and outcome prediction.

These AI and data analytic approaches equip organizations with the tools to understand, diagnose, predict and prescribe actions to enhance the customer experience backed by data-driven insights.

CX insights

After collecting and analysing your data, the crucial next step is to derive insights from it. Customer experience (CX) insights can be broadly divided into three main categories: attitudinal and psychographic insights, behavioural insights and market insights.

Each type provides a unique lens through which to view and understand various aspects of CX:[16]

- **Attitudinal and psychographic insights** explore customers' attitudes and cognitive states regarding their past, present and anticipated future experiences with organizations. Attitudinal insights are concerned with customers' overall dispositions towards their experiences, while psychographic insights explore the psychological aspects that influence how customers relate to these experiences. These insights are critical for organizations to assess customer satisfaction, advocacy and perceived effort. They are typically collected from both structured and unstructured data collected across various customer interaction channels such as contact centres, emails and websites.

  To generate attitudinal and psychographic insights, organizations can employ predictive big data analytics (BDA) and AI techniques like speech emotion analysis to gauge customers' emotions, moods and stress levels. Monitoring online discussions is also vital for identifying emotionally charged touchpoints and detecting highly satisfied or dissatisfied customers who may not directly voice their concerns to the organization. Furthermore, analysing the content that customers share, such as images on social media, can offer deeper insights into their personality traits and how these traits influence their experiences at various touchpoints.

- **Behavioural insights** focus on how customers' actions and decisions are shaped by their experiences. This encompasses understanding the specifics of customer behaviour and decision-making in response to their experiences. Capturing data on consumer behaviour, such as using Google Analytics, provides real-time insights into how customers interact with digital touchpoints. Descriptive BDA helps identify trends and changes in consumer behaviour, while diagnostic BDA, like A/B testing, sheds light on consumer preferences and actual behaviour. Predictive BDA can forecast future behaviours based on past actions, such as ad-clicking behaviour, offering valuable insights for organizations to tailor their customer engagement strategies.

- **Market insights** are crucial for organizations to evaluate and monitor their CX performance relative to their competitors and understand the impact on their overall brand equity. This involves assessing the competitive position and market share by tracking how organizations and their competitors are perceived in terms of CX. Predictive BDA techniques, such as graph mining and social tagging, are instrumental in gathering knowledge on customer-based brand equity, brand positioning and market structure. Analysing online keyword search data from tools like Google Trends can help organizations anticipate product demands, identify emerging trends, and predict potential market disruptions, thereby guiding strategic decisions in product development and marketing.

Effectively categorizing and generating CX insights allows organizations to gain a comprehensive understanding of their customer experience, guiding them in enhancing their strategies across different facets of their business.

CX actions

Armed with a collection of valuable insights, you're now in a position to translate these insights into actionable strategies. This translation may be something within your purview or might require approval from management, depending on your organizational role and structure.

CX actions are fundamentally linked to an organization's capabilities, which are essentially process-driven activities aimed at enhancing the customer experience. Organizations must leverage their CX data, analytics and insights to fuel a dynamic cycle of CX actions. These actions encompass monitoring, prioritizing, adapting and redesigning customer touchpoints and the overall customer journey.

CX actions can be broadly categorized into operational and strategic actions:[17]

- **Operational actions** are short-term and focus on individual touchpoints. They involve activities like *monitoring*, *prioritization* and *adaptation* of touchpoints, often leading to incremental innovations. For instance, operational actions might include deploying a dedicated team to monitor touchpoint performance using insights derived from CX data or employing IoT technology to track and improve physical touchpoint interactions, such as in-field repair services.

  For example, companies like Spotify have cleverly used descriptive and predictive analytics to adapt their touchpoints based on customer behaviour insights, creating highly personalized experiences such as the annual *Spotify Wrapped*, which features users' listening habits and preferences, further personalizing the customer journey by interacting better with the platform.

- **Strategic actions,** on the other hand, are long term and encompass the entire spectrum of potential touchpoints within the customer journey. Actions aimed at altering the design of the touchpoint journey are more inclined to foster radical innovation. For example, strategic actions may involve using CX insights for business planning and cross-departmental co-ordination to innovate and transform the customer journey, significantly altering the business model or industry standards.

  An example of operational action in practice is Caterpillar (CAT) establishing the CAT Connect to help customers, and the CAT dealers' team utilizes predictive and prescriptive BDA to support customers' machinery, enhancing efficiency and reducing repair costs through data-driven insights.[18]

  For strategic actions, John Deere's approach as an agricultural equipment manufacturer exemplifies how integrating sensors and software in agricultural equipment to provide real-time data analysis can transform the customer journey, shifting from a manufacturing-centric to a platform-centric business model and thereby achieving significant industry innovation.[19]

In essence, whether through operational tweaks or strategic overhauls, leveraging CX insights allows organizations to refine customer touch-points and journeys methodically, ensuring a seamless and engaging customer experience that aligns with both immediate and long-term business objectives.

To sum up, this framework plays a crucial role in highlighting the complexities involved in gathering, utilizing and analysing CX data across various touchpoints, encompassing physical, digital and social interactions. Customers often engage with multiple channels at different phases of their journey; for instance, purchasing through one channel and seeking after-sales support via another. Consequently, it is essential for organizations to effectively leverage CX data across these diverse channels and thoughtfully design and administer the customer journey to address these multifaceted interactions.

Put the framework into practice

Let's take a **B2B enterprise** specializing in the sales and servicing of trucks that provides a comprehensive range of products and services to diverse customers, each with multiple branches.[20] With various customer touch-points, including sales, parts service and maintenance service, the company historically relied on net promoter score (NPS) metrics to gauge customer experience. Recently, the company shifted its strategy towards a more predictive model of customer loyalty by harnessing customer data. They now collect and analyse data based on attitudinal, emotional and behavioural factors through a sophisticated machine-learning model.

It's evident how the transition to leveraging comprehensive customer data can illuminate the complexities of customer interactions across physical, digital and social channels. Customers engaging through different channels at various stages of their journey pose a unique challenge; for instance, making a purchase via one channel and seeking post-purchase support through another. This underscores the importance for organizations to proficiently utilize **CX data** across all platforms, ensuring that the design and management of the customer journey are meticulously aligned with these multifaceted interactions.

The data-driven approach to CX underscores a pivotal shift. By analysing over three years' worth of attitudinal, emotional and transactional data, the company has moved beyond traditional NPS metrics. The use of **CX analytics**, such as machine learning and natural language processing (NLP), has enabled them to predict customer loyalty with an impressive accuracy rate, revealing that reliance on NPS alone significantly underestimates potential customer churn.

The insights generated from the analytical efforts have been significant. Despite a high NPS suggesting strong customer advocacy, AI analysis identified a substantial churn risk. Furthermore, a notable discrepancy emerged between customers' qualitative feedback and their NPS categorization, highlighting the limitations of relying solely on numerical scores.

Armed with these **CX insights**, they undertook **targeted CX actions** to address identified pain points and reprioritize touchpoints critical to their customers, such as credit financing and invoicing, which were previously overlooked in favour of sales and service interactions. This strategic realignment, informed by deep data analysis, not only enhances customer satisfaction but also safeguards the company against potential revenue losses attributable to customer attrition.[21]

The example shows how businesses can harness the power of CX data analytics to transcend traditional CX measurement methods, reveal the true complexity of customer relationships, and drive substantive improvements across all touchpoints of the customer journey.

In the B2C sector, many insurance businesses use CX data to enhance customer experience and build loyalty by better understanding customer experience and driver behaviour. They utilize AI to analyse data on how drivers behave and experience driving. For example, Driverly, an insurance tech firm, is dedicated to collecting behavioural data through the phone to offer the most competitive rates for customers, moving away from traditional insurance models that rely heavily on demographic factors and risk assessments. Instead, Driverly focuses on actual driving behaviour to set premiums. Whether you're a young driver with a limited no-claims history or an experienced motorist, Driverly ensures that pricing is competitive, based purely on behaviour.[22]

To continue with the insurance businesses, this industry needs to go beyond selling products to selling experience. Many of them conduct frequent customer surveys to collect CX data on customers' satisfaction levels with various insurance services, such as claims processing and customer support. Ratings are typically on a 1 to 10 scale. Utilize net promoter score (NPS) to gauge loyalty and the probability of customers recommending insurance services to others.

To remain competitive, insurance businesses must transition from merely selling products to delivering exceptional experiences. While many insurers regularly conduct customer surveys to gather insights into satisfaction levels with services such as claims processing and customer support – often using a 1 to 10 rating scale and net promoter score (NPS) to measure loyalty and the likelihood of recommendations – this approach alone is no longer sufficient. The industry needs to elevate its customer experience (CX) analytics by incorporating feedback from diverse channels, including social media and customer support interactions, to better understand customers' emotional connections with their services.

Key recommendations

- **Extract emotional tone**: Leverage advanced analytics, such as natural language processing (NLP), to analyse feedback across channels like social media and customer support. Identify emotional states such as frustration or satisfaction to gain deeper insights into customers' emotional engagement with insurance services.

- **Analyse behavioural data**: Examine customer engagement and activity patterns, including policy renewals, claim submissions and customer support interactions. Detect trends such as renewal rates, claim frequency, and behavioural shifts that could signal dissatisfaction or emerging opportunities.

- **Enhance cross-selling and upselling**: Use transactional and purchase history data to identify opportunities for tailored cross-selling and upselling strategies, maximizing customer lifetime value.

- **Forecast customer behaviour**: Employ predictive analytics to combine emotional, attitudinal and behavioural data for accurate customer behaviour forecasting. This enables insurers to anticipate customer needs, improve retention strategies and deliver personalized experiences.

By adopting a holistic, data-driven approach, insurance companies can move beyond transactional relationships, promoting stronger emotional connections and loyalty with their customers.

INSIGHTS AND ACTIONS FOR CX ENHANCEMENT

- **Attitudinal insights**: Determine the main factors influencing customer satisfaction and loyalty.

- **Behavioural insights:** Develop strategies to mitigate customer churn through targeted retention efforts and customized support initiatives.

This could lead to **CX actions** such as continuous touchpoint monitoring to regularly track the customer journey and behaviour to pinpoint improvement areas and optimize the overall customer experience. Another action is through adaptation and personalization: personalize insurance products and communication to align with each customer's unique preferences, behaviours and emotional needs.

Utilizing AI and customer experience data enables the insurance company to transcend traditional NPS metrics, affording a more nuanced understanding of customer behaviour. This approach facilitates a proactive stance in improving the customer experience, boosting loyalty and driving growth, showcasing a model for integrating CX data analytics into business strategy.

Guidelines for professionals

Some guidelines professionals can follow to assist their organizations in comprehensively understanding which types of CX data and analytics are most effective for producing actionable insights.[23]

1 **Strategize:** Begin by identifying the CX actions your organization aims to achieve. For immediate operational goals, focus on assessing current touchpoints, resource allocation, or modifications to existing touchpoints. For long-term strategic objectives, consider a holistic view of all potential touchpoints and significant changes across the customer journey. Despite the allure of a comprehensive approach, be mindful of the complexities and investments required for big data analytics (BDA). Start with manageable steps, such as monitoring specific touchpoints, to build experience and confidence in CX analytics. Leadership with a clear vision for the strategic importance of CXM is essential for guiding these actions. Preparing the necessary technological and human resources and initiating pilot projects will facilitate organizational buy-in and demonstrate the value of BDA-powered CX insights.

2 **Assess:** Determine the CX insights needed to support your strategic actions and the corresponding analytics techniques. Evaluate whether your organization has the internal capabilities to perform these analytics or if there's a need to develop or outsource these functions. For example,

descriptive analytics can provide initial attitudinal and behavioural insights, which can be enhanced with more advanced analytical methods. Consider the feasibility of taking action based on these insights, especially as you integrate more sophisticated analytics into your strategy.

3 **Examine:** Identify the types of CX data available and needed, considering the digital, physical and social touchpoints. Address ownership issues of the data and how it's managed within your organization. Transitioning from siloed data management to a unified system that accommodates both structured and unstructured data is crucial. This might necessitate adopting a big data infrastructure that meets technical requirements for processing and storing large volumes of complex data.

4 **Decide:** After evaluating your analytic capabilities and data availability, decide whether to enhance in-house resources, outsource, or adopt a hybrid approach. Similarly, determine if leveraging existing data or acquiring new data is necessary. Conduct cost–benefit analyses to guide these decisions, especially when considering third-party solutions to gain CX insights.

5 **Implement:** This stage involves realizing the chosen CX analytics and data strategies. It requires collaboration across various organizational roles and potentially external partners to develop and deploy solutions that align with your CX objectives. Modern UX methodologies, like Agile UX for MVP development and DevOps tools, will be instrumental in this process, ensuring the scalability and reliability of the CX solutions.

6 **Learn:** Establish feedback mechanisms to learn from the CX implementation process. Sharing insights throughout the organization and training employees on their application is vital for fostering a culture that values CX improvement. Consider forming a cross-functional team dedicated to translating BDA-generated insights into actionable strategies and overseeing their execution across departments. Monitoring the business impact of these insights, such as customer satisfaction and operational efficiencies, will highlight the value of your CX initiatives.

By following these guidelines, managers can effectively navigate the complexities of employing CX data and big data analytics (BDA) for customer experience management (CXM), fostering an environment that leverages data-driven insights to enhance customer experiences and achieve business objectives.

KEY TAKEAWAYS

Traditional CX metrics, while useful, often fail to capture the full spectrum of customer experiences and behaviours. Their limitations, including a tendency to oversimplify customer interactions and an inability to fully gauge emotional and psychological customer states, highlight the need for a more nuanced approach to understanding customer experiences.

The discussion in this chapter highlighted the challenges associated with these metrics, such as their reliance on structured data, which may overlook rich insights contained within unstructured feedback from customers. Therefore, we explored a framework designed to help organizations effectively identify and utilize various types of customer experience (CX) data and analytics to create meaningful, actionable insights. Specifically, our findings revealed:

- Traditional customer experience metrics like NPS are limited in capturing the full customer journey. Use a broader set of data points to measure loyalty, satisfaction and engagement more accurately.

- Incorporate big data analytics to combine different types of customer data, including both structured (e.g. surveys) and unstructured (e.g. social media comments), to uncover deeper insights.

- Apply machine-learning models to predict customer behaviour and loyalty. Use these insights to address issues and personalize experiences to meet individual customer needs proactively.

- Implement a CXM framework powered by big data to monitor and adapt customer interactions dynamically, ensuring responses are personalized and timely across all touchpoints.

- Generate CX insights in all business contexts (B2B, B2C, public service) to anticipate needs, resolve issues proactively, and improve satisfaction and loyalty.

- Make a sustained commitment to data analysis and continuously adapt based on actionable insights, ensuring your organization remains competitive in a customer-centric marketplace.

After assessing our CXM maturity, the following chapters will focus on discussing how practitioners can apply AI to predict customer loyalty and engagement and refine our market positioning strategies.

Notes

1 Holmlund, M, Van Vaerenbergh, Y, Ciuchita, R, Ravald, A, Sarantopoulos, P, Villarroel Ordenes, F and Zaki, M (2020) Customer experience management in the age of big data analytics: A strategic framework, *Journal of Business Research*, 116, 356–65

2 Zaki, M (2019) Digital transformation: Harnessing digital technologies for the next generation of services, *Journal of Services Marketing*, 33 (4), 429–35

3 Reichheld, F F (2003) The one number you need to grow, *Harvard Business Review*, December. https://hbr.org/2003/12/the-one-number-you-need-to-grow (archived at https://perma.cc/MU94-EJ22)

4 Wiesel, T, Verhoef, P C and de Haan, E (2012) There is no single best measure of your customers, *Harvard Business Review*, 11 July. https://hbr.org (archived at https://perma.cc/HA8Y-SLW4)

5 Marketing Explainers (2024) McDonald's marketing strategy explained, *The Marketing Explainers*, 5 January. www.marketingexplainers.com/mcdonalds-marketing-strategy-explained/ (archived at https://perma.cc/QR5W-QMFF)

6 Exhibitor Online (2016) How Caterpillar owned the show. www.exhibitoronline.com/topics/article.asp?ID=2480 (archived at https://perma.cc/F929-JLQ4)

7 HubSpot (2024) 9 benefits of customer interviews & how to conduct them. https://blog.hubspot.com/service/customer-interviews (archived at https://perma.cc/9HFS-PP5P)

8 McColl-Kennedy, J R and Zaki, M (2022) Measuring and managing customer experience (CX): What works and what doesn't, in Edvardsson, B and Tronvoll, B (eds), *The Palgrave Handbook of Service Management*, Palgrave Macmillan

9 Slater, D (2024) The imperatives of customer-centric innovation, Amazon Web Services (AWS) Executive Insights. https://aws.amazon.com/executive-insights/content/the-imperatives-of-customer-centric-innovation/ (archived at https://perma.cc/9LUF-96XE)

10 Dixon, M, Freeman, K and Toman, N (2014) The value of keeping the right customers, *Harvard Business Review*, 29 October. https://hbr.org/2014/10/the-value-of-keeping-the-right-customers (archived at https://perma.cc/VC9M-NJZ7)

11 Jackson, S (2023) Tim Cook's daily routine: The schedule of the Apple CEO who wakes up at 4 a.m. and reads hundreds of customer emails a day, *INSIDER*, 9 December. https://uk.news.yahoo.com/tim-cooks-daily-routine-schedule-092101549.html (archived at https://perma.cc/LED4-Z9ZH)

12 Holmlund, M, Van Vaerenbergh, Y, Ciuchita, R, Ravald, A, Sarantopoulos, P, Villarroel Ordenes, F and Zaki, M (2020) Customer experience management in the age of big data analytics: A strategic framework, *Journal of Business Research*, 116, 356–65

13 ibid.

14 ibid.

15 ibid.

16 ibid.

17 ibid.

18 Caterpillar Inc. (2024) With Cat® Connect, you are in control. www.cat.com/en_GB/by-industry/electric-power/product-support/cat-connect.html (archived at https://perma.cc/CL8X-JV48)

19 Deere & Company (2024) Precision agriculture technology: The essentials. www.deere.co.uk/en-gb/industries/agriculture/the-essentials (archived at https://perma.cc/ZF25-47BS)

20 ibid.

21 Zaki, M, McColl-Kennedy, J R and Neely, A (2021) Using AI to track how customers feel – in real time, *Harvard Business Review*, 4 May. https://hbr.org/2021/05/using-ai-to-track-how-customers-feel-in-real-time (archived at https://perma.cc/9KD5-6KZN)

22 Driverly (2024) About us. www.driverly.ai/about (archived at https://perma.cc/VUF8-F4SL)

23 Holmlund, M, Van Vaerenbergh, Y, Ciuchita, R, Ravald, A, Sarantopoulos, P, Villarroel Ordenes, F and Zaki, M (2020) Customer experience management in the age of big data analytics: A strategic framework, *Journal of Business Research*, 116, 356–65

8

Customer loyalty

In the last chapter, we discussed how firms could leverage a wealth of valuable CX data to evaluate and analyse customer journeys and experiences. Building on this foundation, the next objective is to develop a loyal customer base. Customer loyalty is often seen as a crucial measure of a company's performance. To achieve success, companies must grasp their customers' thoughts and feelings. While firms invest substantial time and money in understanding their customers better, many still struggle to listen to them effectively. As highlighted previously, depending solely on single metrics such as NPS can be misleading. These metrics fail to illuminate the deeper issues that contribute to lower ratings. We know that these one-dimensional metrics are easy to apply. Still, they do not sufficiently capture the complex nature of customer loyalty, which cannot be fully evaluated using just one indicator (such as NPS in surveys).[1]

Therefore, I hope you agree that a broader and more nuanced approach is necessary for understanding and predicting customer loyalty. Companies looking to build a loyal customer base should do more than collect and review customer experience (CX) data such as NPS, CSAT and CES. They should also expand their evaluation to better predict actual customer loyalty actions.

In order to achieve this, I will explore the multifaceted nature of customer loyalty, which encompasses various aspects: attitudinal factors such as outstanding performance, appeal and desirability, and effective communication; emotional considerations like admiration; and behavioural components, which cover patterns of purchasing and interaction.

Customer loyalty

Customer loyalty occupies a pivotal role in every firm strategy and is consistently associated with the firm's profitability. It is often defined as a consumer's profound attachment or commitment to a product, service, brand or organization.[2] This loyalty typically stems from the customer's experiences, which integrate customer evaluation of their growing satisfaction with the quality of the product and service. Ultimately, customer loyalty leads to profitability through the reduced costs of acquiring new customers and servicing repeat buyers.

Customer attrition appears in two primary forms – dis-adoption at the category level and inter-firm attrition,[3] often referred to as *churn*. Additionally, distinctions are often drawn between *active* and *inactive* customer statuses before churn occurs.[4] Research highlights several key factors that companies need to consider in predicting customer churn effectively:[5]

- **Attitudinal factors**, such as customer satisfaction, reflect the customer's perception of service quality. Other important predictors could include customer characteristics and social connectivity.

- **Service failures** are present or absent in the relationship between the customer and the company.

- **Switching costs** are the expenses a customer faces when moving to a different service provider.

- **Behavioural factors** such as usage behaviour during interactions between the customer and the company play a crucial role.

For example, telecommunications operators routinely apply data analytics to analyse customers who are likely to churn or retain for contractual services, taking into account factors like the duration of service agreements, promotional influences, variations among subscribers, cohort-wide trends, and seasonal variations in usage patterns. In the e-commerce and online retail sector, factors such as the recency and frequency of purchases are considered alongside variables like spending levels, service disruptions, shifts in the types of items purchased within a category, changes in spending per category, socioeconomic factors, and membership in loyalty programmes.

Today, organizations can leverage a vast array of CX data sources to gain real-time insights into customer loyalty across attitudinal, emotional and behavioural dimensions. The introduction of digitization enables firms to proactively assess customer loyalty using advanced AI and machine learning techniques. These methods are capable of identifying patterns in customer data that correlate with business outcomes.[6]

As discussed, harnessing the power of CX data necessitates a sophisticated AI approach that can integrate insights and extract knowledge from vast quantities of both structured and unstructured data. Machine learning not only aids in predicting customer behaviour but also helps address the challenge of managing the vast amount of information generated in customer feedback scenarios, enabling managers to understand better and respond to customer issues, preferences and behaviours.

Customer loyalty as a multifaceted measure emphasizes the importance of distinguishing between factors that merely predict churn risk and those that cause it. For example, customer behaviours can be seen as predictors (like frequency of purchases or engagement with customer service), while customer satisfaction (e.g. frustration with customer service) may be an actual cause of churn. This distinction is critical as it addresses not only the specific reasons customers may leave but also the broader, often unobserved differences among them.

I will showcase how machine learning-based methods can facilitate the integration of attitudinal, emotional and behavioural data to provide a more comprehensive understanding of customer dynamics.

Customer loyalty elements

Figure 8.1 shows how firms can break down the key components of customer loyalty to enhance their measurement capabilities.

Customer loyalty is a complex concept that encompasses three types of customer responses.[7]

Attitudinal response

This involves customers recognizing and endorsing the company's performance and products as they align with their needs and expectations. The dimension refers to a customer's cognitive and emotional preference or attitude towards a brand as attitudinal responses. To effectively gauge these responses, it's crucial to consider three sub-dimensions: superior performance, desirability, and reach and communication.

SUPERIOR PERFORMANCE
The company delivers high-quality products and services.

This refers to the customer's focus on the performance of a product or service. Firms can consider quality as an indicator of product or service

FIGURE 8.1 Customer loyalty elements

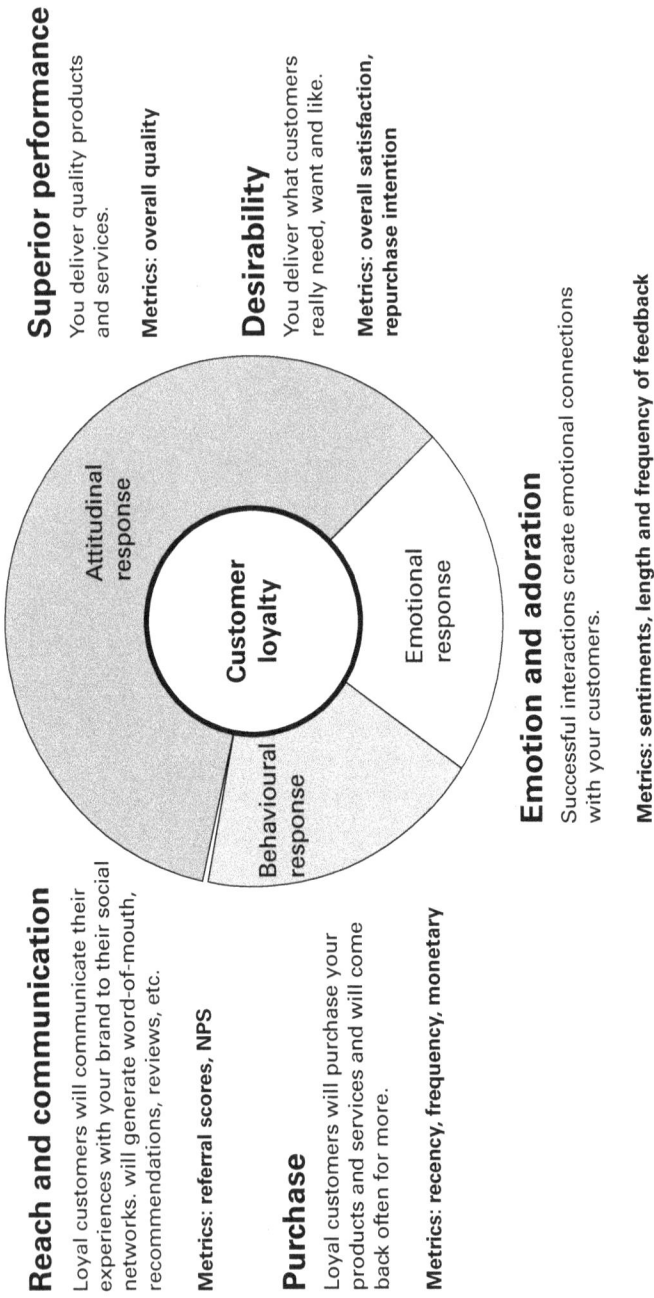

Superior performance

You deliver quality products and services.

Metrics: overall quality

Desirability

You deliver what customers really need, want and like.

Metrics: overall satisfaction, repurchase intention

Emotion and adoration

Successful interactions create emotional connections with your customers.

Metrics: sentiments, length and frequency of feedback

Attitudinal response

Customer loyalty

Emotional response

Behavioural response

Reach and communication

Loyal customers will communicate their experiences with your brand to their social networks. will generate word-of-mouth, recommendations, reviews, etc.

Metrics: referral scores, NPS

Purchase

Loyal customers will purchase your products and services and will come back often for more.

Metrics: recency, frequency, monetary

excellence. Firms create value through the integration of quality resources at various touchpoints, encompassing multiple activities and interactions.

For instance, in a B2B context, customers might assess the quality of resources provided, such as machines, parts, sales personnel and service engineers. They may also evaluate the activities undertaken, including the sale of machines, delivery of parts, and provision of engineering services like machine repairs, breakdown recovery and predictive maintenance solutions. To gauge customer perceptions of these resources and activities, firms conduct surveys that ask customers about their experiences, focusing on factors like quality, responsiveness, availability, and the duration of interactions with employees.

- **Desirability**: The company meets the real needs, wants and preferences of customers.

  This dimension refers to the customer's positive feelings or attitudes toward the brand, which stem from a satisfying usage experience (pleasurable fulfilment). It can be assessed through metrics such as overall satisfaction and repurchase intentions, which are derived from the customer's experiences in purchasing and using a product or service. These measures offer valuable insights into the customer's attitudes towards the brand and their likelihood of remaining a customer in the future. For example, Nike's dedication to research and development exemplifies how a brand can promote desirability among its customers. By consistently focusing on creating high-performance athletic wear and footwear, Nike uses advanced materials and technologies to boost comfort, performance and style.

  For instance, introducing a new line of running shoes featuring innovative cushioning technology is designed specifically to reduce impact and enhance energy return for runners. This commitment to innovation not only meets the functional needs of athletes but also appeals to their desire for the latest advancements in sports technology, making Nike's products highly sought-after. This includes technologies that aim to reduce carbon footprint, such as ReactX technology, aiming to optimize energy return and lower carbon footprint.[8] Feedback could be gathered through metrics like overall satisfaction and repurchase intention.

- **Reach and communication**: Loyal customers share their positive experiences through their social networks, generating word-of-mouth recommendations.

Feedback can be gathered and evaluated from various communication channels. Traditional methods like referral and NPS (net promoter score) surveys provide structured data that firms use to collect and analyse customer feedback. The communication measure relies on the referral metric, which gauges the likelihood of customers recommending a product or service to others. As discussed in Chapter 7, the NPS metric categorizes responses into three groups – promoters, passives and detractors – offering a clear picture of customer advocacy levels. However, firms can define ways to make sure that customers manage to recommend and promote the services to colleagues and friends.

For example, firms can introduce referral incentives where both the existing customer (referrer) and the new customer (referee) receive a benefit. For instance, both might get one month free when the referee signs up for a subscription based on a referral. This creates a win-win situation, incentivizing existing customers to promote the service actively. To make the referral process straightforward and accessible, the service integrates easy sharing options within its digital platform. Customers can share referral links via email, social media, or even through direct messaging apps with a single click. The service might also provide personalized messages or social media-friendly graphics that customers can use to make their referrals more appealing. Firms can track the status of customer referrals through a dashboard that shows which friends have signed up and which rewards have been claimed. Notifications encourage continued engagement, reminding customers of unused referral bonuses or upcoming expiration dates for their incentives. The service should actively promote the referral programme through various channels, such as during the sign-up process, within regular customer communications (like emails and in-app notifications), and during customer service interactions.

KEY METRICS THAT COULD BE USED AS A DATA SOURCE UNDER ATTITUDINAL RESPONSES

- **Quality assessments:** These are evaluations typically done through customer surveys, quality audits, or reviews that measure a product or service's perceived value and effectiveness. Quality assessments help identify areas where a product or service meets, exceeds or falls short of customer expectations. For example, customers might be asked to rate the durability of a product or the responsiveness of a service on a scale from poor to excellent.

- **Overall satisfaction**: This metric gauges the general happiness of customers with a product or service. It's usually measured using a single survey question, such as '*Overall, how satisfied are you with our product/service?*', with responses typically on a Likert scale from very dissatisfied to very satisfied. This metric helps businesses understand the cumulative impact of their product or service experience on customers.

- **Repurchase intentions**: This metric measures the likelihood that a customer will buy a product or service again. It is predictive of future sales and customer loyalty and is often assessed with survey questions like '*How likely are you to purchase our product/service again?*' Responses are usually gathered on a scale from unlikely to very likely. High repurchase intentions suggest strong customer loyalty and satisfaction with the value received.

- **Referral scores (e.g. NPS)**: As discussed in Chapter 7, this metric assesses a customer's willingness to recommend a product or service to others. This score can significantly influence customer behaviour, as personal recommendations are a powerful form of marketing.

As discussed, historically, companies have relied on quantitative surveys. Despite their high cost and increasing unpopularity among customers, who find them intrusive and thus are less willing to respond, these surveys have remained a cornerstone of customer understanding strategies.[9]

It's worth mentioning that qualitative customer insights, such as feedback and reviews, can replace these metrics. By leveraging NLP and LLM technologies, it's possible to identify customer perceptions of product quality ('*the product is flawless*'), intentions to repurchase ('*I would buy this product again*'), general satisfaction ('*I am pleased and satisfied with the service provided*') and likelihood of referral ('*I would endorse this product to my contacts. I convinced my partner to buy it*').

Emotional response

Customers develop a deep affection for the company's offerings, reacting with strong positive emotions and adoration. Adoration plays a vital role in customer loyalty, reflecting the profound bond customers can develop with a product or service. Customers often display emotions like love and joy and essentially become brand fans. Those who experience significant delight in their interactions with a service typically exhibit higher loyalty levels. To raise customer loyalty, companies must design emotional experiences that elicit delight, as discussed in Chapter 5. Gathering qualitative feedback through surveys, emails, social media comments, reviews and phone calls is essential for comprehending the customer's emotional experience. This feedback offers in-depth insights into the crucial aspects that shape it.

Many companies develop their own sentiment analysis models or utilize pre-built sentiment and emotion analysis tools to evaluate qualitative feedback. This enables them to understand customer compliments and concerns better. For example, Tactful AI, a customer engagement platform, allows its customers to understand customer sentiment and emotion in conversation data in its chatbot platform.[10]

KEY METRICS THAT COULD BE USED AS A DATA SOURCE UNDER EMOTIONAL RESPONSES

Attitudinal measures alone often fail to capture nuanced emotional responses and overlook critical feedback. Through my research in this area, we've observed that customers frequently provide high ratings even when they encounter major issues with a product or service, leading companies to overlook substantial customer dissatisfaction.[11] This oversight can result in customer loss without the firm understanding the cause. For instance, in one case, a promotor customer rated their NPS with the repair service in an asset-heavy B2B service as 10 out of 10. However, their comment revealed deeper issues: 'The only thing that we were a bit disappointed with is to do with repairs. It seems that every time they come out, there is over $1,000 in service. The fitters seem to be struggling with diagnosing the issue, and it always seems to be more expensive.'

In scenarios where a customer rates a company highly yet still voices a complaint within the same survey, it highlights a complex aspect of customer feedback that often occurs. This dual-natured feedback can be especially dominant in call centres, where customers might discuss issues yet still award high scores in other channels, such as surveys. Another complexity arises in B2B contexts where the decision maker may be satisfied with the service, but other stakeholders involved, like those who ordered the service, might not share the same sentiment.

To address these challenges and accurately represent the diverse perspectives across different channels, companies need to adopt a strategy that differentiates and aggregates feedback effectively. This involves creating a comprehensive 360-degree view of customer experiences, integrating and analysing feedback from all touchpoints and stakeholders. Such an approach ensures that a business can assess and respond to the various voices of its customers, encompassing both positive ratings and specific complaints, to enhance overall service delivery and customer satisfaction.

This demonstrates that textual data, including direct customer comments, are now produced at numerous touchpoints throughout the customer journey. Open-ended feedback and user-generated content are valuable resources for extracting meaningful insights and identifying specific pain points along the customer journey. Therefore, relying on a structured approach to capture customer feelings and emotions from qualitative feedback is essential. Natural language processing (NLP) and large language models (LLMs) present new opportunities for enhancing the measurement and management of customer experience (CX) from verbatim comments set in many systems, such as customer relationship management systems (CRM), social media, customer reviews, emails, call centre notes, chatbots and others.

Current AI tools often only detect basic positive or negative sentiments. In the customer journey, in Chapter 4, we demonstrate that the CX consists of value creation elements, discrete customer emotions, and cognitive responses at distinct touchpoints, which are essential elements in designing CX. Therefore, firms should adopt this customer-centric approach to evaluate how customers react to their CX designs. Here, the LLM and AI capability can be used to analyse and categorize keywords that describe the customer experience (CX) across several dimensions: resources (e.g. knowledge, systems, products and skills); activities (including fixing, ordering and service delivery); context or scenarios that influence the experience (like weekends); interactions (such as calling or chatting); and customer roles (such as providing suggestions or remaining neutral). This, in addition, identifies both the emotional responses (joy, love, sadness, anger, frustration and surprise) and cognitive reactions (compliments, complaints and suggestions) of customers at various touchpoints.

Therefore, the first and most significant change firms should make is to flip where they're investing in their analysis of customer emotion. They should start with the qualitative comments and then turn to the results of their quantitative surveys. IKEA has shifted its approach by prioritizing qualitative customer feedback to better understand evolving consumer expectations shaped significantly by the rise of online shopping. While IKEA's products have long been central to its brand, the retail landscape demands a shift towards customer-centric shopping experiences.[12] This shift is evident in IKEA's introduction of new physical retail formats like the Design Studios in Manhattan and London, which represent a more tailored approach to customer engagement.[13]

However, managing the customer experience across both physical and digital channels presents significant challenges, particularly given the vast scale of customer interactions at IKEA, which includes over 2.5 billion web visits and 957 million store visits annually, supported by a global staff of more than 200,000. Historically, this has been problematic as feedback often remained siloed within various segments of the company, hindering effective utilization. Therefore, IKEA invested in developing capabilities to capture customer feedback across different channels and integrate insights from every interaction – whether it's an email, phone call or online review – to have a comprehensive view of the customer journey. This helps identify both issues and successes across all touchpoints. To deepen its understanding of customer sentiments, IKEA employs natural language processing (NLP) to analyse the free text from customer comments. This allows IKEA to capture the nuances of customer emotions and experiences in their own words. The solution features a straightforward dashboard that enables employees to quickly identify and address emerging issues, enhancing responsiveness and problem-solving efficiency. By collecting and acting on this data, IKEA not only enhances current operations but also gathers the insights necessary to innovate and introduce improved services. This proactive data strategy marks a significant evolution from traditional retail to a dynamic, customer-responsive model.[14]

The IKEA initiative shows that, with the right AI tools, you can analyse qualitative data, which can be more insightful than surveys. Companies might even consider abandoning traditional quantitative surveys, as these tools enable real-time understanding of customer thoughts and feelings across various touchpoints.

Behavioural response

Behavioural dimensions reflect a buyer's ongoing commitment to repurchase or continually use a specific product or service.[15] Often, the customer's readiness to pay a premium price is used as an indicator of this commitment.

For example, consider a consumer electronics company like Apple. Customers who repeatedly upgrade to the latest iPhone model demonstrate a behavioural response indicating strong brand loyalty. This repeated purchase behaviour, especially given the premium price of Apple products, is a clear indicator of their commitment. Similarly, in subscription-based services like Netflix or Spotify, a customer's willingness to continue their subscription month after month, even as prices might increase, also showcases this behavioural commitment. The ease of cancellation contrasts sharply with their choice to remain subscribed, further underscoring their loyalty.

In each case, the customer's readiness to pay a premium price, not just once but repeatedly, serves as a strong behavioural indicator of their loyalty and satisfaction with the product or service. This ongoing financial commitment helps companies gauge the effectiveness of their customer retention strategies and can guide future product development and marketing efforts.

KEY METRICS THAT COULD BE USED AS A DATA SOURCE UNDER BEHAVIOURAL RESPONSES

The recency, frequency and monetary (RFM) method is a well-established technique for analysing customer purchasing behaviour using past transactional data.[16] RFM metrics effectively predict future customer lifetime value (CLV), customer behaviour patterns, and the likelihood of churn. This dimension assigns profitability scores to customers by analysing their purchase behaviour through transactional data. Of these, recency is regarded as the most indicative of behavioural loyalty, making it a critical metric for assessing ongoing customer engagement.

CLV accounts for the customer's initial purchase, repeat purchases, and the average duration of their relationship with the company. RFM and CLV are instrumental in measuring customers' loyalty and retention rates. Also, they set a benchmark for the maximum amount that should be spent on acquiring a customer, ensuring that acquisition costs do not exceed the potential profit from that customer. But they also encourage companies to prioritize long-term customer relationships over short-term profits. Using these metrics is crucial for enabling businesses to evaluate the financial significance of each customer relationship and strategize ways to maximize retention and profitability over time. Sustainable business growth involves retaining existing customers, which is more cost-effective than acquiring new ones.

In my discussions with various companies, I've often heard that integrating behavioural data with customer experience (CX) data is a significant challenge due to organizational silos. This situation is common in firms with multiple products and brands that operate independently, making it difficult to share data across the organization. This lack of data integration hinders the ability to embrace a truly customer-centric approach. Additionally, firms in, for example, the consumer goods industry often face challenges in gathering customer insights since they typically sell through third-party retailers, and this data isn't always shared. This separation prevents companies from effectively linking behavioural, attitudinal and emotional data to gain a comprehensive understanding of customer loyalty and pinpoint areas for service improvement. As a response, many of these firms are beginning to sell directly through their digital channels to gain better visibility into customer behaviour and preferences.

At one of the Cambridge Service Alliance events, Dr Robert Bates, the head of decision science at Currys, an electronics retail company, highlighted the crucial role of creating a well-defined CLV segment in retail through machine learning models. This approach should leverage historical data that includes purchasing behaviours, customer interactions and potentially demographic information to forecast the future value a customer will contribute to the company. Using machine learning algorithms is vital in uncovering patterns not easily detected by human analysts, leading to more precise customer segmentation.

Additionally, Dr Bates discussed the significance of analysing return rates and transaction counts across customer segments to highlight the effects of a poor net promoter score (NPS). By examining how these metrics correlate with NPS, firms can distinguish the direct financial impact of customer satisfaction. This analysis is vital, as it quantifies the potential loss from missed transactions linked to customer dissatisfaction, providing actionable insights for improving customer experiences and prioritizing business efforts.

These insights can lead to several strategic actions:

- Knowing the impact of customer satisfaction on CLV guides more informed decisions about enhancing customer service, product quality and loyalty initiatives.

- Identifying the most valuable customer segments and understanding how their satisfaction is linked to financial outcomes enables better resource targeting to maximize CLV.

- Detailed insights into CLV segments allow for the customization of marketing efforts to better meet the specific needs and preferences of different customer groups, thus potentially boosting campaign effectiveness.

Let's pause here, and before you turn to the next section, take a moment to reflect and consider the following questions:

- How does your offering stand out from your competitors'?
- How appealing is your offering to customers?
- Do customers genuinely love what you provide?
- Have there been repeat purchases from your customers?
- Have your customers been advocates for your brand?

Put the framework into practice

Let's take a B2B asset-heavy dealer case study.[17] The company specializes in the sale and servicing of trucks and serves a broad customer base, each with multiple branches. The company has several customer touchpoints, including sales, parts service and maintenance. With its complex inter-company relationships and varied customer touchpoints, this setting provides a rich context for examining customer loyalty assessment practices within the service industry.

The company is committed to making customers feel valued, secure and at ease when interacting with the firm. To support this commitment, a customer experience roadmap was developed. This roadmap is envisioned as a journey that ensures the alignment of all business segments with the customer experience strategy and an understanding of its impact on business performance. This includes clarifying what the customer experience entails, how it is implemented, and its importance. They are keen to establish standards for customer interactions and define communication methods, specifying who engages with customers, how and when. This includes facilitating each business segment's input into the broader business strategy, and evaluating the organization's performance in customer experience via monthly telephone surveys conducted by an external party to capture the voice of the customer authentically.

To align with our framework, metrics could be used.[18]

Attitudinal data

Data is gathered monthly through structured customer surveys, addressing various aspects of customer satisfaction and service quality. The company collects comprehensive survey data to enhance its understanding and management of customer interactions. This survey includes both structured and unstructured questions, featuring 12 items that assess various aspects such as overall satisfaction, intent to repurchase and refer, availability of resources, responsiveness, communication, duration of service completion, preparation, quality of service, and timeliness and accuracy of invoicing. Customers provide their ratings on a scale from 1, representing 'Very Dissatisfied', to 10, indicating 'Very Satisfied'. A well-established metrics for attitudinal responses, including *quality scores, overall satisfaction and purchase intention*, could serve as variables to train the machine learning model.

Emotional data

Data is collected via open-ended survey questions, allowing customers to express detailed feelings and suggestions. Additionally, emotional responses are collected via an open-ended question that asks, '*Do you have any other comments or suggestions on how we could improve this service?*' This question enables the company to capture real-time feedback and insights about aspects of the service that may not be covered in the structured survey. Analysing customer feedback using large language models (LLMs) involves breaking down textual comments into sentence-level components to understand the underlying sentiments and specific issues customers are facing.

Here's how to conduct such an analysis.[19] Let's take the example of a loyal customer who rated the service 10/10:

> The only thing that we were a bit disappointed with is field service repairs. It seems that every time they come out, it's over $1,000 in service. The fitters seem to be struggling with diagnosing the issue. It always seems to be more expensive.

While the customer's feedback indicates high overall satisfaction, it reveals a critical gap in expectations versus actual service concerning repair costs and diagnostics. This expressed *disappointment* could potentially lead to customer attrition if not addressed, despite the high ratings. Such insights are invaluable for the company to improve areas like pricing strategies and the technical training of their technicians to better diagnose issues. This detailed feedback emphasizes the need to examine deeper than just numerical ratings to fully grasp and enhance customer sentiment and loyalty.

To do so, first, NLP can help process this comment automatically and divide the customer feedback into individual sentences to focus on specific thoughts or issues mentioned.

This allows for a more targeted analysis of each aspect of the feedback:[20]

- **Identify touchpoints:** Determine which part of the service or product the customer refers to in each sentence. For example, if a customer mentions service, '*parts*', '*sales*', or '*workshop*', this could be classified as a touchpoint. In the example above, '*field service repairs*' is the touchpoint.

- **Categorize resources and activities:** Map each sentence to value creation elements such as resources, activities, context, interactions and the customer's role. For instance, the customer mentions '*fitters*', which would be classified under Resources, and the action '*diagnosing the issue and fitting*' under activities.

- **Analyse context**: LLM models can look for any mention of situations or conditions that affect the customer's experience. This could include time-specific events or particular circumstances impacting the service '*Service cost*'.

- **Assess interactions**: identify how customers describe their interactions with the service or company representatives, including both direct actions and communication methods (e.g. '*Service visits*').

- **Understand customer role**: Consider what role the customer plays in the interaction (active or passive). Are they making suggestions, providing feedback, or merely describing their experience? In this example, the customer could be classified as an '*active*' feedback provider.

- **Detect discrete emotions**: Identify and label any explicit emotions customers express, such as frustration or pleasure. This provides insight into the emotional impact of the CX. In our example, '*Disappointed*' is the negative emotion mentioned by the customer.

- **Determine cognitive responses**: Look for cognitive responses that reflect the customer's thinking, like complaints, compliments or suggestions. These often provide actionable insights. The example above could be classified as a '*complaint*'.

- **Root cause analysis**: Where possible, infer the root causes behind the feedback. In our example, the complaint is about the high service pricing. Therefore, the root cause might be categorized under '*Price Value*'.

By leveraging large language models (LLMs) and NLP for this analysis, we can streamline the text analysis process by automating tasks like sentiment detection, root cause, emotion detection and value creation keyword extraction. This enhances the efficiency of data processing. LLMs are also proficient at identifying patterns and trends within extensive datasets and can explain the reasoning behind the model's classification, as shown in Table 8.1. These capabilities allow for more accurate predictions of customer behaviour and provide valuable insights for shaping business strategies. The ultimate aim is to utilize these insights to not just comprehend but also enhance the customer experience by systematically addressing the issues highlighted in the feedback.

The AI algorithms can recognize the specialized language of customers, seamlessly blending expressed sentiments with established evaluation methods to extract meaningful insights. These insights are powerful, shaping both immediate responses and strategic long-term customer relationship, the model's precision well beyond random guesswork.

The outcome is a model that is not only quantitatively smarter but also emotionally resonant with customer sentiments. When you combine attitudinal and emotional data as features, it boasts a higher accuracy rate. This assures us of a deep understanding of what our customers truly feel. Also, firms can leverage these models by analysing qualitative data generated from customer service and call centres. This tool transforms how practitioners approach customer feedback, moving from a reactive to a proactive stance and replacing uncertainty with accuracy. It's a strategic asset for any business aiming to connect with and retain its customers genuinely.

TABLE 8.1 An illustrative example of using NLP and LLMs for classifying emotional data

Dimension	CX analysis	Reasons
Touchpoints	Repairs	The specific service interaction mentioned by the customer
Resources	Fitters	The personnel involved in the service
Activities	Diagnosing the issue	The service action being critiqued
Context	Service cost	The situation regarding the expense of service
Interactions	Service visits	The occasions when the service is performed
Customer role	Active feedback provider	The customer is providing specific feedback
Discrete emotions	Disappointment	The customer feels let down by the service costs
Cognitive responses	Complaint	Despite a high CSAT score, there is dissatisfaction with the cost and diagnostic service provided
Root causes	Price value	The high service charges and the fitters' apparent difficulty with diagnosis suggest inefficiencies and pricing issues that the company needs to investigate

Behavioural data

This data is sourced from the company's financial system, which records revenue details for parts, installation and maintenance services, as well as labour revenue and other miscellaneous income.[21] These structured records reflect customer interactions documented as product support services. The data includes transaction records, which are systematically organized and detailed with information such as the date, amount, product or service purchased, and associated revenue. Customers engage with the organization through product support (PS) transactions captured in the behavioural sales data of the financial systems. This includes revenues from parts, installation, maintenance and other services, which mirror transactional customer behaviours.

In this case, the aim is to track buying behaviour at specific touchpoints such as sales and services like parts and labour and how much was spent to determine how likely customers will keep doing business with this firm. The recency, frequency and monetary (RFM) method helps to understand customers' buying patterns by looking at their past purchases. Also, this method is good for guessing how valuable a customer will be in the long run and if they might stop buying from us.

Here's how to conduct such an analysis:

1 **Generate the RFM measures:**

   o **Recency:** Identify when the customer last bought something to see how recently their interaction with us was.

   o **Frequency:** Count how often customers buy from us every quarter to see if there are any regular buying patterns.

   o **Monetary:** Calculate how much money customers spend with us each quarter.

2 **Aggregate data:** Summarize total spending across different services for a comprehensive view of overall spending. Even if multiple transactions occur on the same day, count each separately.

3 **Analyse customer behaviour:**

   o Determine the number of services each customer orders annually.

   o Calculate the average time between purchases to understand buying frequency.

4 **Define churn:** Identify potential churn based on inactivity and mark customers who haven't made a purchase over a specific period and identify who is '*at risk*', considering the average purchase interval is n

days, adjusted for variability (standard deviation). In our example, in collaboration with the company, we defined churn customers who haven't made a purchase in over 90 days as at risk, considering the average purchase interval is 22.5 days in this case, adjusted for variability (standard deviation). Every company will be different in defining its customer churn or inactivity.

5 **Segment customers:**

o A clustering algorithm can be used to group customers based on purchasing behaviour, identifying patterns such as frequent buyers or those likely to churn.

o Focus on clusters with high churn risk for targeted retention strategies.

You could look at your customers' buying history for a specific year to see if you could spot any patterns.

6 **Create predictive features from behavioural data:** In the world of data analysis, classification modelling, often known as supervised learning, uses certain data points, or predictive variables, to guess what will happen next or classify things into groups.

o After clustering the data, you would end up with groups, in our case four clusters of customers who bought stuff in similar ways. You can label them following your business practice (e.g. bronze, silver, gold and platinum).

o Pay special attention to the cluster with the least activity, minimal frequent purchases, lowest spending, and most instances of not coming back – that's our *churning* group, meaning these customers might be on their way out.

o Focus on this churning cluster to better predict who might stop buying in the future.

In our case, we found that one specific cluster, comprising about 43 per cent of our customers, was at the highest risk of attrition. The company must monitor this group closely and explore strategies to understand their behaviour before they potentially churn. This examination should include a detailed review of attitudinal and emotional data, with a particular focus on qualitative feedback, which could reveal specific issues customers have with the service. Employing natural language processing (NLP) is vital in this context to uncover the underlying reasons why these customers are considered at risk of leaving.

Machine learning model

You now have the chance to see how machine learning models use data from various sources to enhance customer loyalty predictions. By integrating diverse data points – including attitudinal, emotional and behavioural features – across multiple channels, machine learning algorithms can use these features to predict customer loyalty more accurately. This comprehensive approach allows companies to go beyond simple metrics like NPS, enabling them to make well-informed, data-driven decisions that strengthen customer relationships and drive business growth.

To do so, you need to consider the following:[22]

- **Identify the target variable you want to predict.** In this example, the target variable is identifying customers who are likely to churn in the second year. Use data from the previous year to determine which customers are at risk of falling into this category.

- **Apply a machine learning classification technique** that leverages features derived from the customers' attitudinal, emotional and behavioural information. This approach helps predict the likelihood of customers churning by analysing comprehensive datasets reflecting their interactions and sentiments. In case of the issue of imbalance in your target variable – where a significant majority of customers are not labelled as churners – you should consider adjusting the representation of the minority class. This is a common challenge in machine learning and can impact the performance of your model. There are many practical machine learning techniques that could deal with such challenges. For example, you could increase the size of the under-represented class to help balance the dataset and improve your model's predictive accuracy and reliability. This adjustment ensures that the model is not biased towards the majority class and can effectively identify churn risks among customers.

- **Generate CX insights:** We tested the models, in many cases, on average, solely relying on attitudinal features – factors like quality, NPS, purchase intentions, referrals and overall satisfaction. These models accurately predicted loyalty for 62.2 per cent of customers.

  We then incorporated emotional features derived from qualitative data, including the number of surveys, word counts, sentiment analyses of positive, neutral and negative sentiments, and value creation elements. This approach slightly improved our predictive accuracy to an average of 64.6 per cent.

However, when we shifted our focus to purely behavioural data – factors like recent purchases, number of transactions, total revenue, churn rates, and purchase frequencies for specific quarters – the model's accuracy significantly increased to, on average, 85.4 per cent.

To capitalize on these insights, we combined the three models – attitudinal, emotional and behavioural – into an ensemble model. This ensemble model demonstrated remarkable efficacy, accurately classifying, on average, 93 per cent.

Insights for practitioners

Adopting this framework and a data-driven approach provides several valuable insights for managers. By understanding the complex, multifaceted nature of customer loyalty, roles such as chief marketing officers (CMOs), account service managers and customer experience managers can significantly enhance their strategic initiatives. This depth of insight is crucial for tailoring strategies that effectively address various aspects of customer loyalty and improve overall engagement.

This approach helps address four key questions:[23]

Does your firm offer a service that customers truly value?

Ensuring exceptional service delivery is crucial to increasing customers' willingness to make repeat purchases. It is essential to evaluate services from the customer's viewpoint.

For example, in one of our case studies, attitudinal data indicated that 79 per cent of customers from participating firms rated the service quality between 8.5 and 10, demonstrating a high perceived quality. Additionally, 68 per cent of customers reported high overall satisfaction, and 77 per cent showed a likelihood to repurchase.

However, as discussed, while these metrics provide insights into service performance and repurchase intent, they do not fully capture the emotional and behavioural aspects of customer loyalty.

Our analysis revealed a potential churn rate of 43 per cent among customers. To gain a more comprehensive understanding of customer loyalty, it is beneficial to consider a framework that encompasses attitudinal aspects (like superior performance, desirability and advocacy), emotional connections (such as customer satisfaction) and behavioural indicators (including purchasing patterns). We recommend that firms adopt this holistic framework, which builds on established research, to analyse and enhance customer loyalty thoroughly.

Is there a substantial, loyal segment of customers who purchase from the firm?

Companies know how to segment their customers; however, integrating these segments with attitudinal and emotional data often presents a challenge. While certain segments may exhibit high loyalty through frequent purchases and positive reviews, negative emotional reactions and lower satisfaction scores highlight areas needing attention to boost overall customer loyalty.

For example, in our case:

- **Platinum segment**: This group shows strong loyalty with high ratings in quality (8.4), overall satisfaction (7.4) and repurchase intention (8.4). Yet, 33 per cent express negative emotions, particularly citing delayed deliveries and pricing issues. Behaviourally, they are very active, generating 792 transactions and £6,036,655 in revenue quarterly.

- **Gold segment**: This group ranks second in loyalty, with 972 transactions and £980,037 in annual revenue. They engage moderately and purchase frequently, with an average recency of about six days.

- **Silver segment**: This segment records fewer transactions (240 annually) but maintains consistent quarterly engagement, contributing £162,693 in annual revenue.

- **Bronze segment**: As the least loyal tier, these customers engage the least, with transactions averaging 64 days apart and annual revenue of £37,859, marking the lowest interaction frequency across the customer base.

Enhancing customer loyalty effectively requires addressing each segment's specific needs and concerns, especially where negative feedback indicates dissatisfaction.

Who is churning, and why is there a risk of churning?

Customers have a significant churn risk characterized by a low average number of transactions and revenues. In our B2B case, the model identified

43 per cent, with 16 transactions only and an average total revenue of £14,212 spread throughout the year. Their engagement frequencies are the lowest among all segments, with transactions peaking slightly in the fourth quarter.

To unravel the causes of their churn, it's crucial to investigate customer feedback collected from surveys, customer service and social media. Analysis of this feedback shows that:

- Of our respondents, 63 per cent are dissatisfied, 22 per cent are satisfied, and 15 per cent remain neutral.

- These customers have critical touchpoint issues, such as concerns over high pricing, service shortcomings like unexpected major changes, and logistical issues, including the unavailability of parts as promised. Other noted problems include discrepancies between product labels and contents and invoicing delays during staff absences.

Addressing these specific issues through real-time analysis and targeted interventions could significantly enhance customer retention, particularly among those expressing substantial dissatisfaction and those at risk of churning.

What can the firm gain from applying our machine learning model to predict and retain loyal customers?

Applying a machine learning model can predict and retain loyal customers and offer substantial benefits, as evidenced by our many analyses of customer experience (CX) data:

ATTITUDINAL INSIGHTS

- NPS data showed that 70 per cent of their customers were promoters, 25 per cent were passives, and only 5 per cent were detractors.

- AI analysis indicated that 42 per cent of customers were at risk of churning.

- Despite being labelled promoters via NPS, 43 per cent of these customers expressed complaints in qualitative feedback, highlighting inconsistencies between different data sources.

This highlights the risk of relying solely on a single data source like NPS, which can mask underlying issues like customer churn.[24] Customers often rate services highly in surveys even when significant problems exist, a critical dynamic that traditional surveys may fail to capture. This oversight can lead to customer loss without a clear understanding of the causes.

BEHAVIOURAL INSIGHTS

- The AI-driven analysis helped segment customers into Bronze, Silver, Gold and Platinum categories, revealing that relying only on NPS could overlook a large segment at risk of churning – potentially costing the firm, on average, £14,618,575 in lost revenue.
- This insight helps the firms anticipate sales declines and prevent customer defection by integrating NPS with emotional response data to categorize customers by their monetary value.
- Analysing CX data enables firms to identify customers at risk of defection despite high CSAT or NPS scores due to unresolved issues. These attitudinal and behavioural insights empower companies to take proactive steps to prevent churn, thereby reducing the costs of losing and acquiring customers. By detecting when customers' satisfaction levels drop, companies can intervene to prevent potential defections.

STRATEGIC ACTIONS

AI insights can be utilized to pinpoint and prioritize customer issues needing attention by taking the necessary actions:[25]

- **Real-time monitoring**: AI insights facilitate pinpointing customer issues promptly, allowing immediate action to enhance the customer experience.
- **Training and communication**: Tailoring employee training to focus on empathy and customer interaction and adapting communication strategies based on customer feedback ensure a better service experience.

KEY TAKEAWAYS

Adopting an AI-driven model to measure and manage customer experience is essential in the digital era. Companies can continuously monitor real-time data, gaining insights allowing seamless service delivery or prompt intervention for effective service recovery. Organizations can leverage CX data from both internal and external touchpoints – across digital, physical and social channels – to proactively meet customer needs, retain customers, and achieve sustained loyalty and growth.

In particular:

- Traditional metrics like NPS are insufficient for measuring customer loyalty in today's digital landscape.

- Analytics are vital in CX management for collecting relevant CX data and deriving actionable insights from it.

- CX data varies from structured to unstructured forms and can be integrated for more comprehensive analysis.

- Machine learning models are capable of predicting customer loyalty effectively by using multiple data sources.

- A thorough understanding of the different aspects of customer loyalty, combined with the application of machine learning techniques, can significantly improve customer loyalty management and enhance the overall customer experience.

In the next chapter, we will explore another use case of AI, focusing on how it can enhance the measurement of customer engagement.

Notes

1 Zaki, M, McColl-Kennedy, J R and Neely, A (2021) Using AI to track how customers feel – in real time, *Harvard Business Review*, 4 May. https://hbr.org/2021/05/using-ai-to-track-how-customers-feel-in-real-time (archived at https://perma.cc/4WT6-M6PG)

2 Oliver, R L (1999) Whence consumer loyalty? *Journal of Marketing*, 63, 33–44

3 Libai, B, Muller, E and Peres, R (2009) The diffusion of services, *Journal of Marketing Research*, 46 (2), 163–75

4 Castanedo, F (2014) Using deep learning to predict customer churn in a mobile telecommunication network. www.semanticscholar.org/paper/Using-Deep-Learning-to-Predict-Customer-Churn-in-a-Castanedo/7e2eba72e678ed796cd4c69b53ed0be4736e8b0c (archived at https://perma.cc/QB4S-EX4Q)

5 Zaki, M, Diaz, D, Kandeil, D, Neely, A and McColl-Kennedy, J R (2016) The fallacy of the net promoter score: Customer loyalty predictive model, Cambridge Service Alliance. https://cambridgeservicealliance.eng.cam.ac.uk/system/files/documents/2016OctoberPaper_FallacyoftheNetPromoterScore.pdf (archived at https://perma.cc/KZ2Z-2CSP)

6 Holmlund, M, Van Vaerenbergh, Y, Ciuchita, R, Ravald, A, Sarantopoulos, P, Villarroel Ordenes, F and Zaki, M (2020) Customer experience management in the age of big data analytics: A strategic framework, *Journal of Business Research*, 116, 356–65

7 Zaki, M, Diaz, D, Kandeil, D, Neely, A and McColl-Kennedy, J R (2016) The fallacy of the net promoter score: Customer loyalty predictive model, Cambridge Service Alliance. https://cambridgeservicealliance.eng.cam.ac.uk/system/files/documents/2016OctoberPaper_FallacyoftheNetPromoterScore.pdf (archived at https://perma.cc/SVJ8-892R)

8 Nike (2024) Nike releases its ReactX technology, aiming to optimise energy return and lower its carbon footprint, Product News. www.nike.com/gb/a/reactx-foam-release-info (archived at https://perma.cc/7CSS-V3QN)

9 McColl-Kennedy, J R, Zaki, M, Lemon, K N, Urmetzer, F and Neely, A (2019) Gaining customer experience insights that matter, *Journal of Service Research*, 21 (1), 8–26

10 Tactful (2024) AI chatbot. https://tactful.ai/omnichannel/ai-chatbot/ (archived at https://perma.cc/5S9M-MHUG)

11 Zaki, M, McColl-Kennedy, JR and Neely, A (2021) Using AI to track how customers feel – in real time, *Harvard Business Review*, 4 May. https://hbr.org/2021/05/using-ai-to-track-how-customers-feel-in-real-time (archived at https://perma.cc/Y7PL-4ZA2)

12 Jonzon, M M (2019) IKEA: from flatpacks to actionable insights, Cambridge Service Alliance. https://cambridgeservicealliance.eng.cam.ac.uk/node/1412/future-digital-services-and-platforms (archived at https://perma.cc/CE6P-PRE5)

13 IKEA (2019) IKEA planning studio in Manhattan is now open! Corporate news: People and culture, retail, 15 April. www.ikea.com/us/en/this-is-ikea/newsroom/ (archived at https://perma.cc/98RY-EYVQ)

14 Jonzon, M M (2019) IKEA: from flatpacks to actionable insights, Cambridge Service Alliance. https://cambridgeservicealliance.eng.cam.ac.uk/node/1412/future-digital-services-and-platforms (archived at https://perma.cc/VHK2-M98G)

15 Zaki, M, Diaz, D, Kandeil, D, Neely, A, Diaz, D and McColl-Kennedy, J R (2016) The fallacy of the net promoter score: Customer loyalty predictive model, Cambridge Service Alliance. https://cambridgeservicealliance.eng.cam.ac.uk/system/files/documents/2016OctoberPaper_FallacyoftheNetPromoterScore.pdf (archived at https://perma.cc/V4CR-9CUG)

16 Fader, P S, Hardie, B G S and Lee, K L (2005) RFM and CLV: Using iso-value curves for customer base analysis, *Journal of Marketing Research*, 42 (4), 415–30. https://doi.org/10.1509/jmkr.2005.42.4.415 (archived at https://perma.cc/X2MZ-DGNU)

17 McColl-Kennedy, J R, Zaki, M, Lemon, K N, Urmetzer, F and Neely, A (2019) Gaining customer experience insights that matter, *Journal of Service Research*, 21 (1), 8–26

18 Zaki, M, Diaz, D, Kandeil, D, Neely, A, Diaz, D and McColl-Kennedy, J R (2016) The fallacy of the net promoter score: Customer loyalty predictive model, Cambridge Service Alliance. https://cambridgeservicealliance.eng.cam.ac.uk/system/files/documents/2016OctoberPaper_FallacyoftheNetPromoterScore.pdf (archived at https://perma.cc/6QQH-GAD6)

19 McColl-Kennedy, J R, Zaki, M, Lemon, K N, Urmetzer, F and Neely, A (2019) Gaining customer experience insights that matter, *Journal of Service Research*, 21 (1), 8–26

20 McColl-Kennedy, J R and Zaki, M (2022) Measuring and managing customer experience (CX): What works and what doesn't, in Edvardsson, B, Tronvoll, B (eds), *The Palgrave Handbook of Service Management*, Palgrave Macmillan

21 Zaki, M, Diaz, D, Kandeil, D, Neely, A, Diaz, D and McColl-Kennedy, J R (2016) The fallacy of the net promoter score: Customer loyalty predictive model, Cambridge Service Alliance. https://cambridgeservicealliance.eng.cam.ac.uk/system/files/documents/2016OctoberPaper_FallacyoftheNetPromoterScore.pdf (archived at https://perma.cc/Y8RU-MJLA)

22 ibid.

23 ibid.

24 Zaki, M, McColl-Kennedy, J R and Neely, A (2021) Using AI to track how customers feel – in real time, *Harvard Business Review*, 4 May. https://hbr.org/2021/05/using-ai-to-track-how-customers-feel-in-real-time (archived at https://perma.cc/XP79-YC9C)

25 McColl-Kennedy, J R, Zaki, M, Lemon, K N, Urmetzer, F and Neely, A (2019) Gaining customer experience insights that matter, *Journal of Service Research*, 21 (1), 8–26

9

Customer engagement

The potential of digital technology lies in enhancing customer engagement and gaining deeper insights into their behaviours. To achieve better engagement, organizations must create relevant and compelling content that resonates with their customers. This chapter explores the role of digital platforms like social media in organizations' customer engagement strategies and the challenges they face in driving higher engagement rates.

I will also explore how AI can help organizations identify the types of content that perform best in driving engagement in digital platforms. Also, we will discuss the key challenges in measuring engagement and responses, the volume and diversities of content types, and different contextual factors that drive or deter engagement. By addressing these challenges, organizations can enhance their social media strategies and create engaging content that resonates with their customers.

Customer engagement

Customer engagement has significantly transformed consumer behaviour over recent years, with customers now seeking experiences alongside products. In the early 2000s, content was primarily distributed through traditional channels such as print, television and radio. However, today's marketing landscape has shifted dramatically. Web platforms, mobile apps and social media have become the primary mediums for many brands to engage with their customers. Moreover, the rise of digital platforms has reshaped business channels, enhancing how the company connects with its customers. Additionally, the surge in digital channels has vastly improved the ability to identify customer preferences, determine the most effective marketing channels, and optimize investment returns.

Social media is central to these digital channels for every firm, but its engagement rates are often modest. According to the Social Media Industry Benchmark Report,[1] the average engagement rate on Facebook across various industries is only 0.08 per cent, and the median Instagram engagement rate across industries is less than 1 per cent. Even in industries driven by high passion and enthusiasm, such as sports, Facebook engagement rates barely touch 0.18 per cent of the audience.

Brands design diverse content aimed at capturing consumer attention, enhancing engagement, improving brand perceptions, influencing attitudes, boosting firm performance, fostering customer loyalty and increasing brand equity. Despite marketers' efforts to create diverse content that addresses informational, emotional and commercial needs, aiming to build deeper connections during distinct customer experiences, a significant 61 per cent of consumers still do not interact with brands on these platforms.[2] Consequently, brands face the challenge of adapting their content strategies to strengthen consumer relationships and elevate engagement levels.

While social media channels offer seemingly measurable metrics such as likes, shares, reach and impressions, they fall short of understanding the sentiment and emotion behind interactions. These metrics cannot reveal why certain content resonates more with audiences and how to optimize future content for better engagement. Further, many organizations struggle to derive actionable insights to enhance content and increase engagement.

Although customers can be influenced by various linguistic styles and characteristics of textual content, including its usefulness, interactivity, informality, complexity, emotionality and vividness, market insights, such as HubSpot, reveal that 54 per cent of consumers across various demographics want more video content from brands they follow.[3]

For instance, Instagram has seen an 80 per cent increase in video consumption.[4] In particular, millennials show a stronger preference for visual content like images and videos over textual content. This shift challenges brands to manage content creation and curation across different formats to optimize engagement at various consumer interaction stages (pre-, during and post-experience).

It is also crucial to understand content's specific attributes, frequency and categories (e.g. emotional, informational and commercial) that can enhance engagement. Informational content is non-promotional and provides insights into the latest brand activities, whereas emotional content is designed to elicit sensory or affective responses. Commercial content enhances consumer awareness of the firm's products and services.[5]

For example, emotional content might include highlights of iconic players or significant victories. Informational content could cover topics such as athlete acquisitions or broader updates like new product launches or organizational changes. Commercial interactions often focus on narratives centred on business activities such as collaborations, product promotions, or exclusive offers.

Similarly, consumers are more inclined to interact or share their opinions online when brands distribute content through social media. This ongoing interaction between brands and consumers can foster positive brand-related thoughts, leading to more likes and shares and promoting positive engagement online. Additionally, the sentiment towards brands on social media can greatly differ depending on the situational context, types of experiential events, and the nature of the content, whether informational, emotional or commercial.[6]

If you follow Tesla on any of its social media platforms, you'll notice diverse content. They regularly share informational updates, such as announcements of new models, where they not only provide detailed textual information about performance features but also enhance these updates with images and videos that highlight the sleek design and innovative technology characteristic of the brand. This blend of content helps to inform and visually captivate their customers and fans.

Similarly, Nike effectively leverages emotional content on its social media channels. For instance, Nike might release a content tribute to everyday athletes facing and overcoming personal challenges. Set to inspiring music, combined with motivational quotes like 'You break it, you own it' and 'It's never about how you start', such videos aim to resonate deeply with viewers.[7] By showcasing the transformative power of sports, these videos strive to connect on an emotional level, encouraging viewers to overcome their own obstacles and push their limits.

Coca-Cola's approach to commercial content on social media also highlights the power of personalized engagement. Their successful 'Share a Coke' campaign is a prime example of this strategy in action. By personalizing Coke bottles with names, Coca-Cola fostered a personal connection with consumers, encouraging them to share their experiences online. This campaign not only increased engagement but also highlighted how effectively content can be utilized in commercial campaigns to captivate and engage an audience across various social media platforms.[8]

With the increasing diversity and volume of digital content, practitioners are turning to AI to automatically analyse, process, categorize and generate this content. This leads to an important question: How do AI and GenAI help brands identify key content features and predict which content types will boost engagement in digital platforms?

Let's explore the answer to this question in this chapter.

Market-generated content framework

Marketers can tailor their strategies to align with the experiential event timeline. Experiential events are pivotal moments or periods a brand capitalizes on to connect with its audience.

These can be segmented into three phases:[9]

- **Before:** The anticipation phase, where content is geared towards building excitement, raising awareness and priming the audience for what's to come.

- **During:** The participation phase captures live interactions, real-time marketing and engagement as the event unfolds.

- **After:** The reflection phase, where content extends the experience by offering recaps and highlights, and encouraging sharing of personal experiences.

Most firms, before a product launch, might tease features on social media (before), live-stream the launch event (during), and then share user-generated content featuring the product (after).

During the content strategy development, they must decide on the optimal mix of content volume, types and characteristics for each social media platform. For instance, X (Twitter) may be used for quick, informational updates, while Instagram could be better for visual and emotional storytelling and push commercial promotion through their digital app. This is why content generation is a multifaceted approach that encompasses key dimensions (Figure 9.1):[10]

- **Content volume:** Refers to the quantity of content released. A strategic balance must be maintained to avoid overwhelming or under-engaging the audience.

- **Content types:** This includes a variety of content, such as informational (news, facts), emotional (stories, experiences) and commercial (promotions, calls to action).

- **Content characteristics:** Pertains to the quality and attributes of content, like relevancy, authenticity and appeal, which are tailored to resonate with the audience.

- **Platform type:** Recognizes that different platforms cater to varying content preferences and audience demographics, influencing where and how content should be distributed.

- **Competitor strategy:** This involves analysing what competitors are doing in terms of content creation and distribution. By understanding the strategies employed by competitors, a brand can identify gaps in the market, innovate its content approach, and differentiate itself to capture audience interest. This strategic analysis helps in designing content that not only resonates with the audience but also stands out in a crowded market.

Finally, the success of these strategies is evaluated using engagement metrics, which can help marketers understand which types of content resonate best with their audience and why.

This understanding allows for continual optimization of content strategies, ensuring the highest levels of engagement and a strong ROI on content marketing efforts.

For example, Manchester United is a global football sports brand with 1.1 billion fans, engaging with them through various digital channels, such as online merchandise sales, social media, its ticketing and venue website, and the 24/7 MUTV channel, which distributes content across 195 territories via seven digital platforms.[11] In partnership with HCLTech,[12] Manchester United has digitalized its operations, transitioning from a conventional sports club to a digital sports enterprise. They have developed a digital app that functions as a digital experience platform to deliver seamless and engaging content customized to Manchester United fans across the globe.

FIGURE 9.1 Customer engagement assessment framework

Navigating content types and characteristics proved to be a considerable obstacle for Manchester United, particularly during the Covid-19 pandemic in 2020.[13] The pandemic led to the suspension of football matches and presented a substantial challenge: How can the connection with fans be sustained in the absence of live matches? While Manchester United and other sports clubs have a track record of maintaining high fan engagement during off-seasons and between games, the Covid-19 pandemic dramatically shifted the dynamics of fan interaction and engagement. A pivotal aspect of the club's strategy was shifting from mere 'social' presence to 'social responsibility'.[14] The manner in which businesses reacted to the crisis would profoundly impact their brand image in the long run.

This shift also involved discovering new content and formats to keep fans engaged. Prior to 2019, the club had undertaken a massive project to tag all its digital content, a move that became incredibly beneficial. This enabled them to focus on classic games through *Match Rewind* and package these as box sets. They introduced new formats such as UTD Unscripted long reads, a UTD podcast, and significantly increased activities like competitions, quizzes and fantasy football.[15]

When matches resumed behind closed doors, the club created a fan mosaic for the otherwise empty stadium and showcased video celebrations that fans had recorded and sent in.

Another crucial strategy was content diversification across platforms, with 60 print publications normally available at games moved online, further enhancing opportunities to track fan engagement. The club's app, which was already gathering insights about fans, played a crucial role, and the club capitalized on this by creating more incentives for fans to register. This multifaceted approach helped Manchester United not only sustain but also deepen fan engagement during an unprecedented time.

This demonstrates that consumer engagement is multifaceted, deeply influenced by the linguistic nuances and specific attributes embedded within content, such as its usefulness, interactivity, casual tone, sophistication, emotional impact and relevance. As consumer preferences and cultural narratives shift, it becomes imperative for brands to stay abreast of these changes and tailor their content accordingly to ensure it resonates and encourages engagement.

Key challenges

One of the attractions of social media channels is that they give the impression of being highly measurable, with executives able to use social listening tools that produce eye-catching graphs showing the numbers of likes, shares, reach and impressions.

However, these measures have some challenges:[16]

- First, each social media platform uses **different engagement metrics** and has its own set of metrics that indicate performance. Different platforms prioritize different aspects of engagement, making it difficult to standardize a cross-platform engagement strategy. Social media platforms frequently update their algorithms, which can affect how metrics are calculated. This requires firms to stay agile and adapt their strategies regularly. For instance:

  o **Facebook** focuses on metrics like reach, impressions, engagement rate (likes, comments, shares) and click-through rate.

  o **Instagram** emphasizes likes, comments, story views and engagement on Reels.

  o **X (Twitter)** tracks retweets, likes, replies and impressions.

  o **LinkedIn** measures engagement through likes, comments, shares and impressions, strongly focusing on content relevance for a professional audience.

- Second, these metrics capture only a keystroke, such as likes, failing to capture the underlying sentiments of those actions. While some social listening tools use NLP algorithms to analyse customer sentiments towards brands, they do not necessarily indicate if the content truly resonates with these specific types of customers.

- Third, the volume of the unstructured data is huge. With multiple posts across several platforms, the sheer volume of data can be overwhelming. Analysing this data to derive meaningful insights requires significant time and resources.

- Fourth, these metrics can't tell you in detail why one post appeals more than another and, by extension, how best to drive engagement through future posts. Consider a scenario where a brand releases two posts spaced far apart in time that achieve similar engagement levels, such as likes. Determining the relative success of each post becomes challenging, particularly since the older post might have benefited from a longer period of exposure. To address this, engagement outcomes have to consider these time-related dynamics. This metric relates the engagement rate of a post to the average performance of posts from the previous three or six months or using the number of followers per day. Moreover, adopting this method makes algorithms more precisely assess the success of posts, thereby improving their ability to predict the effectiveness of future content in engaging audiences.

- Last, multimodal content has become the standard on digital platforms. While text has traditionally been a primary mode of communication in content creation, allowing brands to weave narratives around their activities to engage customers, its impact is significantly amplified when integrated with dynamic visual elements such as images and videos.

The realm of visual content has made it clear that such elements are more than mere additions – they are powerful conduits for eliciting cognitive and emotional reactions from consumers. Personalized, tailored content, which speaks directly to the interests and needs of consumers, consistently gathers a more positive engagement than content that lacks personal relevance.

This is where AI's role becomes pivotal. Through advanced analytics and pattern recognition, AI models can analyse large datasets to identify emerging trends and preferences, enabling brands to adapt their content strategies in real time. With the capabilities of machine learning, vision analytics and natural language processing, AI can analyse the keywords of linguistic styles to optimize the text for desired engagement outcomes. Furthermore, in visual content, AI can process, analyse and understand image and video characteristics that most appeal to specific consumer segments. Using techniques such as computer vision, AI can examine visual elements – colours, shapes, text within images – and evaluate how these correlate with consumer engagement metrics. AI-powered tools can then predict which images or video frames are likely to perform better with target audiences.

AI and GenAI also enhance content personalization by tailoring messages and visuals to individual consumer profiles. This hyper-personalization is based on consumer behaviour, past interactions and demographic information, creating content that is not only suitable but also highly relevant to each consumer.

As brands continually seek to deliver content that captivates and engages, AI can provide a crucial toolkit for translating complex consumer behaviours and designing responsive and engaging content strategies. It empowers brands to deliver the right message to the right consumer at the right time across the most effective channels, transforming content into a dynamic asset that actively fosters deeper consumer relationships.

Applying AI to your market-generated content

Taking the football industry as an example, its migration to digital channels mirrors many other sectors. Football clubs and associated brands find themselves in a fierce battle for fan attention, churning out a plethora of diverse content types, from texts and images to videos.

Let's explore this industry to illustrate how data from social media content can be utilized to discern customer preferences and identify the types of content that boost engagement.

By analysing the interactions and engagement metrics of social media posts, we can gain insights into what content resonates most with customers and drives the most interaction. This approach helps to tailor content strategies that effectively capture the attention and interest of the audience, leading to increased engagement on sports-related social media platforms.

The main goal is to predict posts with high engagement ('likes' metric and sentiment of replies). However, as previously discussed, metrics such as 'likes' don't allow for a relative engagement comparison between posts from different dates. Thus, we recommend creating a metric comparing the total likes on a given date to the average total likes of posts from the prior specific number of months (e.g. six months). To simplify, the target variable could be categorized into two outcome variable groups: low and high engagement posts.

The recent capabilities of the multimodal AI algorithm[17] allow it to predict engagement levels with high precision by training on models that incorporate relevant content features. These include experiential and contextual elements, topics and sub-topics in textual content, and various attributes related to audio and video. However, transforming this diverse multimodal data into features that can be predictively utilized by the AI model will require considerable effort.

Social media content

The design of social media and emerging platforms such as the metaverse will hinge on the dynamic interaction between businesses and consumers through content. Therefore, the capability to generate personalized content and engage actively with brand communities will be crucial. These interactions often depend on engagement drivers such as value co-creation, usage intensity, brand strength and content types, which are designed to promote behavioural engagement actions like viewing, reacting or commenting.

Brand communities are essentially groups of admirers that enrich the consumption experience. They are characterized by strong, meaningful brand relationships that motivate members to invest significant personal resources in support of the brand and to cultivate social relationships with fellow members through shared consciousness, rituals and traditions. To nurture these communities, such as football fans, brands need to develop and implement content strategies that not only boost consumer engagement but also strengthen community commitment and enhance financial performance.

Firms use social media monitoring tools such as Brandwatch[18] and many others, which enable brands to manage their digital footprint across different social media channels. Firms can capitalize on their historical dataset since they created their account. In the Facebook dataset, you can have a rich dataset with details like post ID, post link, publication date, content of the post, type of post (including video, photo, link, event, status, question), intended audience (whether global or targeted), target countries and any branded content sponsors (for example, endorsements related to another company such as the brand of a sports kit manufacturer). It also captures the textual captions and hashtags used.

The dataset generated from these social listening tools can track key social media performance metrics such as likes, total and paid reach, total impressions (the total count of users who have seen the post), total interactions, comments and shares per post. These metrics are widely recognized in the industry as indicators of consumer engagement. Similarly, every post elicits responses in the form of comments and replies from users across the platform, each expressing themselves in their unique way. For example, based on their typical frequency of interaction with the official account of the global soccer brand, users should be categorized as either 'top commenters' if they fall within the top 1 per cent of frequent commenters (representing the brand community), or simply as 'users' if not.[19]

Typically, brands try to tailor their content more effectively by segmenting posts that target either a global audience or specific geographic regions. Moreover, they can design a selection of posts written in a specific language. In the sports context, recognizing the international spread of their fan base, clubs often tailor their communications to specific linguistic groups. For example, they might share posts in Chinese during significant cultural events like Chinese New Year to strengthen connections with fans in that region. Similarly, if a team like Liverpool has an Egyptian player like Mo Salah, they could post in Arabic to celebrate a key goal he scores or an impressive tackle in a crucial match, enhancing engagement with Egyptian fans.

The data from the social media monitoring tool typically includes only links to posts, without the actual media content. To address this, firms should maintain an archive of their content or enable their teams to access and download these media files from content management software or similar tools. In this way, brands can have a dataset to train machine learning models with such data.

Each content type – textual, video and audio – constitutes unstructured data. Typically, a social media post consists of a textual post, a collection of images or videos, and associated contextual metadata. Textual posts can be categorized by their topics and sub-topics. In image analysis, the images might either have humans or lack human presence or include one or several individuals, which could increase the number of features that can be extracted from this image data.

For posts that feature videos, the social listening tool can provide enriched metadata with details such as video length, total views, and various viewer retention milestones (such as 3 seconds, 10 seconds, 30 seconds and complete viewings). With this type of data, brands can conduct more in-depth analysis to determine at which points engagement peaks and where fans typically engage most, based on these retention markers.

The video file itself usually contains multiple media components, including visual (image sequences) and auditory elements. Practitioners need to extract the image and audio elements from the video files to analyse them separately. For the visual components, practitioners need to extract images from the video content using a systematic sampling method. By normalizing the length of each video from 0 to 1, you can capture frames at 0.00, 0.25, 0.50, 0.75 and 1.00 intervals, resulting in five images per video, which could be representative enough for video engagement, along with the accompanying audio.[20]

Moreover, brands can tap into external public datasets if they want to enrich their dataset. For example, in the sports context, the football application programming interface (API) available on the Rapid API platform[21] can be leveraged to deepen our understanding of the context and experiential events that could influence the timing of each post. By merging the social media dataset with data from the football API and publication data as a linking key, you can enhance analysis with additional dimensions. For example, these included indicators of whether a post was shared for specific events, such as a match day, the result of the match (win, loss or draw), the ongoing league at the time of the post, the relevant season (active season or off-season), and signposts for other significant events linked to the brand, such as player transfer announcements and the specific players involved. Contextually, considering the publication date and our link with a global football brand, posts can be connected to specific football seasons, ongoing leagues or tournaments, particular match days, and other football-related events.

Machine learning techniques, such as deep learning algorithms, are powerful at processing multimodal raw data as inputs. However, brands should develop a model that a) autonomously processes this data and generates features, thus avoiding the labour-intensive and complex task of manually crafting features, which requires specialized domain knowledge, and b) incorporates a model with explainability capabilities, which helps in understanding the relative importance of various content attributes and their potential impact on engagement. This approach not only streamlines the process but also enhances the effectiveness of predictive analytics, leading to more accurate and insightful outcomes for the business.

The upcoming sections will discuss the analysis of different types of content and the techniques employed for feature extraction to develop an AI model capable of identifying content that can enhance engagement.

Content analysis

Textual contents: Leveraging NLP's capabilities and employing approaches such as topic modelling techniques, brands can process and categorize the vast textual posts into overarching topics and nuanced sub-topics to use as predictive features. Recent advancements in large language models (LLMs) and deep learning techniques significantly eliminate the need for traditional text pre-processing methods. These methods are capable of learning and representing documents with high accuracy. Furthermore, these models have demonstrated superior performance compared to traditional dictionary-based approaches, resulting in more effective outcomes.

In the sports context, applying these models can enable us to segment content, such as emotional content (e.g. match days, fan interactions), informational content (e.g. club news, stats) and commercial content (e.g. club T-shirts). For instance, posts with words like 'goal' or 'premier league' typically aligned with the 'match day' topic. This granular analysis could offer brands an approach to tailor their content, aligning it with specific experiential or contextual events and ensuring maximum resonance with their audience.[22]

Visual content: The aesthetics of images and video content play a pivotal role in engaging and satisfying customers. Extracting multifaceted features from video and image frames will be essential to understanding how these features can drive engagement. Firms can use deep learning capabilities to perform a range of tasks, from image categorization to object tagging and even celebrity recognition.

Companies have the option to create their own models, leverage the many open-source models available on platforms like Hugging Face, or use proprietary models developed by tech giants like Microsoft, Google and Amazon. For instance, the Microsoft Azure Computer Vision APIs use state-of-the-art deep learning models to extract features from each image and video frame.

For **image categorization**, the Microsoft APIs classify each image based on its visual components using a hierarchical taxonomy. This system includes 86 categories with parent–child relationships, allowing each image to be probabilistically linked to one or more of these categories. This classification covers a broad spectrum, from abstract elements and group photos to crowd scenes, portraits and various environmental settings (such as indoor, outdoor, sky views, buildings, etc.).[23]

The **object detection or image tagging** function assigns content tags to thousands of recognizable objects, beings and scenes, with no formal taxonomy connecting the tags to specific objects detected.

Additionally, practitioners can investigate how recognizing **specific individuals** (such as players or sports legends) or notable **places and events** in the frames might affect audience engagement. The API's domain-specific content detection feature can identify up to 808 celebrities, including current and former football players, coaches and prominent audience members, as well as seven significant landmarks, such as famous soccer/football stadiums and cities where matches are held. These features are useful for creating patterns that reveal what fans enjoy and what they do not.

Face attributes and emotions significantly impact consumer engagement; here, you can continue to employ specialized computer vision models capable of providing detailed analysis of facial characteristics in images. These include facial emotion recognition, face image quality, facial count and various other facial descriptors. There are many APIs, such as Face⁺⁺.[24] The face detection API identifies human faces within an image and provides high precision bounding boxes for each detected face. The face landmarks API detects and returns co-ordinates for key facial component points, including the contour of the face, eyes, eyebrows, lips and nose contours. It also analyses various facial characteristics, such as age, gender, smile intensity, head pose, eye status, emotional expression, perceived beauty, eye gaze, mouth status, skin condition, image quality and blurriness. These varied facial features extracted from the images can serve as additional feature dimensions. They enhance the predictive model by identifying which facial characteristics are most likely to increase engagement.

Evidence in psychology research suggests that certain **facial characteristics** might indicate personality traits. Notably, the facial width-to-height ratio (fWHR) has gained significant attention in psychology and management studies.[25] The predominant view is that individuals with a broader facial width are often perceived as more socially assertive, which could explain their favourable reception in social settings. These facial measurements have also been associated with various socio-professional outcomes, including higher salaries, quicker career advancement, and notable academic successes. However, this highlights how such measurements can introduce biases towards certain personality types, which need scrutiny and privacy issues to be addressed. Nevertheless, these features can help explain why customers might be drawn to specific players or legends beyond their achievements. By analysing the landmarks on each face, you can calculate the fWHR and include this measurement in the different sets of features to explore whether a higher fWHR correlates with increased social engagement.

Auditory contents: From the video, you can extract audio and process it through pretrained audio neural networks to detect different sound events and gauge their energy levels, exploring the hypothesis that more dynamic sounds could enhance engagement.

As you would imagine, you will embark on a complex aggregation and clustering process for the myriad features extracted from image and video sub-components to tie everything together. Through a series of data transformations, dimensionality reduction and clustering techniques, you generate clusters where you group these features statistically to recognize patterns that predict specific behaviours or preferences. This structured approach not only streamlines the vast array of data into actionable insights but also enhances the accuracy and relevance of the predictive models, facilitating more informed decision-making based on the intelligence gathered from complex multimedia content.

The goal is to assess various classifier models in terms of their ability to predict high or low engagement, utilizing all generated features from different types of multimodal unstructured data. Additionally, we aim to identify the key attributes that influence the success of posts.

To achieve this, consider employing various training strategies based on the type of content features:[26]

- **Textual content only**: Train your classifier using features derived solely from textual content.
- **Video elements only**: Focus on features from video elements, including both audio and visuals.
- **Textual and visual elements**: Combine features from both textual content and video elements.
- **Textual, contextual and visual elements**: Use a comprehensive approach by integrating textual, contextual and video features.

Each model set, corresponding to these different combinations of input features, will help evaluate their respective impacts on engagement prediction. This systematic approach allows for a detailed analysis of how different types of content contribute to user engagement, facilitating a deeper understanding of effective social media strategies.

During the evaluation phase, consider utilizing complex algorithms that leverage new LLM multimodal techniques or ensembling, which typically yield better performance on classification metrics compared to simpler models. This often indicates a preference for models that, while delivering high accuracy, might sacrifice transparency for improved performance.

Despite their effectiveness in making predictions, these complex 'blackbox' models often lack operational transparency. To address this, you might utilize explainable AI techniques to enhance transparency, providing a way to assess the general importance of features and individual predictions. On a broader level, the model can illuminate key content traits that drive engagement, while at a more granular level, it can pinpoint specific attributes that significantly impact individual posts. By integrating these explainable AI values, you ensure that the models are not only predictive but also transparent, satisfying the growing need for clear, understandable algorithmic decision-making.

We found, in general, that the top-performing algorithm that integrates textual and visual elements generally yielded the most effective results regarding model prediction accuracy. This combination of textual content and video features harnesses the strengths of both modalities: textual elements provide context and detailed information, while visual elements capture attention and convey emotions that might not be fully expressed through text alone.[27]

By blending these two types of content, the models can access a richer dataset that enhances their ability to recognize patterns and nuances related to user engagement. This multimodal approach leverages the complementary nature of text and visuals, allowing for a more comprehensive analysis of the factors that drive engagement. This synergy is particularly powerful in environments where user interaction is influenced by both the informativeness and aesthetic appeal of the content, making it a robust choice for predicting engagement outcomes effectively.

What we learnt

Multiple factors significantly influence content engagement levels. Some of these findings are intuitive, while others challenge conventional wisdom. For brands and practitioners, understanding these nuances is critical for designing content that truly resonates with customers.

Insights into content that have a positive impact on engagement[28]

- **Creating emotional content** plays a crucial role in driving engagement in videos. For example, in the context of sports, in-game actions, which often showcase players in their prime moments on the field, particularly those that resonate deeply with football enthusiasts, highlight the audience's feeling towards comprehensive game highlights rather than isolated incidents.

- **The sentiment of replies** has a direct positive correlation between the average sentiment score of replies and the number of likes, indicating that positive reactions in replies reflect higher engagement.

- **Visuals of celebrities** or mentions of prominent figures from image content have an effect. In our context, specific footballers can spike engagement, hinting at the audience's interest in current experiential events or the dynamics of their favourite teams. This celebrity influence extends to exposed visuals, with the audience demonstrating a preference for raw and emotional moments. A clear example in our data is images of players or personalities in unguarded moments, perhaps expressing surprise or shock – moments that offer a genuine glimpse behind the scenes.

- **Strengthening the importance of authenticity.** For example, visuals related to fans – the very lifeblood of the sport – have also been shown to impact engagement. This fan effect, while significant, could be influenced by various factors and may vary in different contexts or sectors.

- **High-octane commentary** from the audio component during pivotal moments like goal celebrations is another notable driver of engagement. It seems that audiences are not merely seeking information but an emotional connection, craving authentic reactions that amplify the intensity of the live experience.

- **Segments of clear and concise commentary** from audio data. It's not just the content but its presentation that matters. Especially when minimally interrupted by background music, it appears to be highly valued. It suggests that, for audiences, a clear narrative without distractions enhances their engagement with the content.

- **Surprisingly, posts with images** generally perform better than those with videos, highlighting a preference among users for still imagery over video content.

Here, several content features appear to decrease the likelihood of high engagement. **The insights from our research** are highlighted below.

- **Close-up visuals:** Extreme close-up shots, especially of faces, seemed to reduce engagement. For example, while one might expect pivotal moments like goal celebrations to be a highlight, the model suggests viewers prefer wider shots that capture team dynamics and audience reactions.

- **Blurred visuals:** Images with subtle blurring, hinting at depth, reduced engagement. This suggests that viewers might prioritize clarity and sharpness over artistic depth effects. In our video data, we found this negative effect typically prominent in the fifth shot, which might be perceived as a quality lapse. Similarly, in still images, especially those evoking nostalgic moments from the past (like significant team victories from the 1970s), the poor image quality compared to contemporary standards negatively impacted engagement.

- **Promotional content:** Textual content centred around media commercial promotions and sponsor-related topics was less engaging. Additionally, videos featuring informational logos on plain white backgrounds were not captivating, emphasizing the importance of clear and effective branding.

- **Black screens:** The appearance of a black screen, especially in the middle of a video, decreased engagement. Such interruptions might disrupt viewer immersion, suggesting the importance of seamless colour content presentation.

- **Redundant information:** Surprisingly, sharing specific related details (e.g. match dates) in videos led to decreased engagement. This may indicate that such information, while timely, isn't always of primary interest to the viewers.

- **Background noise:** Commentary overlaid with noise (e.g. stadium or training shouts) had a negative impact. This mix might be seen as chaotic or distracting, highlighting the importance of clear audio for effective engagement.

- **Specific themes:** Behind the scenes and CSR activities, for instance, do not perform as well, suggesting that the mass communication of certain topics might not always resonate with the audience.

- **Certain topics within customer replies:** Replies such as those discussing controversial club decisions or player performances were negatively associated with the number of likes. This suggests that posts generating discussions around these contentious topics tend to be less liked.

- **Posts dominated by top commenters:** These correlated negatively with engagement metrics. This may be because these commenters are more active in general, possibly using the platform to boost traffic to their own channels rather than engaging meaningfully with the content.

Moving forward: The role of AI in content strategy and customer engagement

As we enter a digital era marked by an overflow of content, AI's capability to make content stand out and resonate with your target audience becomes increasingly invaluable. This is particularly evident in dynamic fields such as the sports industry, where passion, pivotal moments and a consistently engaged audience create an ideal setting for AI-enhanced content optimization.

- **AI in sports content optimization:** Take, for example, a football match – a single event can generate a massive amount of content, with upwards of 10,000 photos captured. Yet, not all of these photos will engage the audience effectively. This is where AI steps in, armed with insights and features that can spark engagement with your fans and customers. Machine learning models can sift through these thousands of photos, ranking them based on their potential to engage audiences. AI extends beyond mere selection; it can refine content strategy, advising on optimal cropping, captioning and even the sequencing of posts to maximize audience resonance.

- **Contextual sensitivity of AI:** In sports, context dramatically influences the impact of content. A goal scored during a high-stakes match elicits more excitement than one from a friendly match. AI can be harnessed to understand these nuances, incorporating real-time contextual data to ensure that content is not only timely but also contextually resonant. This enables brands to synchronize their content release strategies with moments of peak audience anticipation and excitement.

- **Personalization through AI:** AI's ability to personalize content is perhaps its most powerful feature. By analysing individual user behaviours, AI can personalize content feeds, tailoring them to match personal preferences – whether that's a focus on a specific player, type of play, or even particular auditory cues. This ensures that every piece of content delivered is highly relevant and engaging to each viewer.

- **Dynamic feedback loops:** Integrating AI into content strategies also facilitates a dynamic feedback loop. By continuously monitoring engagement metrics and user feedback, AI can adapt and refine its strategies. This agile approach allows content strategies to remain responsive and aligned with changing audience preferences.

- **Democratization of content optimization:** For smaller firms without the resources of their larger counterparts, an AI-driven approach democratizes content optimization. It enables these smaller entities to achieve maximum engagement without a proportional increase in resources, levelling the playing field in content creation and distribution.

- **Future synergy:** The future synergy between AI and human creativity will significantly shape content strategies. While AI offers tools, metrics and recommendations, the human touch ensures the emotional resonance of content remains intact. The transformative potential of AI extends across various sectors – sports, retail, fashion, automotive, beauty, food, healthcare and beyond – optimizing content for maximum customer engagement. This not only removes the guesswork from content strategy but also drives engagement, significantly improving a brand's social media ROI.

As content continues to proliferate across digital platforms, the strategic integration of AI in content creation and optimization will become a cornerstone of successful digital marketing, enhancing both the efficiency and impact of content strategies.

KEY TAKEAWAYS

AI holds immense potential, providing avenues to improve customer engagement and obtain deeper insights into what content is relevant, captivating and resonates with audiences. We explored how digital platforms, including social media strategies, play a role in engaging customers and the obstacles they face in achieving higher engagement levels.
Here are the key takeaways:

- Brands need to create diverse and high-quality content to capture consumer attention and drive engagement. This includes informational, emotional and commercial content tailored to meet customers' distinct experiences and interactions at different stages – before, during and after a particular event.

- Practitioners are encouraged to utilize AI tools to analyse, process and categorize content effectively. AI can help identify the types of posts that perform best, predict future content performance, and tailor content strategies based on deep insights into customer preferences and behaviours.

- It is crucial to understand and adapt to each social media platform's unique characteristics and metrics. The days of posting identical content across all platforms, including your apps, are over. Each platform draws distinct customer segments with unique expectations and uses different methods to measure engagement. Therefore, strategies must be tailored to align with these metrics to maximize effectiveness.

- Engagement metrics such as likes, shares, reach and impressions are important, but they need to be supplemented with qualitative data that can capture the sentiment and emotion behind interactions. This provides a more complete understanding of what drives engagement.

- Additionally, comparing today's post responses with follower numbers or calculating the average performance of similar posts from the past three to six months provides a more effective solution to overcome the cumulative effect of posts. This strategy enables the AI to accurately determine the engagement percentage at that time and improve its understanding of which content performs best.

- The use of AI, including GenAI, not only helps in content creation but also in personalizing content to match consumer profiles and behaviours. This hyper-personalization ensures that the content delivered is relevant and engaging for each individual, which can significantly enhance engagement rates.

- There is a strong consumer preference for visual content over textual content, particularly among younger demographics. Video content, for example, has been shown to significantly increase engagement, particularly when it is high quality and emotionally compelling.

- Brands should strive for agility in their content strategies, making real-time adjustments based on ongoing engagement metrics and consumer feedback to keep content strategies aligned with audience preferences.

In the next chapter, I will discuss how AI, including generative AI, can be utilized to create personalized experiences in customer service.

Notes

1   Rival-IQ (2021) *2021 Social Media Industry Benchmark Report*. www.rivaliq. com/resources/social-media-industry-benchmark-report-download-2021 (archived at https://perma.cc/D5MP-T6LK)

2   Ritson, M (2011) Hard evidence of social media's failings, *Marketing Week*, 23 November. www.marketingweek.com/hard-evidence-of-social-medias-failings/ (archived at https://perma.cc/FW4D-9Z2L)

3   HubSpot Blog (2018) Content trends & preferences. https://blog.hubspot.com/ marketing/content-trends-preferences (archived at https://perma.cc/6TZE-K6TE)

4   Bump, P (2024) How video consumption is changing in 2024, HubSpot. https:// blog.hubspot.com/marketing/how-video-consumption-is-changing (archived at https://perma.cc/346Z-UEY5)

5 Meire, M, Hewett, K, Ballings, M, Kumar, V and Van den Poel, D (2019) The role of marketer-generated content in customer engagement marketing, *Journal of Marketing*, 83 (6), 21–42

6 ibid.

7 Nike (2022) Never done inspiring, Department of Nike Archives, 17 May. www.nike.com/gb/a/never-done-inspiring-ad-revolution (archived at https://perma.cc/UL4R-N6AK)

8 Fisher, L (2013) Debranding: Why Coca-Cola's decision to drop its name worked, *The Guardian*, 6 August. www.theguardian.com/media-network/media-network-blog/2013/aug/06/coke-debranding-name-dropping (archived at https://perma.cc/L4K5-HDAV)

9 Lemon, K N and Verhoef, P C (2016) Understanding customer experience and the customer journey, *Journal of Marketing* (JM-MSI Special Issue), 1–62

10 Zaki, M and Diaz, D (2021) 'Likes' guaranteed: How AI can revolutionise your social media and customer engagement strategy, in *Cambridge Service Alliance Annual Report 2021*. https://cambridgeservicealliance.eng.cam.ac.uk/files/annual_report_2021.pdf (archived at https://perma.cc/D2VM-GRER)

11 Salt, P (2020) Digital engagement in the era of Covid: At the forefront of service transformation in the digital era, Cambridge Service Alliance. https://cambridgeservicealliance.eng.cam.ac.uk/IndustryDay/2020 (archived at https://perma.cc/9HS6-AETY)

12 HCLTech (2018) Manchester United shoots for success with a 'digital experience platform' powered by HCL. www.hcltech.com/press-releases/manchester-united-shoots-success-digital-experience-platform (archived at https://perma.cc/BA26-2J6V)

13 Salt, P (2020) Digital engagement in the era of Covid: At the forefront of service transformation in the digital era, Cambridge Service Alliance. https://cambridgeservicealliance.eng.cam.ac.uk/IndustryDay/2020 (archived at https://perma.cc/3MWP-6ARN)

14 ibid.

15 ibid.

16 Zaki, M and Diaz, D (2021) 'Likes' guaranteed: How AI can revolutionise your social media and customer engagement strategy, in *Cambridge Service Alliance Annual Report 2021*. https://cambridgeservicealliance.eng.cam.ac.uk/files/annual_report_2021.pdf (archived at https://perma.cc/7RTF-R7D2)

17 ibid.

18 Brandwatch (2024) Our data and network coverage. www.brandwatch.com/datanetworks/ (archived at https://perma.cc/EX3C-3UG2)

19 Zaki, M and Diaz, D (2021) 'Likes' guaranteed: How AI can revolutionise your social media and customer engagement strategy, in *Cambridge Service Alliance Annual Report 2021*. https://cambridgeservicealliance.eng.cam.ac.uk/files/annual_report_2021.pdf (archived at https://perma.cc/KYM5-R8DV)

20 ibid.

21 API-FOOTBALL (n.d.) API-Football – documentation, RapidAPI. https://rapidapi.com/api-sports/api/api-football/details (archived at https://perma.cc/7PMR-8C4J)

22 Zaki, M and Diaz, D (2021) 'Likes' guaranteed: How AI can revolutionise your social media and customer engagement strategy, in *Cambridge Service Alliance Annual Report 2021*. https://cambridgeservicealliance.eng.cam.ac.uk/files/annual_report_2021.pdf (archived at https://perma.cc/CYK4-8URY)

23 Microsoft (2024) Azure AI Vision, Microsoft Azure. https://azure.microsoft.com/en-gb/products/ai-services/ai-vision (archived at https://perma.cc/C355-BXJ6)

24 Face++ (2024) Face++. www.faceplusplus.com (archived at https://perma.cc/8RA2-PR4P)

25 Paredes Haz, V, Pino Emhart, F and Díaz, D (2019) Does facial structure explain differences in students' evaluations of teaching? The role of perceived dominance. https://repositorio.uchile.cl/handle/2250/168496 (archived at https://perma.cc/WYV2-W498)

26 Zaki, M and Diaz, D (2021) 'Likes' guaranteed: How AI can revolutionise your social media and customer engagement strategy, in *Cambridge Service Alliance Annual Report 2021*. https://cambridgeservicealliance.eng.cam.ac.uk/files/annual_report_2021.pdf (archived at https://perma.cc/LVK5-LLBW)

27 ibid.

28 ibid.

10

Personalized experience

At some point in our lives, we are all likely to encounter significant frustration with customer service. I recently experienced this while travelling from Birmingham, UK, to Kristiansand, a charming city in Norway, to speak at an academic conference on information systems. My original itinerary with Scandinavian Airlines (SAS) involved flying from the UK to Copenhagen and then on to Kristiansand. However, the evening before my departure, I received an automated message informing me that my flight was cancelled and I had been re-booked on a different route, which increased my layovers from three to four. I was supposed to arrive in Kristiansand by 3.00 p.m., travelling at 9.00 a.m.

Upon arriving at the airport and clearing security, I awaited my flight in the lounge. An hour before departure, the flight was delayed, and at the original departure time, I received another automated message: my flight to Copenhagen was cancelled. I was now re-booked to travel from Birmingham to Dublin, then Dublin to Amsterdam, and finally to Kristiansand, with no information provided about my luggage. Upon boarding, the airline's customer service at the desk informed me that they did not have my luggage and needed the pilot's permission for me to board. Great!

I arrived in Amsterdam and approached the KLM check-in desk for information about my luggage. They were helpful as they said, '*It is SAS issue, not ours*'! And I should follow up with them. Meanwhile, KLM announced another delay for their flights!

I finally reached Kristiansand at 3.00 a.m., only to discover that many passengers, including myself, did not receive their luggage. In the small airport, there was no customer service available at that hour, but there was a paper note hanging at the desk instructing passengers to fill out a form if their luggage was lost.

I managed to send the required form and call them the next morning, but no one replied – it went straight to voicemail – as if to say, '*Don't bother us and fill out the form*'! I sent an email, and the agent on duty replied that we didn't have any information and would update the portal if we received any.

I later learnt that my luggage had stayed in the UK and had been sent to my home. I had to travel without my belongings for two weeks due to this mix-up and the careless handling by the customer service. This nightmare service highlighted the importance of effective communication and care responsibility in customer service.

Furthermore, this example shows the numerous challenges customer service faces, highlighting the need for significant CX transformation. This chapter will explore these challenges in detail and demonstrate how companies can bridge the gap between automation, AI and conversational, personalized care with a human touch to enhance customer experience management. I will present a comprehensive framework that considers various conversation styles that influence the emotional customer experience in text-based interactions. This framework incorporates psychological factors, individual customer knowledge and contextual elements to personalize conversation styles, resulting in improved customer satisfaction, well-being, and reduced churn. I will provide industrial examples of customer service handling from multiple companies, demonstrating how businesses can harness AI not just for automation but to truly understand and engage with their customers on a deeply personal level.

Customer service challenges

The rise of digitization and the reduction of human contact in customer service are creating challenges in personalizing interactions and maintaining a personal touch.[1] This issue is becoming more acute as companies increasingly abandon traditional telephone-based customer service. As customer service moves to digital platforms, utilizing text-based communication through live chats, email ticketing systems, social media or chatbots, the element of personal touch is frequently lost.

Companies are shifting towards a customer-centric approach to build long-term customer relationships and facilitate social elements of the customer–company relationship. However, offering a personal touch with increased contactless service imposes immense challenges on the company and frontline service agents. For example, the lack of in-person conversations in in-store or physical environments could impede customers from feeling cared about. Because customers are most often emotionally loaded when facing a service failure, service agents might be able to detect these negative emotions and respond accordingly. While this is easier with face-to-face interactions, it becomes challenging when dealing with unstructured textual or vocal data. In particular, text-based interactions make understanding customer emotions and conveying empathy difficult.

According to Zendesk,[2] more than half of all consumers report feeling increasingly stressed and exhausted when interacting with customer support. A customer reaches out and indicates they are already facing a problem. Failing to resolve customer problems efficiently and a lack of empathized agents can lead to further frustration. For example, according to Ofcom,[3] telecom and broadband customers often experience significant frustration with their providers due to their desire to quickly connect with the right person over the phone and resolve their complaints on the first attempt. As switching providers becomes easier in these sectors, those who fail to maintain high standards should anticipate churning customers.

This leads to another challenge: in many cases, agents cannot resolve the issue because of a lack of customer data accessibility. Zendesk[4] reported that six out of ten customer service agents report that insufficient consumer data frequently leads to negative experiences. Agents' ability to address customer issues effectively is directly linked to how well equipped they are with relevant customer information. Organizations lacking comprehensive or accurate customer data may find it challenging to resolve consumer concerns efficiently.

The Customer Service Benchmark Report for Travel and Hospitality[5] presents some interesting statistics. It reveals that omnichannel support is uncommon for the travel and hospitality industries, with only 12 per cent of companies offering support across various digital channels. Additionally, 70 per cent of customer emails go unanswered, and 46 per cent of direct messages on social media receive no response. Empathy in customer service within these two sectors is notably low; only 11 per cent of interactions show empathy, 97 per cent of email responses fail to provide meaningful answers, and 70 per cent of customers expect a conversational care experience. Two-thirds of consumers are more likely to become repeat customers if they feel that a business cares about their emotional state.[6] Consumers seek to be treated as valued members of an organization, not just as statistics. Companies that demonstrate genuine concern for their customers' needs and emotions tend to retain more customers over the long term.[7]

Companies' average response time to customer queries varies significantly. For example, for established service providers in the travel and hospitality sector, average response time is around 27 hours, though they tend to respond quicker on social media platforms such as X (Twitter previously), within 5.8 hours.[8] Furthermore, 28 per cent of companies do not personalize email responses with the customer's name. The accessibility of finding contact support teams on websites is also lacking; 38 per cent of companies do not offer email support, and 55 per cent do not have an X (Twitter) account.[9] This creates the impression that firms do not care about their customers' issues, effectively sending the message, 'Don't bother talking to us!'

Therefore, customer behaviour is shifting from call centres towards automated digital omnichannel customer service interactions relying on more text-based interactions (digital self-service), such as live chats, which is evident in customer services. Zendesk[10] noted that 72 per cent of customers across various industries reported a significant improvement in service quality after interacting with chatbots, particularly with the advancement of technologies like AI and generative AI. However, the chatbot industry remains highly fragmented, with a mix of major players and small startups, making it challenging to identify a single leader with a strong brand presence in this space. However, 40 per cent of customers consider having access to multiple communication channels as the most crucial feature of a customer service department.[11]

Generally, consumers have a positive perception of chatbots, appreciating their ability to offer 24/7 support, quick responses and a degree of autonomy. Consequently, chatbots often receive higher satisfaction ratings than direct interactions with human agents or other digital communication channels.[12] However, a Forrester Consulting survey cited by *Forbes*[13] reveals that 50 per cent of consumers frequently feel frustrated during their interactions with chatbots, and nearly 40 per cent of these interactions are perceived as negative. Furthermore, a single negative chatbot experience can drive away 30 per cent of customers. This is because chatbots struggle with complex questions and frequently fail to respond accurately. Over half of those surveyed find it challenging to obtain solutions to their issues using chatbots. Furthermore, almost half of the respondents reported that chatbots often offer answers or solutions that are irrelevant or nonsensical in relation to their questions. Over half of the respondents indicated that they frequently find it difficult to connect with a human agent after exhausting all responses from the chatbot. Additionally, 29 per cent of customers express frustration with scripted and impersonal responses encountered during live chat sessions.[14]

This illustrates that customer service, including many contactless options, often lacks personalized care and a human touch, leading to negative customer experiences. There is an increasing demand for 'conversational care', where customers seek personalized and empathetic interactions. This demand is particularly relevant with the advent of new technologies like generative AI and large language models (LLM) capable of producing human-like conversations. However, these technologies have their limitations. In the limited time available, untrained customer service agents may struggle to grasp all the necessary individual and psychological aspects of customer knowledge and adjust their conversational style accordingly. Off-the-shelf AI solutions often lack emotional depth and typically do not achieve high accuracy. Additionally, generative AI models are prone to errors known as 'hallucinations' and 'inaccuracies', which can create safety concerns and complicate their implementation. These errors occur when the AI generates information that is not based on factual data, creating misleading or completely incorrect outputs. As discussed in Chapter 6, such inaccuracies can not only confuse customers but also pose serious safety concerns, especially in sensitive industries like healthcare or finance, where incorrect information can have dire consequences. Additionally, the lack of contextual understanding in generative models can lead to responses that are irrelevant or fail to align with the brand's voice and values, making it harder for organizations to use these models effectively in customer-facing roles.

Relational personalization

As evident from various challenges and statistics, customers increasingly rely on digital channels for customer service and are eager for conversational care. To meet these expectations, companies must focus on affective communication, which involves expressing and interpreting emotions in interpersonal interactions through digital channels. Customers desire to be heard and valued, necessitating communication that resonates on an emotional level – where relational personalization becomes crucial.

Traditionally, companies have excelled in personalizing websites, advertising, product recommendations and email messages. For instance, companies like Google and Amazon have achieved significant success with personalized product recommendations and tailored advertising based on customer demographics and browsing history. However, personalization has been less explored in building relationships and interacting with customers at different touchpoints, such as customer service.[15] Therefore, customer service should go beyond informative personalization to achieve deeper relational personalization and increase emotional loyalty through genuine customer engagement.[16]

Relational personalization in customer service hinges on an agent's ability to demonstrate empathy, recognize customer emotions, and respond appropriately. However, firms focus primarily on the agents' (human or bot or hybrid) productivity and guide them through designing conversational scripts or flows to answer questions quicker so they can move on to the next one in line. This is partially achieved through an integrated design that combines automated chatbot channels with human agents. Chatbots can handle frequently asked questions using a traditional functional and scripted intent-and-response design, providing quick responses to common customer queries. For more complex inquiries, human agents can step in, offering human engagement. This combination ensures productivity, automating routine tasks while human agents address more complex issues. Additionally, many companies outsource these services to specialized providers, often at lower costs, or to cover 24/7 requests across different geographical locations.

Companies are leveraging platform thinking by using services such as Tactful AI, an AI-driven solution designed to help firms connect with customers across various channels, including email, social media and call centres.[17] This omnichannel communications platform ensures the delivery of consistent experiences for every customer, facilitating meaningful and personalized interactions. By adopting this technology, customer service agents can utilize a centralized inbox for all channels, enabling effortless channel switching while maintaining conversation continuity. This approach enhances collaboration for unified customer service, ensuring smooth information sharing and issue resolution from a single inbox. It reduces response times, showcases attentiveness, and demonstrates customer care while gathering real-time feedback for continuous improvement.

Relational personalization is inherently affective and interactional. It aims to fulfil the need for social connection and a sense of belonging by establishing social interactions and interpersonal relationships with customers.[18] It focuses on creating social bonds by making customers feel understood and providing relevant solutions. This approach can take various forms, including computer-mediated interpersonal communication. The goal is to enhance the efficiency and effectiveness of interactions through personalized communication, addressing both emotional needs and problem-solving.[19]

Here is where artificial intelligence (AI) can bridge the gap by detecting customers' emotions and personalizing responses to recover from service failures. AI can provide a personalized touch beyond automating simple inquiries or product recommendations, which many digital channels, including chatbots, often fail to achieve based on statistics.

Synchronous communication between the customer and either human or digital agents is vital for building customer relationships. Effective two-way interactions – whether verbal (text or voice) or non-verbal (emojis or gestures) – are crucial. On the company's side, customer service can be managed by human agents (e.g. in call centres), digital conversational AI agents (e.g. chatbots), or a hybrid approach (e.g. AI-assisted human agents). For customer service agents with varying levels of AI integration, both verbal and non-verbal communication are essential for building relationships.[20] Relational personalization should be integrated into synchronous communication to allow agents to tailor their interactions and create a personalized communication style, which can be achieved by applying capabilities like generative AI.

The rise of conversational AI applications in business, which encompass technologies enabling human–computer communication, is noteworthy. These technologies use natural language processing techniques like intent detection, classification, language modelling and text generation. In text-based customer service, conversational AI applications differ in their collaboration with human agents, underlying technology and role in customer service.

Market research indicates a potential 136 per cent growth rate for chatbot adoption in service organizations[21] and that 79 per cent of contact centre leaders plan to invest more in AI capabilities over the next two years. This impending automation of customer service through conversational AI necessitates a thoughtful approach to how AI and human agents can collaboratively personalize customer service conversations by providing a personal touch.[22]

The digital nature of customer service communication can delay the development of customer relationships. Moreover, shifting interactions to digital platforms allows frontline employees to manage multiple conversations simultaneously. With AI support, partial automation (e.g. auto-complete, conversational coaching) often leads to more pre-written templates or scripted responses where customers can detect these scripted responses, making them feel less personally attended to.

Together, conversational AI and service agents can enhance relational personalization, improving the customer service experience. HCLTech stated that chief experience officers (CXOs) see improvement in personalization by using AI and cloud capabilities. Personalized and scalable experiences are shown in this survey by HCLTech to provide substantial benefits to customers, users and employees. Leaders are distinguishing themselves from others by their proactive use of generative AI (GenAI). Unlike traditional machine learning, GenAI excels at quickly understanding data, processes and natural language without needing extensive training or data labelling. Consequently, two-thirds of leaders stated that they are implementing GenAI to gain real-time insights from large volumes of unstructured data, such as conversational data. GenAI's key strength lies in its creative capabilities and in enabling personalized chatbot interactions. For customers, firms report improvements such as higher quality of customer service (47 per cent), which is expected to increase to 57 per cent over the next three years, along with greater customer loyalty (46 per cent), improved customer satisfaction (44 per cent), and an enhanced ability to attract new customers (27 per cent), projected to rise to 44 per cent. Employees also benefit from these experiences, with reports of increased engagement and morale (46 per cent), better talent attraction (46 per cent), improved teamwork (44 per cent), and higher productivity (43 per cent), which is expected to grow to 52 per cent as new work methods are implemented. Different industries emphasize various outcomes; for instance, life sciences prioritize high-quality customer service (54 per cent), financial and consumer firms focus on customer loyalty (51 per cent and 48 per cent, respectively), financial firms also emphasize improved productivity (40 per cent), while tech firms and manufacturers highlight talent attraction (60 per cent) and productivity (51 per cent) as key advantages.[23]

Ashish Kumar Gupta – Chief Growth Officer, Europe and Africa, Diversified Industries, HCLTech – stated in this report that you have to look at different kinds of customers, different kinds of employees with different workflows, and then at different kinds of users for the product or service itself. But then you have to see that all of these are mutually reinforcing. For example, if you have some automation that provides a good customer experience, it will likely provide a better experience for the employees and free them up from mundane tasks. The key is how the organization actually brings it all together so that you have a truly integrated vision of experience leadership.[24]

The challenge is to design conversational AI to enable relational personalization, either automatically or by assisting service agents. The question is *how*?

The following section explores the essential elements for conversational AI to effectively implement relational personalization.

Guided framework: Relational personalization elements in customer service

Personalization goes beyond understanding the customer intent and profile and capturing further elements such as the journey step (pre-purchase, purchase and post-purchase) or other experiential factors.

Therefore, relational personalization focuses on four key pillars: controlling entity, customer knowledge, conversation style and CX effects.[25]

Controlling entity

Controlling entity refers to the type of agent or system that manages and interacts with customers. This is depicted as a continuum from entirely human-operated to fully digital, highlighting varying degrees of AI integration. Types of agent or system include:

- **A human agent** (e.g. call centre) involves customer service representatives or agents who manage interactions personally. Human agents handle various tasks ranging from simple to complex inquiries and provide assistance to customers. An example is traditional call centres where agents respond to customer queries via phone in many service providers.

- **A digital agent** (e.g. chatbot) refers to fully automated systems that use NLP and AI to manage customer interactions without human intervention. Digital agents handle routine inquiries, automate responses, and engage in scripted interactions based on AI algorithms. An example is chatbots on websites or social media that answer FAQs, guide users through processes, and provide information autonomously.

- **A hybrid** (e.g. routing, coaching, analytics) is a blend of human agents and AI tools. Hybrid systems often include routing mechanisms where customer service supervisors can transfer interactions from bots to human agents when more complex or nuanced handling is required. For example, as discussed in Chapter 6, the Tactful AI platform allows supervisors to easily set and adjust routing rules based on demand, ensuring inquiries are distributed among agents for optimal workload balance and shorter wait times. Also, priority-based routing caters to high-value customers, offering advanced support. With skill-based, queue-based and priority-based routing options, Omniengage empowers supervisors to manage customer engagement with maximum efficiency and satisfaction.

Additionally, AI supports human agents for tasks like natural language processing (NLP), data analysis, customer behaviour prediction, and providing insights or coaching to improve service. An example is Salesforce's Einstein AI, a customer service platform that connects to various systems like CRM, enabling human agents to receive real-time suggestions from AI to enhance interactions based on information from the CRM systems.[26]

From the customer's perspective, the preference to interact with a frontline employee or a chatbot often depends on the type of service or product offered. Affective elements also play a role in this preference; in some cases, frontline employees are perceived as more competent and warmer than chatbots. Delegating to a human, based on an understanding and contextualization of a customer's affective profile, can help provide a personal touch on a relational level.

One significant challenge is the chatbot's ability to recognize when human intervention is necessary accurately. This decision is not always straightforward and relies on the chatbot's programming and the complexity of the customer's issue. Chatbots might prematurely escalate simple queries to human agents or fail to escalate complex issues, leading to customer frustration. Maintaining a consistent service experience during the handover from a chatbot to a human agent is crucial. Customers might find it irritating or inconvenient if they have to repeat information or if the context of their query is lost in the transition.[27]

Customer knowledge

This involves understanding and gathering information about the customer to build a comprehensive knowledge base about them. To build relationships through conversation, personalization efforts must address the customer on an affective level. This involves gathering information about the customer, enabling companies to act on this level. Knowledge about the customer helps to understand their experiences and allows for personalization on a relational level.[28]

To achieve this, firms need to capture the following elements through an NLP-enabled system that can enrich the digital agent with insights to design a conversational flow that suits the customer's experiences and emotions or by providing these insights to human agents to help them manage the conversation in an affective way.

EXPERIENCE CONVERSATION CONTEXT (INTENT)

From a temporal perspective, a distinction can be made between the customer's past and current enquiries and experiences with the company, which influence their perception, attitudes and behaviours when interacting with the agents.[29] The customer's current experience is influenced not only by their affective and emotional reactions during the conversation but also by their previous experiences with the company.[30]

Prior interactions along the customer journey provide essential context for the current interaction. Understanding the customer's past behaviour or attitude towards various aspects of the company helps personalize the current customer service interaction appropriately. This knowledge offers critical insights necessary for resolving customer service issues effectively and building long-term relationships. Acquiring this information can be challenging for customer service agents, but it is a promising area for AI solutions that can extract these insights from existing customer experience (CX) data.[31] For example, generating insights from CX data (e.g. surveys, reviews, social media, CRM, etc.) is essential, as discussed earlier in Chapter 7. It can inform agents about attitudinal insights such as customer satisfaction, advocacy, or behavioural insights to reveal customers' purchasing behaviour.

While the context from previous experiences is crucial for the current interaction, customer relationships are also built over time. Customer emotions are shaped by evaluating the consequences of events, such as subsequent steps in their journey. It is important to consider the development of emotions throughout the conversation. Current experiences are vital for resolving the present issue, not previous ones. There should be a distinct approach for a customer who has complained multiple times about an unresolved issue compared to a customer encountering a problem for the first time. The design and flow of the conversation should reflect these differences.

In many cases, a customer might initially contact a brand through one channel, such as email or a call, but if they remain unsatisfied, they may turn to a chatbot to voice their concerns. It's crucial for agents to have access to this information to guide the conversation effectively. Omnichannel platforms such as Tactful AI are vital in these situations. A centralized inbox that tracks customer experiences and journeys in one place helps firms understand both current and past interactions and experiences, allowing them to provide a more consistent and informed conversational response.

EMOTIONS

Relational personalization aims to enhance customer service experiences, which are significantly influenced by customers' emotional and affective state. Emotions play a crucial role in relationship building by fostering trust, understanding preferences and desires, and making customers feel valued and cared for. Also, it influences how firms better design a conversational flow that can help solve customer problems and leave a positive gesture that elevates customer satisfaction. Emotions emerge as reactions to three factors: the consequences of events (such as issue resolution or past interactions with the company), agents' actions (such as the manner in which a service agent addresses the customer), and elements of objects (such as a chatbot UX interface).[32]

While emotions are short-lived and event-triggered, moods are not event-specific and can last for extended periods, with emotions being more intense. Emotions are particularly relevant to customer experiences and service due to their high intensity and event-specificity, e.g. customer service. On an interpersonal level, proactively managing and addressing customer emotions strengthens the customer–employee relationship.

It is necessary to distinguish between different emotions to accurately determine and respond to a customer's emotions during interactions. Applying NLP emotion models can help extract the customer's affective states from the conversation data, including Ekman's six basic discrete emotions (anger, disgust, fear, happiness, sadness and surprise).[33]

As discussed earlier, a customer experiencing intense frustration is entirely different from a neutral customer with a calm tone who is asking specific questions. The conversation flow cannot be scripted and standardized in these cases.

PERSONALITY

The customer's personality is fundamental for enabling and maintaining relationships, affecting behaviour and emotional processes. In customer service, personality traits influence how service quality is perceived and deemed satisfactory. Customers' personality traits impact their preferences when interacting with agents. Also, their characteristics provide context that significantly influences their decision-making process, preferences, behaviours and experiences. Customers with different personality traits perceive service outcomes differently and thus require varied CX strategies to meet their needs.[34]

Personality can be expressed through written and verbal communication. Consequently, AI models can be trained to identify users' personalities from digital channels, and generative AI can also be trained to generate responses specific to certain personality traits by using the common five-factor model, which identifies five distinct personality traits: openness (complex vs. conventional, uncreative), conscientiousness (dependable, self-disciplined vs. disorganized, careless), extroversion (outgoing, enthusiastic vs. reserved, quiet), agreeableness (sympathetic, warm vs. critical, quarrelsome) and neuroticism (calm, emotionally stable vs. anxious, easily stressed).[35]

People are naturally drawn to those who are similar to themselves. Consequently, we can expect in the future an increase in humanized voice assistants like ChatGPT, Alexa or Google Gemini incorporating personality traits to create a more personalized experience when interacting with users. Leveraging large language models (LLMs) can facilitate this personalization. However, companies must address trust and privacy concerns associated with using AI agents to manage personality traits, as these issues can influence the relationship between personality and customer experience.

For example, Scarlett Johansson recently voiced concerns over OpenAI's use of an AI voice in the latest version of ChatGPT, which she claimed closely resembles her own voice from the 2013 sci-fi movie *Her*. After OpenAI's demo, it seemed the company aimed to enhance personalized interactions by using a voice that felt familiar or appealing to specific user profiles and contextual conversation. Although OpenAI had previously approached Johansson to license her voice – a proposal she declined – the company later apologized and discontinued the voice's use, clarifying that it was modelled on a different actress. Johansson expressed her shock and frustration, citing the rising concerns about deepfakes and the protection of personal identities. OpenAI's CEO, Sam Altman, denied any intentional mimicry of Johansson's voice and emphasized their commitment to improved communication and transparency in the future.[36]

Conversational style

The personalization effort is delivered and designed by creating a suitable personalized conversational style. Based on the information gathered about the customer, agents (humans or bots) can design and personalize communication styles. Language can impact the customer's experiences. Furthermore, communication styles are essential to building relational personalization by empathizing and reacting appropriately to customers' emotions if required. Emotions can be conveyed from the customer service agent to the customer, and the role of verbal and non-verbal communication is to address the need for socialization and a sense of belonging in some cases. The type of response given by the customer service agent (scripted vs. natural) impacts the relational personalization capability, determining the level of human likeness and its effect.[37] Ultimately, personalized conversations based on acquired customer knowledge should enable customer service agents to promote relational personalization and achieve desired customer experience outcomes such as higher engagement, loyalty and satisfaction.

SOCIAL

One quality required for enabling relational personalization in customer service stems from the human need for socialization. The social context of a conversation (human–human and human–machine) and the role of social others are crucial in the decision-making process along the customer journey, improving customer experience and overall satisfaction. Customers pay attention to emotional cues used in social interactions or recommendations and use them as information to form their reactions. Personalized solutions can signal social interaction, positively impacting the relationship between a customer and the AI recommendation system. In this context, service agents or AI agents can act as surrogates for social others.[38]

Therefore, conversations need to go beyond task-oriented communication to act as social others and include personal chit-chat. Customers appreciate this and see it as socially engaging communication, demonstrating proactivity, a positive attitude, or courtesy. This suggests that the ability to design an engaging dialogue and workflow to interact socially (chit-chat) is required when needed to support building customer service relationships. We discussed this in the social interaction in Chapter 2.

EMPATHY

Responding to a customer empathetically indicates emotional intelligence and can lead to higher customer satisfaction. As discussed, if we recognize the customer in a specific emotional state, like frustration, the response needs to be designed in a specific way to handle this emotion. An empathetic response can be cognitive (taking the perspective of another person) or affective (understanding and potentially sharing the same emotion as another person).[39]

Language is critical for conveying emotions in all customer service conversations (e.g. online chats, phone calls, or in-person interactions). Therefore, verbal cues such as voice and text can significantly influence the customer's emotions. In addition to verbal cues, a service agent's or virtual agent's presence can also significantly impact the customer's emotions. Besides verbal communication via text or speech, this includes non-verbal communication with facial expressions or gestures. There are various ways and strategies for displaying emotions (e.g. emojis).[40]

Advancements in AI, LLM and robots for customer service interactions have shifted the focus to the role of empathy in digital or human-to-non-human interactions, as discussed in Chapter 2.

RESPONSE TYPE

Customer service agents and digital agents such as chatbots or virtual avatars either communicate with natural responses or utilize scripts with pre-written responses. Both of them allow for synchronous communication.[41] Natural responses have a higher degree of freedom and enable customer service to adjust responses dynamically. However, they are also more prone to inappropriate and harmful responses (e.g. hallucination, rigid response, inaccuracy). For example, DPD disabled its AI chatbot after a customer managed to make it swear and write a poem criticizing the company. Frustrated by the chatbot's inability to provide information about their missing parcel or connect them to a human agent, the customer experimented with the bot, leading to it making inappropriate remarks and self-deprecating statements.[42] The customer shared the conversation on social media, which quickly went viral. DPD acknowledged the issue, attributing it to an error following a system update, and has since disabled the chatbot for further updates. The customer found the incident amusing but emphasized the need for AI tools to improve customer experiences rather than complicate them. Despite the viral post, DPD had not contacted him, and his parcel remained missing.[43] This incident clearly puts DPD at

FIGURE 10.1 Relational personalization elements framework in customer service

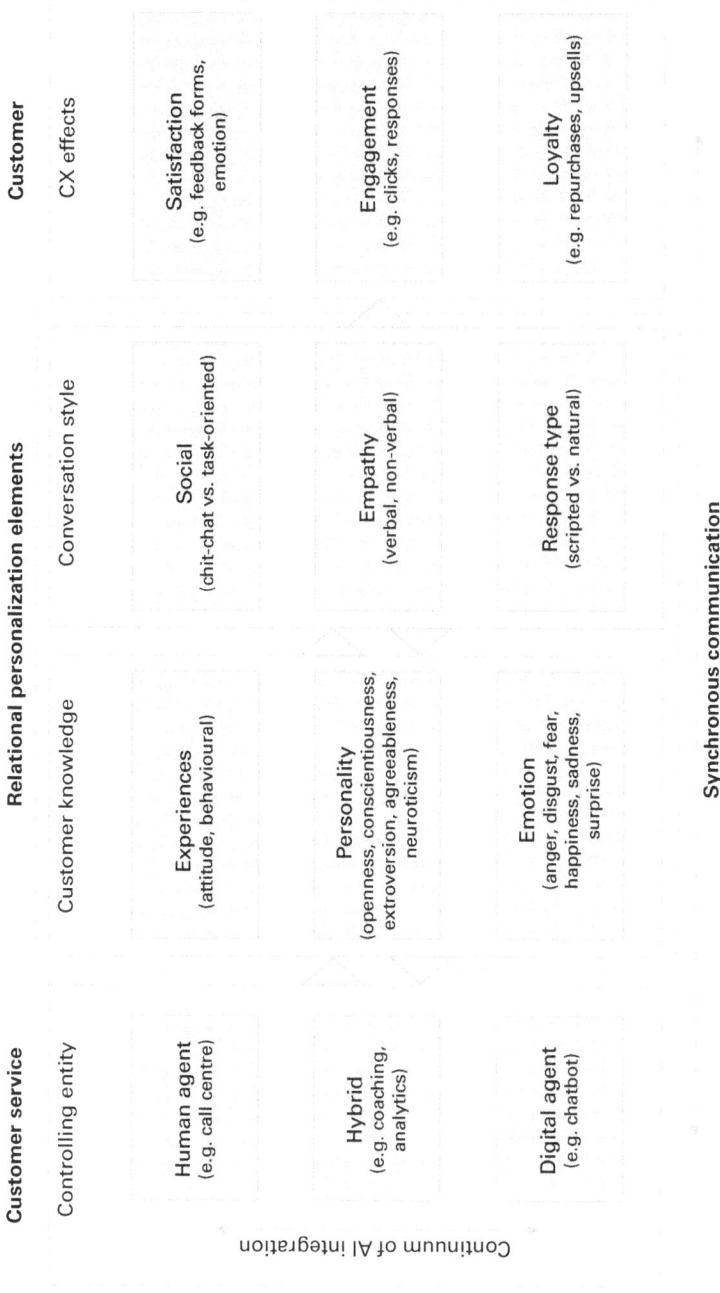

Customer service	Relational personalization elements		Customer
Controlling entity	Customer knowledge	Conversation style	CX effects
		Social (chit-chat vs. task-oriented)	Satisfaction (e.g. feedback forms, emotion)
Human agent (e.g. call centre)	Experiences (attitude, behavioural)		
Hybrid (e.g. coaching, analytics)	Personality (openness, conscientiousness, extroversion, agreeableness, neuroticism)	Empathy (verbal, non-verbal)	Engagement (e.g. clicks, responses)
Digital agent (e.g. chatbot)	Emotion (anger, disgust, fear, happiness, sadness, surprise)	Response type (scripted vs. natural)	Loyalty (e.g. repurchases, upsells)

Synchronous communication

Continuum of AI integration

reputational risk, especially with their B2B customers who rely on them to deliver products to their end consumers.

Generating natural responses automatically is more challenging without human involvement. Practice and academics are still investigating the potential of LLM models and their effectiveness in using natural versus scripted language in customer service.[44]

CX effects

As part of synchronous communication, customers receive relational personalization efforts, which can significantly influence their overall experience. In the framework,[45] implementing such relational personalization using AI can positively impact customer satisfaction, engagement and loyalty by shaping how effectively customer knowledge is utilized and how personalized the interactions feel. Firms could use these metrics as a way to explore how personalization can achieve the following outcomes:

- **Satisfaction:** Timely and relevant responses improve customer satisfaction.
- **Engagement:** Interactive and responsive systems keep customers engaged with humans or AI agents.
- **Loyalty:** Personalized and empathetic interactions promote customer loyalty towards the brand.

Personalization in digital channels can achieve the desired effects. Through synchronous conversations between an agent and a customer, six proposed elements of relational personalization can lead to improved customer experience outcomes in customer service.

In the following section, I will discuss the current landscape of conversational AI technology providers in customer service and assess the extent to which they offer relational personalization experiences based on the proposed elements.

Conversational AI in customer service

Many companies have already implemented chatbots or are planning to introduce conversational AI. Conversational AI has three levels of technological advancement and automation, each impacting its ability to enable relational personalization. These levels of automation can be categorized as conversations augmented by analytics, conversational coaching and conversational agents.

Conversational analytics

Analytics-enhanced conversations leverage natural language understanding (NLU) technology to extract cues such as customer intents, emotions or stress from interactions with service agents. These insights are derived from various data sources, including voice calls, transcripts, emails, live chats, SMS, chatbots and social media.[46] By analysing conversational data, businesses can gain a deeper understanding of the customer journey and tailor their services accordingly.

As discussed in Chapter 7, relational personalization hinges on providing service agents with data about a customer's historical experiences, encompassing attitudinal, emotional and behavioural patterns.[47] Many solutions, such as Amazon Connect Contact Lens, Awaken and Verint, prioritize sentiment analysis to identify customer feelings as a first step towards understanding their needs.

Advanced technologies like Awaken's speech analysis offer detailed emotion detection through vocal cues, distinguishing between emotions such as anger, sadness, happiness, neutrality, anxiety, vulnerability and misunderstanding.[48] Similarly, solutions like Uniphore go beyond basic detection, analysing facial expressions and micro-expressions to uncover deeper emotional states and intentions.[49] This integrated approach allows organizations to identify subtle signs of frustration or confusion that might not be evident through speech or text alone, enabling real-time adjustments to service delivery.

For instance, detecting anger or anxiety in a customer's voice enables service agents to adopt an empathetic tone or escalate the matter to a supervisor. Likewise, facial expression analysis can empower virtual assistants or chatbots to personalize interactions based on the customer's mood, making the experience feel more human. By combining facial and vocal emotion detection, businesses can construct a comprehensive view of the customer's emotional journey, fostering more effective responses and improving satisfaction.

These technologies also support proactive interventions. Detailed emotion analysis provides insights into underlying sentiments like vulnerability or misunderstanding, helping agents adjust their communication strategies to address the root causes of customer concerns. As a result, organizations can personalize interactions, strengthen customer loyalty, and enhance overall service quality.

Beyond emotional insights, solutions such as CallMiner's Eureka integrate data from multiple touchpoints to provide a holistic view of the customer journey. This enables agents to adapt their conversations based on the context of previous interactions.[50] Meanwhile, platforms like Tactful AI apply deep learning, large language models and generative AI to extract nuanced behavioural insights, driving personalization in chatbot interactions. However, gaps remain in some solutions, particularly around identifying customer personalities and tailoring conversation styles to enhance relational personalization.[51]

Conversational coaching

This enhances conversational analytics by utilizing technologies from recommendation systems. In this context, conversational AI transforms extracted cues into actionable insights. AI-based conversational coaching combines natural language understanding (NLU) and automated speech recognition technologies to guide service agents on the best ways to handle customer inquiries and conversations. In text-based communication, conversational coaching can include features like message auto-completion or suggesting next-best responses. Additionally, it can be used to simulate conversations and train new agents.[52] This approach enables relational personalization by not only providing relevant information about customer knowledge factors but also recommending adjustments to conversation styles based on emotion, experience and personality.

For instance, providers such as Nuance and Uniphore offer personalized coaching services using natural language processing (NLP) models that automatically detect and retain specific conversation contexts, including changing intents, topics, issues and named entities, and recommend the next-best actions. Cogito focuses on analysing voice signals and emotions in call centres, offering guidance to help service agents be more empathetic in specific situations by slowing their speech or asking open-ended questions for better engagement.[53]

Although these AI-based conversational coaching tools cover some elements of relational personalization (customer knowledge) and provide recommended actions to service agents, they have not yet been able to automatically generate the most appropriate conversation styles that impact customer experience outcomes. Additionally, they lack the integration of personality-based elements and socially appropriate responses.[54]

Conversational agents

The third and most prominent application of conversational AI in text-based customer service is chatbots, which are designed to free up agents and provide quicker service to customers. Unlike the previous two types, chatbots automatically and directly engage with customers using human-like language, utilizing natural language for both input and output. Each conversational AI application, depending on its level of industry maturity and automation, enhances different aspects of human intelligence for collaborative service provision. However, there is still limited understanding of how these conversational AI applications, in collaboration with customer service agents, can personalize customer interactions and provide a personal touch.[55]

A conversational agent is a technological entity capable of engaging in both reactive and proactive behaviours, interacting with users through natural language inputs and outputs. These agents interact with customers using a variety of modalities. For example, Poly AI's assistant utilizes voice communication (voice bots), facilitating natural, fluid conversations, whereas Aisera's and Tactful AI's chatbots rely on text-based communication.[56]

Personalizing text-based interactions demands sophisticated NLU (natural language understanding) and natural language generation models, as the chatbot must craft suitable words and sentences tailored to specific contexts. Voice bot interactions introduce added complexity by requiring adjustments in tone and speech tempo. Moreover, the design aesthetics of conversational agents, such as choosing between embodied and anthropomorphic forms, adds further complexity.

Embodied agents like Amelia, a three-dimensional conversational agent, can display suitable emotions during interactions by reacting to emotional and personality-based cues. These emotional expressions aid in training conversational agents to convey emotions authentically through facial expressions and gestures.[57]

Conversational agents that utilize emotive expressions and personality traits are seen as having higher emotional intelligence. However, developing an agent that can accurately respond to customers' emotional states presents a considerable challenge due to diverse preferences and interpretations of how emotions are displayed.[58]

Mohamed Elmasry, the CEO of Tactful AI, stated that they are developing a Khepri co-pilot product that aims to transform customer data into strategic insights, driving operational efficiency and revenue growth. By automating customer engagement and providing deep analytics on customer behaviour and team performance, Khepri helps managers make data-driven decisions, optimize processes, and identify new opportunities for business expansion and customer satisfaction enhancement. The Khepri co-pilot for agents automates routine tasks, enhances customer interactions, and boosts sales with AI-driven insights and personalization, increasing agent productivity and customer retention. This synergy between support and sales drives business success and fosters customer loyalty. Additionally, Khepri streamlines AI deployment for system admins, offering easy set-up, smart maintenance, and scalable customer engagement solutions, allowing system admins to focus on innovation and strategy to stay competitive. For supervisors, Khepri offers real-time oversight of customer interactions for quality assurance and strategic insights into team performance metrics. This enables more informed decision-making, optimizes resource allocation, and identifies training opportunities, ensuring a consistent and high-quality customer experience.

Applying AI to customer service channels

AI can be applied in different customer service channels – social media, chatbots and call centres – to understand the extent to which personalized experience elements have been applied by firms. The controlling entities are **human** and **bot agents** responding to customers' enquiries and issues through different customer service settings. The different AI and NLP techniques capture these elements from text-based interactions in these channels, allowing us to assess and enhance personalization efforts across various customer touchpoints.[59]

CX effects

Firms can use a deep learning model to assess whether personalized conversation styles enhance customer experience by tracking sentiment changes during conversations. *Positive experiences* were identified when customer sentiment improved or stayed positive, while *negative experiences* were noted when sentiment decreased or remained negative throughout the conversation. We used this as an outcome variable.[60]

Additionally, you can employ service recovery success as a metric to gauge whether customer inquiries were resolved. Three distinct customer service scenarios could be applied: 1) customers being redirected to another communication channel such as direct messages, phone or email following initial contact; 2) issues resolved during the interaction; and 3) issues remaining unresolved. NLP techniques can be applied to analyse the final two messages of each conversation, classifying them as *referred*, *unresolved* or *resolved*.[61]

Customer knowledge

To assess a customer's attitude towards the company, you can operationalize *past customer experiences* by analysing the sentiment of each customer's previous messages, especially in channels such as social media. In a ticketing or chatbot scenario, this could be achieved by accessing a dataset such as CRM systems. Firms employed the same approach used in measuring affective customer experiences. If the majority of a customer's past messages were negative (or positive), this could classify their past experience accordingly as negative (or positive). In cases with no prior interactions, only neutral messages, or an equal number of positive and negative messages, the past experience can be classified as neutral. Like sentiment analysis, the *emotion classification* NLP model can be applied to extract the six fundamental discrete emotions. For *personality*, you can apply LLM to define the personality traits of each customer.[62]

Conversation styles

In customer service interactions, agents' responses may focus on task resolution or include *social* elements such as small talk. To measure the prevalence of small talk in these conversations, a classifier can be trained to differentiate between responses centred on task resolution and those engaging in social exchange through small talk. Then, you can fine-tune the LLM model using datasets of small talk and task-oriented dialogues. The amount of small talk in each conversation can be quantified by assigning +1 for responses identified as small talk and -1 for those deemed task-oriented, averaging these scores across the conversation. This scoring was also segmented by the different stages of the conversation: the *greeting*, *middle* and *closing remarks*.[63]

An LLM model can be used for detecting *empathy* in text-based communication to identify three ways empathy is expressed, categorized into cognitive (interpretations and explorations) and affective (emotional reactions) dimensions. We simplify these into a single category to more effectively identify the presence of these empathy types. We quantified empathy by assigning +1 for each empathetic response from an agent and calculated an average score for the entire conversation. Additionally, empathy scores were specifically analysed at different stages of the conversation, including the first and last responses from the customer service agent and an average for the mid-conversation responses.[64]

The *response type* and *lexical diversity* can be assessed through the lens of similarity, specifically focusing on lexical rather than semantic similarity, which relates to the actual use of words rather than their meaning. Lexical similarity measures how much customer service text overlaps, examining whether agents reuse specific text snippets. Lexical similarity can be computed by comparing a given response to all prior responses by customer service agents. This can be categorized into three types: 1) general similarity across various customer service accounts; 2) company-specific similarity within the same account; and 3) agent-specific similarity for responses by the same agent within their account. This categorization helps us identify patterns of repetitive language, standardized text snippets, and common phrases in customer service. To derive a similarity score for each conversation, you can average the sum of the similarity scores from the agent's responses within that conversation, further breaking down the scores by conversation stages.[65]

Insights from social media customer service

Many brands are using social media as a customer service, using text-based modality to interact with their customers. We gathered data from 15 customer service accounts across sectors such as telecommunications (Vodafone, UK, BT UK, Three UK, Virgin Media), airlines (British Airway, Ryanair, EasyJet), fashion retail (Zara, H&M, Nike, JD) and banking (Metro, Klarna, Chase, Virgin Money) from August to November 2022. The final dataset for analysis included 34,323 conversations. The aim was to evaluate to what extent these accounts are using our key elements of personalization in customer service.

I will discuss the key insights gained from social media customer service data on the impact of various conversation styles on affective customer experiences. Our analysis has provided several critical findings for practitioners aiming to enhance customer interactions using personalized experience.[66]

- **Cognitive empathy: The cornerstone of positive experiences** – Cognitive empathy emerged as the most consistently positive factor. It universally enhances customer experiences across different scenarios (resolved, unresolved and referred). This indicates that when customer service agents understand and reflect the customers' thoughts and perspectives, it significantly improves the overall interaction. This suggests that training agents to focus on cognitive empathy can be highly beneficial.

- **Affective empathy: A double-edged sword** – In contrast to cognitive empathy, affective empathy – where agents emotionally align with customers – proved to be generally detrimental, particularly in unresolved situations. This insight is crucial as it challenges the conventional wisdom that empathy, in all its forms, is always beneficial. Affective empathy, if not carefully managed, can lead to negative customer experiences, especially when issues remain unresolved.

- **Small talk: Less is more** – Small talk has a generally negative impact on customer experiences, particularly when issues are referred to higher levels. This suggests that customers prefer direct and task-oriented conversations, especially when their problems are pending resolution. Therefore, minimizing small talk and focusing on resolving the issue at hand can lead to better customer satisfaction.

- **Lexical diversity: The value of varied language** – The analysis highlights the importance of lexical diversity rather than scripted text – using varied language and avoiding repetitive phrases. High lexical similarity, where agents use similar or standardized language, negatively impacts customer experiences. This is particularly true in the middle and closing stages of conversations. Encouraging agents to personalize their language and avoid overly standardized responses can improve customer satisfaction.

- **The role of customer emotions: Pinpoint their emotional state** – Initial customer emotions play a significant role in moderating the effects of conversation styles. Negative emotions such as anger or fear can intensify the negative impacts of affective empathy and lexical similarity. On the other hand, positive emotions like joy can mitigate some of these negative effects. This highlights the importance of personalizing communication strategies based on the customer's emotional state at the beginning of the interaction.

- **Previous customer experience: A significant moderator** – Previous customer experiences significantly influence current interactions. A positive past experience enhances current customer satisfaction, even if certain conversation styles might generally have a negative effect. Equally, a negative past experience can intensify negative reactions to similar conversation styles. This finding highlights the need for a holistic approach to customer service that considers the customer's entire journey with the company.

Insights from chatbot

We highlight the key insights from the chatbot-led service interaction experiment. We were keen to understand how different conversation styles, previously identified in human–agent interactions, affect customer experiences when applied by a chatbot. Participants interacted with a chatbot over an imaginary flight cancellation scenario and rated their experiences. Here are the insights.[67]

- **Cognitive empathy: Effective across mediums** – Cognitive empathy continues to be highly effective, even in chatbot interactions. Chatbots that employed cognitive empathy, especially during greetings and mid-conversation, received higher net promoter scores (NPS) and customer satisfaction (CSAT) scores. Participants also reported more positive emotions. This reinforces the importance of designing chatbots that can understand and reflect the customer's perspective, enhancing the overall customer experience.

- **Affective empathy: Less effective for chatbots** – Chatbots using affective empathy – showing emotional alignment with customers – were less effective. These interactions resulted in lower NPS and CSAT scores and increased negative emotions compared to those using cognitive empathy. This suggests that affective empathy might not translate well in chatbot interactions, where the emotional expression may seem less genuine or effective.

- **Small talk: Minimal benefit in chatbot interactions** – Incorporating small talk into chatbot conversations did not improve customer satisfaction. Chatbots using small talk received lower NPS and showed higher levels of negative emotions. This indicates that customers interacting with chatbots prefer conversations that are more focused on resolving their issues rather than engaging in casual chit-chat.

- **Lexical similarity: Mixed results** – The impact of lexical similarity – using similar phrases and language – varied depending on when it was applied:
  - **Standardized greetings**: When chatbots used standardized greetings, there was an improvement in CSAT scores and a reduction in

frustration levels. This suggests that consistency in greetings can create a positive initial impression.

o **Middle and closing stages:** High lexical similarity during these stages did not perform well, leading to decreased NPS scores and higher negative emotions. This highlights the need for more varied and personalized language as the conversation progresses.

• **Emotional states: Importance of cognitive empathy** – The analysis further highlighted the role of cognitive empathy in moderating negative emotions. Chatbots using cognitive empathy significantly reduced feelings of frustration, irritation and sadness among customers. Conversely, chatbots that did not use cognitive empathy or relied on affective empathy instead saw higher levels of these negative emotions. This finding highlights the critical role of cognitive empathy in managing customer emotions effectively.

Insights from call centre

This section shows the critical insights gained from analysing customer service calls at a call centre, focusing on effective communication elements. We discuss how the call centre can enhance the personal touch in digital customer service interactions by analysing conversation styles and their impact on customer experience.

• **Empathetic communication: Essential but underutilized** – Although empathetic communication is infrequently used in customer service interactions, empathy, particularly cognitive empathy, is crucial for building customer rapport and trust. Using empathetic responses can significantly enhance customer satisfaction and deepen relationships. Training agents to better express understanding and concern for customer issues can lead to more positive outcomes.

• **Strategic use of small talk: Building rapport early** – Small talk is most effective when used strategically to build rapport at the beginning of conversations. While it can set a positive tone and make customers feel more at ease, overuse or inappropriate timing can negatively impact customer experience. Small talk should be minimized during the middle and closing stages of conversations, where the focus should be on resolving customer issues efficiently.

- **Lexical diversity: Personalization matters** – Consistent with other channels, increasing lexical diversity is essential to enhance customer interactions. Standardized, repetitive responses are less effective, especially in conversations' middle and closing stages. Personalized greetings, acknowledgements of customer history and varied language throughout the interaction contribute to a more engaging and satisfying customer experience.

- **Data-driven communication: Balanced use** – Data-driven communication, which includes using numbers and statistics to support the conversation, is effective when used strategically. It should be integrated mainly in the middle of the conversation to provide personalized advice and solutions. However, its use at the beginning and end of conversations should be limited to avoid overwhelming customers with information.

- **Emotional intelligence and adaptability: Key to success** – Understanding and adapting to customer emotions and personality traits are vital for successful interactions. The analysis emphasized the importance of training agents in emotional intelligence, particularly in empathy and adaptability. Agents who can recognize and respond to different emotional states and personality traits can significantly improve the effective customer experience.

KEY TAKEAWAYS

In this chapter, we discussed the importance of personalizing relationships in customer service by applying key elements such as customer knowledge, emotion and personality. These factors impact conversation styles and determine the extent to which agents (human, bot, hybrid) become social or use response types that are scripted, natural or empathetic to customers. Additionally, we explored the importance of conversational AI in analytics, agent performance and coaching, and the potential of AI and generative AI to offer personalized experiences to customers.

- **Training and development**:
  - Cognitive empathy: Develop cognitive empathy skills among agents. Encourage agents to use empathetic language to build rapport and trust.
  - Affective empathy: Train agents (human or bots) on the pitfalls of affective empathy, especially in unresolved cases. Enhance training programmes to focus on cognitive empathy skills.

- Small talk: Train agents to minimize small talk and focus on issue resolution. Train agents to use small talk effectively at the beginning of conversations and minimize small talk during issue resolution phases to maintain focus.

- Emotional intelligence development: Focus on skills such as active listening, empathy and adaptability to different customer personalities.

- **Conversation strategies**:

  - Varied language: Use varied and personalized language. Encourage personalized greetings and acknowledgements of customer history.

  - Adaptive communication: Adapt communication styles based on the customer's initial emotional state.

  - Balanced data-driven communication: Integrate data-driven elements, primarily during the problem-solving phase, and avoid excessive use of data at the beginning and end of conversations.

  - Feedback loops: Continuously refine and personalize customer service through feedback.

- **Customer experience management**:

  - Data utilization: Use previous customer interaction data to tailor conversational flow and understand better your customer profile.

  - Emotional tracking: Track and analyse customer emotions to better prepare agents.

- **Chatbot design**:

  - Empathy integration: Prioritize cognitive empathy and avoid over-reliance on affective empathy.

  - Focus on issue resolution: Limit small talk and ensure conversations are task oriented.

  - Language use: Use standardized greetings and maintain varied, personalized language.

  - Emotional management: Employ strategies to reduce negative emotions and monitor the customer's emotional state.

In the following chapter, we will explore how to leverage CX data to gain insights into your market positioning.

Notes

1   Blümel, J H, Zaki, M and Bohné, T (2024) Personal touch in digital customer service: A conceptual framework of relational personalization for conversational AI, *Journal of Service Theory and Practice*, 34 (1), 33–65

2   Court Bishop (2024) 51 customer service statistics you need to know, Zendesk, Contributing Writer. www.zendesk.co.uk/blog/customer-service-statistics/ (archived at https://perma.cc/D4SN-5LQW)

3   Ofcom (2023) Numbers up: Best and worst telecoms customer service revealed, Ofcom. www.ofcom.org.uk/news-centre/2023/numbers-up-best-and-worst-telecoms-customer-service-revealed (archived at https://perma.cc/9WCP-QM3L)

4   Court Bishop (2024) 51 customer service statistics you need to know, Zendesk, Contributing Writer. www.zendesk.co.uk/blog/customer-service-statistics/ (archived at https://perma.cc/7JWA-M3UZ)

5   Ozdoruk, C (2021) How do the world's largest travel companies deliver customer support?, Netomi. www.netomi.com/hospitality-travel-cx-benchmarks (archived at https://perma.cc/6HPA-WQDV)

6   Press, G (2023) One negative chatbot experience drives away 30% of customers, *Forbes*, 1 February. www.forbes.com/sites/gilpress/2023/02/01/one-negative-chatbot-experience-drives-away-30-of-customers/ (archived at https://perma.cc/VSM8-WVUQ)

7   Court Bishop (2024) 51 customer service statistics you need to know, Zendesk, Contributing Writer. www.zendesk.co.uk/blog/customer-service-statistics/ (archived at https://perma.cc/NZV2-D5HY)

8   ibid.

9   Ozdoruk, C (2021) How do the world's largest travel companies deliver customer support?, Netomi. www.netomi.com/hospitality-travel-cx-benchmarks   (archived at https://perma.cc/TT7T-8E47)

10 Court Bishop (2024) 51 customer service statistics you need to know, Zendesk, Contributing Writer. www.zendesk.co.uk/blog/customer-service-statistics/ (archived at https://perma.cc/ZR7L-W77W)

11 ibid.

12 Press, G (2023) One negative chatbot experience drives away 30% of customers, *Forbes*, 1 February. www.forbes.com/sites/gilpress/2023/02/01/one-negative-chatbot-experience-drives-away-30-of-customers/ (archived at https://perma.cc/6HT3-T8C3)

13 ibid.

14 Kayako (2024) Live chat statistics: Trends and insights from 400 consumers and 100 businesses, Kayako. https://kayako.com/live-chat-software/statistics/ (archived at https://perma.cc/PVN2-YNTR)

15 Blümel, J H, Zaki, M and Bohné, T (2024) Personal touch in digital customer service: A conceptual framework of relational personalization for conversational AI, *Journal of Service Theory and Practice*, 34 (1), 33–65

16 Blümel, J and Zaki, M (2024) Providing a personalised service experience using artificial intelligence, *Handbook of Service Experience*, Edward Elgar Publishing

17 Tactful AI (2024) AI chatbot: Omnichannel AI for customer service. https://tactful.ai/omnichannel/ai-chatbot/ (archived at https://perma.cc/V68A-CQ82)

18 Blümel, J H, Zaki, M and Bohné, T (2024) Personal touch in digital customer service: A conceptual framework of relational personalization for conversational AI, *Journal of Service Theory and Practice*, 34 (1), 33–65

19 Blümel, J and Zaki, M (2024) Providing a personalised service experience using artificial intelligence, *Handbook of Service Experience*, Edward Elgar Publishing

20 Bluemel, J, Zaki, M and Bohné, T (2024) Cambridge Service Alliance. https://cambridgeservicealliance.eng.cam.ac.uk (archived at https://perma.cc/QTH2-AAUQ)

21 Salesforce (2021) *State of Service*, 5th edition. www.salesforce.com/content/dam/web/en_sg/www/documents/pdf/state-of-service-5th-edition.pdf (archived at https://perma.cc/Z9TL-QAQJ)

22 Blümel, J H, Zaki, M and Bohné, T (2024) Personal touch in digital customer service: A conceptual framework of relational personalization for conversational AI, *Journal of Service Theory and Practice*, 34 (1), 33–65

23 HCLTech (2024) The blueprint of total experience: Achieving experiences beyond the frame. www.hcltech.com/sites/default/files/documents/resources/brochure/files/hcltech-the-blueprint-to-total-experience-full-report.pdf (archived at https://perma.cc/EE9G-V9DG)

24 ibid.

25 Blümel, J H, Zaki, M and Bohné, T (2024) Personal touch in digital customer service: A conceptual framework of relational personalization for conversational AI, *Journal of Service Theory and Practice*, 34 (1) 33–65

26 Salesforce (2024) *Artificial Intelligence*. www.salesforce.com/uk/artificial-intelligence/ (archived at https://perma.cc/DSW7-7Q3D)

27 Blümel, J and Zaki, M (2024) Providing a personalised service experience using artificial intelligence, *Handbook of Service Experience*, Edward Elgar Publishing

28 Blümel, J H, Zaki, M and Bohné, T (2024) Personal touch in digital customer service: A conceptual framework of relational personalization for conversational AI, *Journal of Service Theory and Practice*, 34 (1) 33–65

29 Blümel, J and Zaki, M (2024) Providing a personalised service experience using artificial intelligence, *Handbook of Service Experience*, Edward Elgar Publishing

30 ibid.

31 Zaki, M (2019) Digital transformation: Harnessing digital technologies for the next generation of services, *Journal of Services Marketing*, 33 (4), 429–35

32 Blümel, J and Zaki, M (2024) Providing a personalised service experience using artificial intelligence, *Handbook of Service Experience*, Edward Elgar Publishing

33 Ekman, P (1992) An argument for basic emotions, *Cognition and Emotion*, 6 (3–4), 169–200

34 Blümel, J H, Zaki, M and Bohné, T (2024) Personal touch in digital customer service: A conceptual framework of relational personalization for conversational AI, *Journal of Service Theory and Practice*, 34 (1) 33–65

35 Roccas, S, Sagiv, L, Schwartz, S H and Knafo, A (2002) The big five personality factors and personal values, *Personality and Social Psychology Bulletin*, 28 (6), 789–801

36 Allyn, B (2024) Scarlett Johansson says she is 'shocked, angered' over new ChatGPT voice', NPR, 20 May. www.npr.org/2024/05/20/1252495087/openai-pulls-ai-voice-that-was-compared-to-scarlett-johansson-in-the-movie-her (archived at https://perma.cc/2B98-3M92)

37 Blümel, J H, Zaki, M and Bohné, T (2024) Personal touch in digital customer service: A conceptual framework of relational personalization for conversational AI, *Journal of Service Theory and Practice*, 34 (1) 33–65

38 ibid.

39 ibid.

40 Blümel, J and Zaki, M (2024) Providing a personalised service experience using artificial intelligence, *Handbook of Service Experience*, Edward Elgar Publishing

41 Blümel, J H, Zaki, M and Bohné, T (2024) Personal touch in digital customer service: A conceptual framework of relational personalization for conversational AI, *Journal of Service Theory and Practice*, 34 (1) 33–65

42 Sky News (2024) The DPD customer service chatbot swears and calls the company the 'worst delivery firm', Sky News, 20 January. https://news.sky.com/story/dpd-customer-service-chatbot-swears-and-calls-company-worst-delivery-service-13052037 (archived at https://perma.cc/T2H8-U66X)

43 ibid.

44 Blümel, J and Zaki, M (2024) Providing a personalised service experience using artificial intelligence, *Handbook of Service Experience*, Edward Elgar Publishing

45 Blümel, J H, Zaki, M and Bohné, T (2024) Personal touch in digital customer service: A conceptual framework of relational personalization for conversational AI, *Journal of Service Theory and Practice*, 34 (1) 33–65

46 Zaki, M and McColl-Kennedy, J R (2020) Text mining analysis roadmap (TMAR) for service research, *Journal of Services Marketing*, 34 (1), 30–47

47 Holmlund, M, Van Vaerenbergh, Y, Ciuchita, R, Ravald, A, Sarantopoulos, P, Villarroel Ordenes, F and Zaki, M (2020) Customer experience management in the age of big data analytics: A strategic framework, *Journal of Business Research*, 116, 356–65

48 Awaken (2024) Speech analytics. www.awaken.io/products/speech-analytics (archived at https://perma.cc/Z2RL-5KLU)

49 Uniphore (2023) Conversational AI Intelliview. www.uniphore.com/resources/analyst-reports/opus-research-2023-conversational-ai-intelliview/ (archived at https://perma.cc/UGJ9-TATR)

50 CallMiner (2024) Eureka. https://callminer.com/products/eureka (archived at https://perma.cc/28EV-R8DZ)

51 Blümel, J H, Zaki, M and Bohné, T (2024) Personal touch in digital customer service: A conceptual framework of relational personalization for conversational AI, *Journal of Service Theory and Practice*, 34, (1) 33–65

52 ibid.

53 Cogito Corporation (2024) Cogito: Human-aware AI for better customer interaction. https://cogitocorp.com (archived at https://perma.cc/54Q7-JJ6A)

54 Blümel, J H, Zaki, M and Bohné, T (2024) Personal touch in digital customer service: A conceptual framework of relational personalization for conversational AI, *Journal of Service Theory and Practice*, 34 (1) 33–65

55 ibid.

56 ibid.

57 ibid.

58 ibid.

59 Blümel, J H and Zaki, M (2023) From small-talk to empathy: How social media can inform the design of chatbots for personalized customer service experience, Frontiers in Service Conference 2023

60 Blümel, J H (2024) Providing personalised experience in text-based customer service conversations, Apollo – University of Cambridge Repository. https://doi.org/10.17863/CAM.109982 (archived at https://perma.cc/6J7G-8XPF)

61 ibid.

62 ibid.

63 ibid.

64 ibid.

65 ibid.

66 ibid.

67 ibid.

11

Brand equity

When firms invest in their brands, designing delightful experiences and ensuring seamless journeys across various channels – digital, physical, and social – they aim to secure a competitive advantage and enhance their market positioning. Designing and managing customer experience not only meets diverse consumer expectations but also drives brand loyalty and market growth. Companies try to communicate their brand identity in a way that resonates with customers, leading to increased customer engagement and business growth.

For example, when you think about purchasing furniture, which brands come to your mind first – IKEA or Amazon?

This immediate association with certain brands highlights the critical role of brand and market positioning in attracting customers. Effective brand positioning ensures that a company stands out in consumers' minds, influencing their purchasing decisions. By strategically positioning themselves, brands like IKEA become top-of-mind furniture choices, demonstrating the importance of cultivating a strong, distinct brand identity that resonates with target markets and aligns with consumer expectations. IKEA's brand attributes include affordability, sustainability, design, functionality and quality. Affordability is the primary focus during product development. Unlike many companies that start product development by analysing consumer trends or identifying gaps in the market, IKEA begins with setting a target price.[1]

In today's highly competitive market, understanding firms' market positioning and how to maximize customer spending is crucial for any business aiming for long-term growth. As mentioned in Chapter 7, a significant insight that can be derived from CX data is market intelligence. Two vital metrics – brand equity and share of wallet (SoW) – are integral to this understanding. Brand equity is the additional value a recognized brand name gives to a product or service, enabling companies to command premium prices and secure a market edge.

Apple, for example, exemplifies this concept. Its organized ecosystem, including products like iPhones, iPads, MacBooks, and services like Apple TV+, integrates seamlessly across both digital platforms and physical stores. This integration creates a compelling value proposition, drawing in customers with its superior experiences and prestigious brand image. Consequently, customers are more likely to spend a significant portion of their budget on Apple products, thereby boosting Apple's share of wallet for technology and entertainment services. Therefore, brand equity is built through strategic investments in marketing, consistently delivering on the brand promise and developing positive consumer experiences and associations over time.

Share of wallet, meanwhile, quantifies the percentage of a customer's spending within a specific category that goes to a brand, directly revealing customer loyalty and preference. For example, Amazon Prime is a standard example of increasing share of wallet through strong brand equity. Amazon strengthens their brand loyalty by providing an array of benefits, such as free shipping, exclusive deals and streaming services. Due to the perceived value and convenience, customers are more inclined to spend a larger portion of their shopping budget on Amazon, thus significantly increasing Amazon's share of wallet.

Strong brand equity enables a brand to secure a larger share of wallet, as customers tend to spend more with brands they trust, which offer a better customer experience and provide better-value products and services. The customer journey, including designing a consistent interaction across digital and physical channels, significantly influences both brand equity and share of wallet.

According to McKinsey, adopting a strategy focused on delivering a standout customer experience (CX) is key to profitable growth and is difficult for competitors to imitate. This approach transforms growth goals based on CX into redesigning customer journeys, supported by a cross-functional operating model for effective implementation. It attracts loyal customers, altering their buying behaviours, which is evident in share of wallet. Effective CX strategies, increasing customer satisfaction by at least 20 per cent, can notably boost cross-selling rates by 15–25 per cent and improve wallet share by 5–10 per cent.[2]

This chapter explores the concept of share of wallet to assess firms' market positions and to demonstrate the use of AI in analysing customer experience (CX) data. By identifying key customer journeys and touchpoints that influence the share of wallet, firms can design superior customer experiences, positioning themselves as the top choice for consumers. Leveraging AI models, companies can analyse customer feedback to optimize their strategies to enhance brand equity, maximize customer lifetime value and strengthen customer relationships, ensuring long-term success in a competitive market.

Measuring market position

Brand equity

Financial performance indicators tied to market positioning include factors such as brand equity, which encompasses metrics like price premiums over competitors, market share, revenue growth rate and customer lifetime value. These metrics offer valuable insights into the financial impact of a brand's equity. Additionally, firms use various attitudinal measurements to understand their brand equity through customer experience (CX) surveys. These surveys gather consumer perceptions, satisfaction and loyalty data, providing a comprehensive view of a brand's equity beyond just financial performance.

BRAND AWARENESS

This is where firms measure how recognizable and familiar your brand is to consumers. Building brand awareness involves ensuring that customers understand your brand's products, values, and image. It goes beyond mere recognition and includes a deeper connection that aligns with brand association. This can be measured through various methods such as surveys, focus groups, website traffic analysis and social media monitoring.[3] Key metrics include unaided brand awareness (the ability to recall a brand without prompts) and aided brand awareness (the ability to recognize a brand with prompts).

For example, over the years, Unilever has developed significant brand equity through steady investment in advertising, maintaining high product quality, and engaging in purpose-driven brand campaigns that connect with consumers. Since its beginnings in 1929, the company has expanded to become a leader in the fast-moving consumer goods (FMCG) industry, boasting around 400 brands. Some of its most prominent brands are

Lifebuoy, Dove, Axe and Sunsilk. Unilever became a fully British company, and it was listed as the sixth-largest FMCG company worldwide in terms of sales.[4] In 2019, the Unilever brand was valued at approximately $4.16 billion. The brand's valuation was $3.97 billion in 2021.[5] Unilever developed the first cross-media measurement model to help their brands evaluate campaign brand awareness across various social media channels.[6]

BRAND ASSOCIATIONS

To evaluate the specific qualities, attributes and values consumers associate with your brand, use brand perception surveys, social media sentiment analysis and focus groups. These methods help understand your brand's personality and positioning in the market.

Let's continue with Unilever's example. Unilever is actively transforming its brands and advertising to promote values such as a more diverse, inclusive and unstereotypical society. As a global company with over 400 brands used by 3.4 billion people daily, Unilever recognizes its influence and responsibility in shaping societal norms.[7]

Unilever's initiatives include breaking down harmful stereotypes that limit individuals' potential and reinforce inequality. By leveraging its advertising and industry partnerships, Unilever aims to create a more representative and inclusive society. This effort involves challenging outdated stereotypes, promoting diversity and integrating inclusive thinking across all aspects of marketing.

For example, Unilever's commitment to *Act 2 Unstereotype* seeks to drive systemic change by embedding diverse and inclusive practices throughout the marketing process. This includes consumer insights, product development, advertising production, and ensuring diverse representation both on-screen and behind the camera. Unilever has also pledged to ban digital alterations to models' body shapes, sizes and skin colours to maintain authenticity.[8]

Unilever's efforts have shown tangible results. Research indicates that progressive advertising can deliver significantly better brand performance, increased purchase intent and greater credibility. The company has also launched resources like the Inclusive Production Toolkit and the 10 Ways to Unstereotype Influencer Brand Content guide to support industry-wide adoption of inclusive practices.[9]

Furthermore, Unilever is addressing disability inclusion by ensuring representation and creating opportunities for people with disabilities in advertising and production. The company mandates that every high-budget production must include at least one crew member from the disability community. Unilever's initiatives demonstrate a commitment to using brand power to drive positive social change and create a fairer, more inclusive world.[10]

PERCEIVED QUALITY

This involves assessing consumers' subjective judgements about a brand's excellence or superiority compared to competitors. This can be done through customer satisfaction (CSAT) surveys, product/service ratings and reviews, and brand reputation studies; check Chapters 7 and 8 for more details.

For example, the LEGO Group has consistently ranked as one of the most reputable companies worldwide, excelling in various reputation metrics, including product quality, governance, leadership, financial performance, innovation and corporate citizenship.[11] The global brand value of LEGO from 2015 to 2023 has seen significant growth. As published by Statista on 22 March 2024, the brand's value was approximately $13 billion in 2023. This marks a substantial increase from its valuation of about $5.4 billion in 2015.[12] One of LEGO's core brand values is product quality, which reflects a dedication to continuous manufacturing, product and design improvement. This commitment ensures the provision of the best play materials, robust support for children's development, and exceptional service to the community and partners. LEGO's reputation for manufacturing excellence has earned customers' trust, delivering products that stand out for their quality.[13] This dedication has positioned LEGO as the go-to choice for children worldwide, surpassing competitors and gaining widespread recognition and recommendations.

BRAND LOYALTY

Brand loyalty is measured by examining customer attachment and repeat purchase behaviour. Important metrics include the customer retention rate, net promoter score (NPS), repeat purchase rate and average order value. Again, as discussed in Chapter 7, NPS and CSAT are common metrics to evaluate customer loyalty and have been used to measure brand loyalty.

This brand loyalty persists regardless of price or competitors' offers, showcasing how loyal consumers repeatedly purchase and recommend their preferred brand. In economic downturns, maintaining customer trust and devotion is crucial. Good customer service is essential for brand loyalty. A

2022 survey revealed that nearly 8 out of 10 global consumers consider it vital for maintaining loyalty. Poor customer service not only generates negative perceptions but also hinders sales. Over 60 per cent of US consumers are unlikely to buy from a brand they cannot contact.[14]

Consumers develop emotional connections to brands that align with their values and local practices. In a 2021 survey, over half of respondents in the US and Western Europe felt emotionally connected to local businesses, while one-third bonded with companies whose practices matched their values.[15]

Younger consumers, especially Gen Z and millennials, show greater loyalty to brands that address social issues. In 2022, nearly 60 per cent of these demographics in the US expressed loyalty to brands that took a stand on social issues.[16]

Loyalty programmes play a significant role in maintaining customer loyalty. A late 2022 survey indicated that 7 out of 10 US shoppers considered these programmes important for staying connected to their favourite brands. Loyalty programmes that offer discounts, rewards or early access to products make customers feel valued. Nearly 80 per cent of American consumers in a 2022 poll said these programmes influenced their decision to continue doing business with a brand. Additionally, 80 per cent of respondents purchased more frequently, and over half talked more often about the brand after joining a loyalty programmes.[17]

Digitalization has enabled brand owners to expand into new markets directly or through aggregators at minimal cost. Consumers now enjoy numerous shopping options, including direct purchases from businesses or through intermediary marketplaces like Amazon. Aggregation models are present in nearly every sector, from food to financial services. While intermediaries can generate new revenue streams for brand owners, they also complicate efforts to build customer loyalty, as seen in the food delivery market.[18]

Initially, food delivery platforms were popular among young, tech-savvy individuals, but the pandemic mainstreamed this service, with over 50 per cent of US consumers ordering food online and 38 per cent using services like Uber Eats, Grubhub or DoorDash. Post-pandemic, both restaurants and aggregators compete for customer loyalty, with customers often showing platform loyalty due to menu variety and convenience. Aggregators charge high fees, sometimes up to 30 per cent, impacting profit margins but offering marketing tools and broader reach. Research shows 75 per cent of restaurants believe DoorDash has helped them reach new customers. In response, larger restaurants are developing their own apps and delivery services to maintain control over customer interactions.[19]

Large restaurant chains are increasingly using loyalty programmes to attract and retain customers. For example, McDonald's new US loyalty programmes enrolled 30 million members within six months, resulting in a 10 per cent increase in digital customer frequency. Loyalty programmes help businesses become data-driven, allowing them to track customer preferences and behaviours and offer targeted promotions and rewards to enhance retention, visits and order size.[20]

Amazon, the world's largest aggregator, has a brand value estimated at $345 billion. Amazon Prime, initially offering free shipping for an annual fee, has expanded its benefits, making it one of the most successful loyalty programmes, with over 60per cent of US households subscribing. Amazon's success demonstrates how digital technologies can disrupt market dynamics, gain market positioning and create new business models. While Amazon is a trusted brand for many consumers, its marketplace provides small suppliers access to markets that would otherwise be unreachable. However, it can result in losing direct customer relationships.[21]

Share of wallet

Companies must prioritize strategies that enhance their competitive rank and share of wallet (SoW).[22] Traditional metrics like satisfaction and NPS are valuable but insufficient on their own. By focusing on what truly drives SoW, companies can achieve significant financial gains and stronger customer loyalty. A brand may have high satisfaction scores, but if customers also favour competitors, the brand's SoW may still be low. This involves understanding why customers choose competitors and addressing those reasons directly.

Researchers[23] developed the Wallet Allocation Rule, which calculates SOW by considering both a brand's rank among competitors and the number of brands a customer uses:

1 **Identify the number of brands:** Determine how many brands (or stores or firms) customers use in the product category you want to analyse.

2 **Survey and rank:** Survey customers to obtain satisfaction or loyalty scores for each brand and convert these scores into ranks. In the case of a tie, take the average rank. For example, if two brands tie for first place, assign each a rank of 1.5.

3 **Calculate share of wallet:** To determine a brand's share of wallet for a given customer, use the Wallet Allocation Rule formula with the brand's rank and the number of brands:[24]

$$1 - \frac{Rank}{total\ number\ of\ brands + 1}$$

with the brand's rank and the number of brands. Repeat this calculation for each customer and brand. To find a brand's overall share of wallet, average the share of wallet scores across all customers. For example, if a customer uses three brands, rank them first, second and third.

o For the top-ranked brand, the calculation is:

$$1 - \frac{1}{3+1} = 75\%$$

o For the second-ranked brand, it is:

$$1 - \frac{2}{3+1} = 50\%$$

o For the third-ranked brand, it is:

$$1 - \frac{3}{3+1} = 25\%$$

Many firms use this rule as it has shown strong correlations with SOW, significantly more than other metrics such as satisfaction or NPS. For instance, being a customer's top choice out of two brands can significantly boost financial returns compared to being the second choice. This suggests that to increase their share of wallet, businesses should focus on improving their rank among consumer choices rather than merely tracking satisfaction levels.

Key challenges

Measuring brand equity and metrics such as share of wallet to understand a brand's positioning from the customer's perspective presents numerous challenges.

Behavioural data is limited

There is a lack of customer-level spending data across competitors. It is difficult for companies to know exactly how much a customer spends with other providers in the same category, as this data is usually difficult to obtain. Without actual customer data, companies often have to rely on generic industry averages for wallet size and share calculations, which may not accurately reflect individual customer situations. With numerous options available to customers, tracking competition for share of wallet is complex in fragmented markets.

Survey fatigue from attitudinal questions

Customers are becoming overwhelmed by the growing number of questions in surveys, which has led to a decrease in response rates, as we discussed in Chapters 7 and 8. The addition of supplementary questions to traditional surveys, aimed at collecting share of wallet information and demographic information such as age, income level and household size, as well as gauging customers' perceptions of how the brand stacks up against competitors in terms of price, variety and product quality, compounds this issue. Answering these comprehensive questions is challenging for many customers, contributing to an increase in incomplete datasets.

As surveys expanded from a brief 5-minute questionnaire to a more detailed 15–20-minute effort, survey fatigue began to set in among respondents. The detailed questions required customers to provide thoughtful responses on various aspects of their shopping experiences and compare these with those offered by competing retailers. This depth and the required time investment led many customers to abandon the survey partway through, significantly impacting the completion rates and resulting in a large number of incomplete responses.

CX factors are missing from these surveys

These metrics do not address the customer experience (CX) factors that elevate a brand to the top position, nor do they consider variables beyond traditional ones like demographics and market intelligence attributes. There is a lack of integration between the customer journey and experience factors with the traditional share of wallet factors. In general, firms ask the customers again why they would rank them in this position compared to their competitors. *Do we need another detailed question to be added to traditional surveys?* Customers might already report this in their unstructured data (comments, customer service, social media, etc.).

Here is an example of a customer saying this in a survey comment:

I love stopping by [coffee chain] for my morning brew! The baristas are always smiling and the service is quick, which is perfect during my busy mornings. However, I wish the seating area felt a bit more inviting and comfortable like [competitor coffee shop]. I find myself going there when I want to meet up with friends or work on my laptop because of the atmosphere, even though I prefer your coffee.

Customer relationships are complex

B2B industries frequently encounter difficulties in measuring brand equity and share of wallet due to the lengthy sales and service lifecycles, which extend over long periods and complex contracts in many cases. For example, in the construction and mining sectors, companies like Caterpillar and Volvo Group provide machinery to large clients who may also procure equipment from other competitive brands, such as JCB or Mitsubishi Heavy Industries (MHI). This diversification complicates the assessment of a single brand's share of wallet and brand equity from this enterprise customer with a site operated using many vendors. The direct nature of B2B transactions often results in a lack of transparent customer spending data, complicating comprehensive share of wallet analysis from a behavioural point of view. Additionally, in many B2C markets, the competitive and fragmented landscape, with numerous options available to consumers, further complicates tracking competition for brand equity and share of wallet.

Loyalty programme bias

While loyalty programme data is valuable for brands, as discussed above, it often falls short in providing an accurate picture of brand equity and share of wallet due to the inherent self-selection bias among members. This bias occurs because loyalty programmes typically attract a specific subset of customers who are already inclined to favour the brand and its offerings, leading to skewed data that does not represent the broader customer base.

Consider a retail brand that uses loyalty programme data to assess its share of wallet. The data indicates that members spend 70 per cent of their total category budget with this brand. However, this figure might not account for casual shoppers who do not participate in the loyalty programme and who might only spend 20–30 per cent of their budget with the brand. Relying solely on loyalty programme data could lead the brand to overestimate its market dominance and customer loyalty, potentially resulting in misguided strategic decisions.

Applying AI to your brand equity data

The volume and complexity of textual data from diverse sources such as surveys, customer service, surveys, reviews, conversational data and social media are expected to rise significantly in the future. According to the International Data Group, by 2025, the global data volume will reach 163 zettabytes, with approximately 80 per cent of business-relevant information coming from unstructured sources, mainly text. This growth is driven by firm-generated content, as well as customer experience data on websites and user-generated content on social networking platforms.[25] This is where natural language processing (NLP) and machine learning techniques are employed to process textual documents, identify patterns, and present the information in a structured format, facilitating the evaluation and interpretation of the output to gain valuable insight.[26]

To build on our previous discussions in Chapters 7 and 8, it is crucial to understand the various customer journey touchpoints – digital, social and physical – as well as the contextual and CX quality factors that influence brand loyalty metrics like share of wallet. Firms can leverage their data to assess the impact of customer responses to key CX and customer journey dimensions of customer experience (CX) quality across these touchpoints. This exploration also focuses on how different market contexts affect the share of wallet position (Figure 11.1).

A service encounter occurs at a specific *touchpoint* or moment of interaction between the customer and the brand or company, directly or indirectly influencing perceptions and evaluations of both the brand and the *customer journey* itself. Critical touchpoints and their sequences either positively or negatively impact a customer's service evaluation during their journey.[27]

Customer experience (CX) characteristics, corresponding to CX *quality dimensions* – cognitive, emotional, sensorial, physical and valence – reflect how customers react to the customer journey.[28] As discussed in Chapters 7 and 8, this aspect of CX management entails acquiring and applying specialized data science techniques to understand customer journeys and adopt a customer-centric approach.[29]

Context significantly influences how customers perceive interactions with a brand or firm, considering all specific factors related to time and place, typically temporary. These influences span individual, social, market and environmental factors.[30] Firms should consider evaluating *market context* when it comes to brand equity, given their global operations, including dynamics from market-related entities interacting with customers and how different touchpoint paths lead to varied outcomes across market contexts, and how brands can systematically use these insights to enhance customer experience.

FIGURE 11.1 Customer experience factors that can predict the share of wallet

Customer journey

Touchpoint   Market context   → Share of wallet

CX qualities

Let's take the retail industry as an example to guide AI in extracting CX factors that can predict the share of wallet using qualitative feedback without the need to ask customers extra detailed questions.[31]

CX and share of wallet data

The data covers two contextual markets, the UK and USA, between 4 January, 2021 and 30 June 2022. The data includes 13,887 comments, 6,316 from the UK and 7,571 from the USA.[32] The data involves a traditional CX survey and a share of wallet survey:[33]

- **The traditional CX survey**: Conducted post-interaction with the brand in digital or physical channels, the survey mainly collects:
  - **Customer satisfaction (CSAT) scores**, where customers rate their experience on a scale from 1 to 5.
  - **Free-text feedback**, collected after a product purchase in-store or a service purchase, with customers encouraged to provide detailed comments about their last interaction.
- **The share of wallet survey**: This is prompted after the traditional CX survey and gathers additional demographic information and perceptions of the competitive landscape through questions about customer interactions, expectations, interests and brand preferences. The questions aim to understand customers' motivations and preferences, which can provide

valuable data for strategic decision-making. Here are some of the questions included in the survey:

- **Main reason for interacting:** *What was your main reason for interacting with the brand?* This question seeks to understand the primary motivation behind the customer's visit or interaction, which can help identify the main drivers of footfall and engagement.

- **Expectations met during last interaction:** *Did the brand meet your expectations during your last interaction?* This question assesses customer satisfaction by comparing customers' expectations with their actual experiences. It helps identify areas where the brand is performing well and where improvements are needed.

- **Interest in products:** *How interested are you in our products?* Understanding the level of interest in the products can help tailor marketing strategies and product offerings to match customer enthusiasm and engagement levels.

- **Product categories shopped for during last visit:** *What product categories were you primarily shopping for last time you visited our store?* This question identifies the specific product categories that attract customers, enabling the brand to focus on popular items and optimize inventory and displays.

- **Companies typically purchased from:** *Which companies do you typically purchase from when shopping in these product categories?* By identifying competitors, the brand can better understand its market position and strategize accordingly to attract customers who might otherwise shop elsewhere.

- **Satisfaction with competitor brands:** *In general, how satisfied are you with these brands when shopping for similar products?* This question gauges customer satisfaction with competitors, providing insights into what they are doing well and areas where the brand might have an advantage.

- **Deciding factors in choosing brands:** *When shopping for similar products, what tends to be the deciding factor in choosing one brand over the other?* This question seeks to uncover the key factors influencing purchasing decisions, such as price, quality, design and customer service. These insights can help align the brand's offerings with customer priorities.

○ **Demographic data:** *i.e. postcode, age, gender, income bracket, etc.* Collecting demographic data helps understand the customer base, enabling segmentation and more targeted marketing efforts. It can also highlight demographic trends and shifts.

The responses to these questions are processed to quantify and analyse the content, providing the brand with detailed insights into customer preferences, competitive dynamics and market trends. This information is crucial for making informed decisions about product development, marketing strategies and customer service improvements.

Using this data, firms can reveal some descriptive statistics, such as:

- The average customer satisfaction score (CSAT) is 3.59, and the average share of wallet (SoW) is 0.63.

- The share of wallet distribution indicates that 65.77% of comments reflect a high SoW. In comparison, 32.03% are medium, and 2.19% are low, with medium and low categories classified together as low for analysis purposes.

- The highest average CSAT scores are observed in February (3.87) and March (3.75), with a downward trend from April to August and the lowest score in September (3.47).

- The scores slightly recovered in October (3.56) and November (3.55) before dipping again in December (3.41).

- Most customers rank this brand second (64.36%) or third (28.11%) in brand positioning, with minimal lower rankings.

- The highest average share of wallets is observed in February and March, and most customers rank the brand second or third, indicating strong brand loyalty and positioning.

This descriptive analysis offers insights into customer sentiment, brand positioning, and seasonal variations in customer satisfaction, aiding strategic planning and improving customer engagement.

NLP and LLMs can be applied for feature engineering

Firms can leverage natural language processing (NLP) and large language models (LLMs) to extract journeys, touchpoints, CX factors and market context from customer feedback.[34]

- **Journeys**: Large language models (LLMs) can classify customer comments to extract experiences across different interaction types with a brand, breaking down the journey into five categories:

  o **Overall (48.68%)**: Customers reported no issues and were satisfied with their overall experience.

  o **Physical (21.42%)**: Feedback related to in-store experiences.

  o **Social (12.42%)**: Highlighted exceptional customer service with personal mentions, enhancing the feeling of being valued.

  o **Digital (9.42%)**: Comments on digital interactions, such as website or app experiences.

  o **Digital and physical (4.66%)**: Evaluate the journey sequence, either starting digitally and ending physically or vice versa.

- **Touchpoints**: LLMs can classify the touchpoints mentioned in customer comments, identifying key areas of interaction, such as:[35]

  o **Marketing**: Feedback on marketing efforts and reaching out to customers.

  o **Catalogue**: Comments on the catalogue content and usability.

  o **Website, app and social media**: Evaluations of the digital platform and its content.

  o **Parking**: Reviews of parking facilities.

  o **Store**: Evaluation of customers' physical and sensorial journey.

  o **Customer support**: Feedback on customer service interactions.

  o **Play area**: Evaluation of the children's play area within the store.

  o **Restaurant**: Reviews of the hospitality service within the physical store.

  o **Self-serve**: Evaluations of self-service options.

  o **Checkout**: Comments on express checkout experiences.

  o **Home delivery**: Comments on home delivery service.

  o **Assembly service**: Feedback on product assembly services is provided.

  o **Returns and exchange**: Feedback on return and exchange processes.

The touchpoints with the highest mentions are Store (5.1k) and Customer support (2.7k), followed by Checkout (1.3k), Restaurant (1.2k) and App (1.0k).

- **Valence**: Firms can leverage sentiment NLP models to extract how customers feel about the experience: neutral (77%), positive (20.79%) and negative (2.21%). It is worth checking whether the CSAT score aligns with the valence scores. Higher CSAT scores (4 and 5) should align with more positive sentiment. If this is not the case, as discussed in Chapter 8, the firm better rely on the valence scores. Also, you can do the same with share of wallet categories. Higher SoW should have more positive sentiments.[36]

- **Emotion**: As discussed in Chapters 8 and 9, emotions are a better predictor of customer loyalty and can train machine learning models to understand customer feelings towards the experience. Here are the top emotions that could be extracted.[37]

  - **Admiration (4.9k mentions)**: Customers express high satisfaction and enjoyment with their experience.

  - **Annoyance (4.0k mentions)**: Customers express frustration and dissatisfaction.

  - **Disappointment (2.6k mentions)**: Customers express unmet expectations and dissatisfaction.

  - **Approval (1.5k mentions)**: Customers express satisfaction and positive feedback.

- **Cognitive:** The factors affecting customer experience need to be extracted from their comments. Firms can leverage NLP topic modelling to cluster the common factors expressed by customers. This approach helps identify prevalent themes and insights, allowing companies to better understand and address customer needs and preferences. Here are some examples in the retail sector.[38]

  - **Accessibility:** Ease of accessing the store and facilities.

  - **Affordability:** Perceived cost-effectiveness of products.

  - **Atmosphere:** Store ambiance and environment.

  - **Digital experience:** Online interactions and digital services.

  - **Ease of shopping:** Convenience and simplicity of the shopping process.

  - **Eating:** In-store dining experience.

  - **Experience:** Overall customer experience.

  - **Findability:** Ease of finding products.

  - **Health and safety:** Safety measures and cleanliness.

  - **Brand affinity:** Loyalty and connection to the brand.

  - **Inspiration:** Inspiration drawn from product displays and layouts.

  - **Loyalty programme:** Effectiveness of the loyalty programme.

- o **Payment:** Ease and efficiency of payment process.
- o **Product offering:** Variety and availability of products.
- o **Quality:** Product and service quality.
- o **Service staff:** Interactions with store employees.
- o **Stock availability:** Availability of desired products.
- o **Store:** Overall store experience.
- o **Waiting time:** Time spent waiting in queues or for service.

- **Market context:** Firms need a way to define each customer's geographical location from the source of the data to compare whether any contextual market factors have a different influence on the share of wallet.[39]

- **Share of wallet as a target variable:** Firms need a method to define the target outcome for their brand equity. In this case, we categorized customers' share of wallet (SoW) into three segments: high, medium and low. This segmentation helps assess and enhance brand equity by focusing on customer spending patterns and aligning marketing strategies accordingly.[40]

  - o **High (47%):** Customers with a significant portion of their spending allocated to the brand.

  - o **Low (combined medium and low for simplicity):** Includes medium (6%) and low (46%) spenders, together making up 53%.

Combining the medium and low categories balances the data, simplifies analysis, and makes it more effective for training machine learning models. This approach helps better understand customer spending patterns and improve predictive accuracy.

Prediction model

The NLP models can successfully extract many features that can be used for modelling. In this case, 24,135 features are generated, encompassing sentiment, emotion and topic modelling. Subsequently, firms can employ several machine learning techniques, including deep learning or traditional ones such as Random Forest, Gradient Boosting and XGBoost, to predict low and high share of wallet (SoW) categories. In our case, the XGBoost algorithm outperformed other techniques, achieving an F1 score of 84 per cent.

F1 is a measure of a test's accuracy in binary classification problems and is commonly used in machine learning to evaluate a model's performance. Finally, for the explainability of the AI prediction model, firms can use Shapley Additive Explanation (SHAP) analysis to identify the top CX factors that impact the share of wallet for business insights.[41]

What we learnt

Key insights into customer experience factors impact share of wallet (SoW).[42]

Valence

The most significant predictors in our model are the valence dimensions within the qualities category: positive sentiments (35 per cent), neutral sentiments (32 per cent) and negative sentiments (3 per cent).

- **Positivity valence sentiment (35%):** Positive sentiments have the most substantial impact on the model's predictions. A high positive sentiment is heavily associated with a higher share of wallet (SoW). This indicates that customers who express positive feedback are more likely to allocate a larger portion of their spending to the brand. Positive sentiments typically include praise for product quality, exceptional service, enjoyable shopping experiences, and satisfaction with the overall brand interaction. For instance, comments such as 'I love shopping here; the staff are always helpful, and the products are top-notch' reflect a high positive sentiment. This type of feedback not only enhances the customer's likelihood of returning but also promotes word-of-mouth recommendations, further boosting the brand's reputation and customer base.

- **Neutral valence sentiments (32%):** Neutral sentiments are the second most influential factor. This suggests that even when feedback is not overtly positive or negative, it still plays a crucial role in understanding customer behaviour and predicting SoW. Neutral feedback often includes factual statements without emotional charge, such as 'The store was clean and well organized'. Such comments, while not enthusiastic, indicate a level of satisfaction that supports steady spending patterns. Neutral sentiments can provide a baseline of customer expectations and help identify areas where improvements can turn neutral experiences into positive ones, thereby increasing SoW.

- **Negativity valence sentiments (3%):** While negative sentiments have a relatively lower impact compared to positive and neutral sentiments, they still influence the model's predictions. Negative feedback typically highlights areas of dissatisfaction, such as poor customer service, product issues, or an unpleasant shopping environment. Comments like 'I was disappointed with the long wait times at the checkout' or 'The product quality did not meet my expectations' reflect negative sentiments. Addressing these concerns promptly and effectively can mitigate their impact on customer spending and loyalty. Companies must have robust mechanisms for managing and resolving negative feedback to prevent it from significantly affecting SoW.

Market features (context)

Market context also plays a crucial role, with the USA and UK markets contributing 7 per cent and 6 per cent to SoW predictions. These features indicate that the geographical market of the customer (USA or UK) significantly affects SoW. This highlights the importance of considering regional differences in customer behaviour and market dynamics when developing marketing strategies. For example, customers in the USA might prioritize different aspects of the shopping experience compared to those in the UK. Understanding these regional preferences allows firms to tailor their offerings and marketing efforts to meet the needs of different customer segments better. This can involve localized promotions, culturally relevant products, and region-specific customer service enhancements.

Touchpoints and journeys

- **Physical store (6%):** The interaction at the physical store is a major factor influencing SoW. Customers' in-store experiences, whether positive or negative, heavily impact their spending behaviour. Positive in-store experiences, such as helpful staff, easy navigation and appealing store layout, can enhance customer satisfaction and increase spending. Conversely, negative experiences, such as long wait times, unavailability of products or poor service, can deter customers from future purchases. Companies should focus on optimizing in-store touchpoints to ensure a seamless and enjoyable shopping experience.

- **Digital (4%) and social (4%):** Digital and social touchpoints also play a significant role. Customers' online interactions and social engagements with the brand are critical in shaping their overall experience and spending patterns. Digital touchpoints include the usability of the website or app, ease of online transactions, and the availability of product information. Social touchpoints involve interactions on social media platforms, where customers might engage with the brand through posts, comments or customer service queries. Ensuring these touchpoints are positive and responsive can enhance customer engagement and loyalty

Cognitive factors

- **Ease of shopping (3%):** Ease of shopping is a key factor in customer satisfaction. Customers who find the shopping process straightforward and hassle-free are more likely to spend more. This includes factors such as intuitive store layouts, easy product findability and efficient checkout processes. Simplifying the shopping journey can significantly enhance the customer experience and encourage repeat purchases.
- **Atmosphere and affordability (2%):** These factors also contribute to SoW, indicating that a pleasant shopping environment and perceived value for money are important to customers. A welcoming store atmosphere, characterized by clean and well-organized spaces, pleasant décor and ambient conditions, can make shopping more enjoyable. Affordability, on the other hand, ensures that customers feel they are getting good value for their money, which can increase their likelihood of returning and spending more.

Value creation (resources) features

- **Restaurant (2%):** The specific facilities associated with customer interactions, such as stores and restaurants, are influential. Positive experiences in these facilities can significantly boost SoW. For instance, a well-maintained store with helpful staff can leave a lasting positive impression on customers. Similarly, a pleasant dining experience in the in-store restaurant can enhance the overall shopping experience. These facilities play a crucial role in creating a comprehensive and satisfying customer journey, which can drive higher spending and loyalty.

Actionable recommendations

The insights derived from our analysis offer several actionable recommendations for firms aiming to enhance their customer experience and boost SoW:

1 **Integrate customer journeys:** Develop a seamless experience that integrates digital, social and physical interactions. Consistency across all touchpoints is crucial for maintaining customer loyalty and increasing SoW. Utilize integrated platforms that allow customers to switch between online and offline channels without losing their progress or preferences. This could include synchronized shopping carts, customer profiles and loyalty programmes accessible both online and in-store. Ensure that branding, messaging and service standards are consistent across all touchpoints. This involves training staff to provide a unified customer experience and ensuring that digital interfaces reflect the same values and quality as physical stores.

2 **Optimize in-store experience:** Given that most complaints are associated with in-store experiences, focus on improving customer support and checkout processes. Enhancing the in-store experience can significantly impact customer satisfaction and spending. Train employees to be knowledgeable, courteous and proactive in assisting customers. Employees should be equipped to handle various customer needs and resolve issues promptly. Streamline checkout processes by implementing technologies such as self-checkout kiosks, mobile payment options and express lanes. Reducing wait times can enhance the shopping experience and increase customer satisfaction.

3 **Prepare for seasonal trends:** Anticipate and plan for seasonal spikes in feedback, such as stock availability issues in September. Proactive management of these trends can prevent negative customer emotions and improve overall satisfaction. Use historical data and predictive analytics to forecast demand and adjust inventory levels accordingly. This can help prevent stock shortages and ensure product availability. Develop targeted marketing campaigns to manage customer expectations and drive sales during peak periods.

4 **Focus on accessibility and shopping ease:** Address customer suggestions related to accessibility and ease of shopping. Simplifying the shopping process can lead to higher customer satisfaction and increased spending. Implement clear signage and store maps to help customers find products easily. Digital tools like store apps with indoor navigation can also enhance the shopping experience. Offer services such as click-and-collect, home delivery and kerbside pickup to provide customers with flexible shopping options.

5 **Capitalize on positive feedback:** Leverage positive feedback to identify and reinforce successful aspects of the customer experience. Use these insights to improve areas where SoW is perceived as medium and enhance aspects that receive lower satisfaction scores.

6 **By contextualizing external factors** such as the pandemic and stock levels, firms can stay agile and responsive, adjusting their service strategies to meet changing customer needs. Recognizing that complaints, compliments and suggestions each require different response strategies is essential for effective customer relationship management.

KEY TAKEAWAYS

In this chapter, we explored how firms are investing in enhancing their market positioning and brand equity, including metrics such as share of wallet (SoW). We demonstrated how firms can leverage qualitative data to extract customer experience (CX) factors, which are essential if they are to become predictive variables using large language models (LLMs) and natural language processing (NLP). Firms can use these factors to predict a better share of wallet using machine learning models. By understanding the key factors influencing customer spending, firms can develop targeted strategies to improve customer satisfaction, loyalty and brand equity.

- Utilize qualitative measurements from customer experience (CX) surveys to gain a holistic understanding of brand equity and avoid intrusive survey questions for customers to provide specific responses to SoW measurements.

- Employ explainable AI and machine learning techniques to analyse customer feedback and extract valuable insights. These technologies help identify key factors affecting brand loyalty and SoW, enabling more targeted and effective CX strategies.

- Don't rely solely on traditional attributes such as product, demographics and price. Focus on creating integrated customer experiences across digital, social and physical touchpoints. Consistency in branding and service quality across all channels is crucial for enhancing customer loyalty and increasing SoW.

- Customer experience qualities (cognitive, emotional, sensorial and physical) and market context (geographical differences) significantly impact SoW.

In the next chapter, we will discuss leveraging data as a key asset to drive new revenue streams.

Notes

1 Yohn, D (2015) How IKEA designs its brand success, *Forbes*, 10 June. www.
forbes.com/sites/deniselyohn/2015/06/10/how-ikea-designs-its-brand-success/
(archived at https://perma.cc/Y74X-KBCM)

2 Bough, V, Ehrlich, O, Fanderl, H and Schiff, R (2023) Experience-led growth: A
new way to create value, McKinsey & Company. www.mckinsey.com/
capabilities/growth-marketing-and-sales/our-insights/experience-led-growth-a-
new-way-to-create-value (archived at https://perma.cc/8593-NEPP)

3 Qualtrics (2024) Brand equity: What it is and how to measure it. www.
qualtrics.com/uk/experience-management/brand/brand-equity/ (archived at
https://perma.cc/HX4X-WS8S)

4 Statista Research Department (2024) Unilever: statistics & facts, Statista, 28
May. www.statista.com/topics/1397/unilever/#topicOverview (archived at
https://perma.cc/H52Q-CHZL)

5 Petruzzi, D (2023) Global brand value of Unilever from 2012 to 2021, Statista,
8 June. www.statista.com/statistics/984317/brand-value-of-unilever-worldwide/
(archived at https://perma.cc/2Z5L-WUKJ)

6 Unilever (2019) Unilever leads efforts to develop a cross-media measurement
model for brands. www.unilever.com/sustainability/equity-diversity-and-
inclusion/transforming-our-brands-transforming-our-advertising/ (archived at
https://perma.cc/Y9LU-G7UJ)

7 Unilever (2024) Transforming our brands, transforming our advertising. www.
unilever.com/sustainability/equity-diversity-and-inclusion/transforming-our-
brands-transforming-our-advertising/ (archived at https://perma.cc/X92B-9FV9)

8 ibid.

9 ibid.

10 ibid.

11 Qualtrics (2024) Brand equity: What it is and how to measure it.
www.qualtrics.com/uk/experience-management/brand/brand-equity/ (archived
at https://perma.cc/K3RG-5S6S)

12 Tighe, D (2024) Global brand value of LEGO from 2015 to 2023, Statista, 22
March. www.statista.com/statistics/984317/brand-value-of-unilever-worldwide/
(archived at https://perma.cc/2ZS7-2GXT)

13 LEGO Group (2024) Transforming our brands, transforming our advertising,
LEGO. www.unilever.com/sustainability/equity-diversity-and-inclusion/
transforming-our-brands-transforming-our-advertising/ (archived at https://
perma.cc/4A7B-AVSH)

14 Statista (2022). How to build brand loyalty: Insights and strategies. www.
statista.com/statistics/984317/brand-value-of-unilever-worldwide/ (archived at
https://perma.cc/F5A2-CFJA)

15 ibid.

16 ibid.

17 ibid.

18 Legters, B (2022) Brand loyalty in the digital age: the battle for customer attention, *Forbes*, 3 June. www.forbes.com/sites/boblegters/2022/06/03/brand-loyalty-in-the-digital-age-the-battle-for-customer-attention/ (archived at https://perma.cc/B98C-Q9RG)

19 ibid.

20 ibid.

21 ibid.

22 Cooil, B, Keiningham, T L, Aksoy, L and Hsu, M (2011) Customer loyalty isn't enough. Grow your share of wallet, *Harvard Business Review*, October. https://hbr.org/2011/10/customer-loyalty-isnt-enough-grow-your-share-of-wallet (archived at https://perma.cc/89YQ-CAHT)

23 ibid.

24 ibid.

25 Shacklett, M (2017) Unstructured data: A cheat sheet, *TechRepublic*, 15 July. www.techrepublic.com/article/unstructured-data-the-smart-persons-guide (archived at https://perma.cc/X32J-REZT)

26 Zaki, M and McColl-Kennedy, J R (2020), Text mining analysis roadmap (TMAR) for service research, *Journal of Services Marketing*, 34 (1) 30–47

27 De Keyser, A, Verleye, K, Lemon, K N, Keiningham, T L and Klaus, P (2020) Moving the customer experience field forward: Introducing the touchpoints, context, qualities (TCQ) nomenclature, *Journal of Service Research*, 23 (4), 431–48

28 ibid.

29 Holmlund, M et al, (2020) Customer experience management in the age of big data analytics: A strategic framework, *Journal of Business Research*, 116, 356–65

30 ibid.

31 Zaki, M and Witell, L (2024) Customer experience: How can firms use AI to predict share of wallet?, Frontiers in Service Conference 2024

32 ibid.

33 ibid.

34 ibid.

35 ibid.

36 ibid.

37 ibid.

38 ibid.

39 ibid.

40 ibid.

41 ibid.

42 ibid.

12

Data-driven business models

Just over a year since the launch of ChatGPT, OpenAI's chat interface that uses sophisticated large language models (LLMs) to interact with users in human-like text, significant discussions have arisen about data usage in the AI era and its potential to drive new business models. OpenAI, a startup that has successfully trained its models using both publicly available data and private data from data partnerships, collaborates with various partners to access non-public content, such as archives and metadata. These partnerships include a major private video library for images and videos to train Sora, as well as the Government of Iceland to help preserve their native languages. OpenAI does not pursue paid partnerships for purely publicly available information and has developed new ways of interacting with chatbots, enhancing user experiences in information retrieval.[1]

The company primarily monetizes its business through a subscription model, offering services like ChatGPT Plus, which provides users with enhanced features, faster response times, and priority access during peak times. Additionally, OpenAI licenses its application programming interface (API) to businesses, developers and other organizations, enabling them to integrate advanced AI capabilities into their applications and services. This model supports a wide range of uses, from customer service automation to content generation. OpenAI also engages in B2B partnerships and collaborations with various companies and institutions to develop and deploy AI solutions tailored to specific industries, often involving custom AI model development and deployment. This approach exemplifies a successful data-driven business model that uses data as a key resource to drive innovation and new business opportunities.[2]

Cazoo, a British online automotive marketplace, was founded in 2018 and launched its used car marketplace in 2019. Cazoo built its business model around convenience and transparency, offering thoroughly inspected used cars with detailed descriptions, high-quality images, a seven-day money-back guarantee and free home delivery within 72 hours. It provided financing options, extended warranties and a car subscription service that included maintenance, insurance and tax. Rapid growth, fuelled by investments, enabled Cazoo to expand into Europe.

However, despite its early success, the company faced significant challenges that ultimately led to financial difficulties and administration. The BBC[3] reported that Cazoo has faced significant challenges leading to its administration after an initially rapid rise during the Covid pandemic. The company, which became popular as consumers shifted to online car buying, struggled to raise funds from investors and transitioned from a dealer model to a marketplace model. This shift resulted in 728 redundancies as Cazoo aimed to offer its platform to the fragmented used car market, providing access to over 13,000 existing car dealers in the UK.

Despite its mission to create a seamless online car buying and selling experience and conduct over 185,000 car valuations monthly, Cazoo has never achieved profitability. The company's losses increased, and it faced intense competition from established car dealers who adapted to offer similar digital and e-commerce experiences.[4]

Cazoo's business values emphasize being customer-obsessed, data-driven, fast-moving and responsible. Cazoo's business model evolved from a direct retailer of used cars to a comprehensive marketplace platform. Initially, Cazoo bought and sold cars itself, but it has since shifted to facilitating transactions between buyers and sellers, including both individual consumers and car dealers. This transition leverages Cazoo's strong brand and advanced technology to connect a fragmented market. The platform generates revenue through subscription and listing fees paid by sellers, including car dealers, to showcase their vehicles to a broad customer base. Additionally, Cazoo conducts over 185,000 car valuations monthly, attracting sellers by offering a streamlined listing process. Central to Cazoo's strategy is creating a seamless digital experience for consumers, allowing them to complete the entire car buying journey online, from browsing and financing to home delivery, supported by robust customer service features like a seven-day returns policy. Strong brand recognition, built through extensive marketing and partnerships, enhances the platform's visibility. Cazoo's operations are data-driven, using AI to optimize customer experience and decision-making, ultimately aiming to revolutionize the used car market by providing a user-friendly, efficient and trusted marketplace.[5]

However, the rapid expansion into European markets, significant marketing expenditures, and the inability to establish a foothold in the highly competitive car dealership industry ultimately led to its financial struggles.

The combination of these factors, alongside the inability to raise sufficient funds and adapt quickly enough to market conditions, resulted in its dramatic decline from a peak valuation of $7 billion in 2021 to its current financial problems.[6]

In these two contrasting examples, it becomes evident how many established firms and startups are moving towards utilizing data generated from using data as a key resource to create new revenue streams, enhance experiences, and offer innovative services. In this chapter, we discuss our final topic, focusing on business models and the potential of data to generate new revenue streams. Following the data-driven customer experience (CX) transformations covered in previous chapters, executives will naturally question how to capitalize on these initiatives to build a successful business model. While ensuring our customers are satisfied or delighted with the designed and managed CX, we must consider how to utilize data as a key resource to drive new data-driven business models (DDBMs).

The exponential increase in data generated from different digital, physical and social channels, from various systems, service encounters and channels, has become crucial. Businesses must access, process and analyse data to stay competitive and ensure survival. It's no surprise that many organizations are striving to develop DDBMs. Established firms with entrenched structures, cultures and traditional revenue streams often find it difficult to innovate, potentially leading to a decline in market position and financial performance if they fail to adopt data-driven practices.

This chapter examines a framework with a DDBM design toolbox to help you position your services and customer experience activities in the current market landscape. We explore six types of DDBMs with examples and provide a set of questions to consider when implementing a DDBM.

Business models

Business model concepts have broadened to encompass value creation in e-business, strategy and innovation management. However, there is no academic consensus on the precise definition or representation of a business model within the fields of innovation management, entrepreneurship or strategic management theory. A useful starting point is to examine their classification. Business model frameworks can be categorized into static and dynamic approaches.[7] Both perspectives are valuable in understanding a company's strategies, operations and adaptation to market dynamics. A static approach describes the current state of a company. A dynamic approach examines the evolution of a business model.

To illustrate the difference, consider the example of Cazoo:

- **Static approach:** At a given point in time, Cazoo's business model involved being a direct retailer of used cars. This model focused on purchasing cars, refurbishing them, and then selling them directly to consumers through a digital platform. The static approach captures this snapshot of Cazoo's operations and strategy, emphasizing its role as a digital-driven car dealer with a strong online presence.

- **Dynamic approach:** Over time, Cazoo's business model evolved to address market challenges and opportunities. Initially thriving during the Covid pandemic with a direct sales model, Cazoo later transitioned to a marketplace model due to financial pressures and changing market conditions. This dynamic approach highlights the company's ability to adapt by shifting from buying and selling cars to facilitating transactions between buyers and sellers, thereby leveraging its platform to support a wider range of customers and dealers.

We have seen various business model frameworks and theories from different scholars.[8] The first notable framework is Chesbrough and Rosenbloom's, introduced in 2002. This framework focuses on the functional aspects of a business model. According to this framework, a business model comprises three key elements: the value proposition, the target market and the value chain. By focusing on these elements, companies can design business models that are well aligned with the needs and preferences of their customers while also maximizing efficiency and profitability.[9]

To make various business model frameworks more accessible and applicable in both startup and corporate contexts, some authors, such as Osterwalder and Pigneur,[10] have attempted to integrate and unify them. The resulting framework, based on business model ontology,[11] is widely adopted by practitioners and is known as the Business Model Canvas. This canvas consists of nine essential elements for understanding and designing a successful business model: value proposition, key resources, key activities, key partners, customer relationships, channels, customer segments, revenue streams and cost structure.

Value proposition refers to a company's unique value to its customers, which could be a product, service, or a combination of both. It should communicate why the company's offerings are superior to those of its competitors. For example, the value proposition for an airline is that it provides a safe, secure and seamless travel experience.

Key resources are the critical assets required to deliver the value proposition to the target market. For airlines, these include:

- A modern, fuel-efficient fleet of aircraft.
- Comprehensive customer relationship management (CRM) systems.
- Skilled workforce, including pilots, cabin crew and ground staff.
- Strategic partnerships with other airlines and service providers.
- Advanced IT infrastructure to support digital transformation and IoT applications.

Key activities are essential to operate successfully and deliver the value proposition. For airlines, these activities include:

- Fleet management and maintenance.
- Route planning and network expansion.
- Customer service and in-flight experience management.
- Marketing and sales to promote services and attract customers.
- Continuous digital innovation and system upgrades.

Key partners are external entities that help the company deliver its value proposition. For airlines, these partners include:

- Aircraft manufacturers like Airbus and Boeing.
- Technology providers for CRM and IoT solutions.
- Strategic alliances with other airlines for code-sharing and network expansion.
- Partnerships with entertainment and retail giants to enhance in flight offerings.
- Suppliers for in-flight meals and amenities.

Customer relationships describe how a company interacts with and maintains its customer base. Airlines foster strong relationships through:

- Personalized services, such as tailored meal and entertainment options.
- Loyalty programmes that reward frequent flyers.
- Exceptional customer service at all touchpoints.
- Transparent communication and proactive problem-solving.

Channels refer to how a company delivers its value proposition to customers. For airlines, these include:

- Direct sales through its website and mobile app.
- Travel agencies and online travel platforms.
- Customer service centres and airport counters.
- Marketing campaigns through digital, print and broadcast media.

Customer segment refers to the group of customers the company aims to reach. It should be clearly defined based on demographics, psychographics and geographic location. This helps tailor offerings to meet specific needs and preferences. For example, Singapore Airlines targets premium customers, including business professionals and high-income travellers who prioritize comfort, service quality and a seamless travel experience. The airline focuses on providing exceptional service that appeals to frequent flyers who value personalized attention and high standards of in-flight amenities.[12]

Airlines focus on:

- Premium customers, including business professionals and high-income travellers.
- Frequent flyers who value high standards of service and personalized attention.
- International travellers seeking seamless connectivity and premium in-flight experiences.

Revenue streams are the various ways a company earns money. Airlines generate revenue through:

- Ticket sales from premium and economy class passengers.
- Ancillary services, such as in-flight shopping and extra baggage fees.
- Loyalty programmes and partnerships with credit card companies.
- Cargo services for shipping goods.
- Onboard sales of meals and beverages.

Cost structure outlines the major expenses required to operate the business. These costs include:

- Aircraft acquisition and maintenance.
- Fuel costs and airport fees.

- Employee salaries and training programmes.
- Marketing and sales expenditures.
- Technology investments and digital transformation initiatives.

By understanding and optimizing these elements, Singapore Airlines can ensure that its business model remains robust and capable of delivering superior value to its customers while achieving financial sustainability.

To summarize, two essential aspects contribute to a successful business model:

- **Value creation:** Organizations must identify crucial resources and activities to effectively articulate a clear value proposition.
- **Value capturing:** Organizations must identify the customer segments that need the value proposition and develop a revenue model to generate returns from the cost structure.

Business models are crucial to the success of any organization, regardless of its size or industry. A well-crafted business model provides a clear roadmap for how a company creates and delivers value to its customers while generating revenue and achieving profitability. Here are key reasons to understand the importance of having a robust business model:

- **Alignment with strategy:** A robust business model aligns a company's resources, capabilities and activities with its strategic goals. A business model provides a foundation for decision-making, resource allocation and risk management by clearly defining the value proposition, target market and revenue streams.
- **Differentiation:** A well-designed business model helps a company differentiate itself from competitors and build a sustainable competitive advantage. This is especially important in highly competitive industries or those experiencing rapid technological change, where companies must continually adapt to stay ahead.
- **Attracting investments:** A strong business model can attract investors and partners by demonstrating the potential for long-term growth and profitability. A business model can inspire confidence and support from stakeholders by presenting a clear picture of how the company creates and captures value.

The airline industry is a prime example of a sector facing significant challenges: intense competition, geopolitical concerns, the rise of low-cost airlines, and the urgent need to reduce its carbon footprint are all forcing airlines to change their operations. In response to these demanding market conditions, Singapore Airlines initially focused on upgrading their assets and infrastructure, adopting a new fleet of lighter, more fuel-efficient planes and expanding their network of hubs to more countries. However, it soon became evident that more drastic measures were needed; the outdated mainframe system hindered the airline's ability to understand and respond to customer needs effectively.[13]

The solution was a comprehensive digital transformation strategy aimed at delivering exceptional customer experiences. Digital is not just about the technology, it's about understanding the problem, knowing what customers and staff need and being able to anticipate that and not just react to problems. It took Singapore Airlines many years to implement a digital transformation process that touched every aspect of the business. A crucial factor in their success was the commitment to developing a data-driven mindset and fostering innovation across all functions and levels of the company. Collaborative efforts, such as sharing data with different sales platforms, partnering with entertainment and retail giants, and working with innovative startups, were integral to this process.[14]

A cornerstone of this transformation was investing in a next-generation customer relation management system designed to capture all aspects of the customer experience, ensuring a seamless service. Frequent flyers on Singapore Airlines now receive their preferred drinks and newspapers without asking, and meals are served at their convenience rather than when it is most convenient for the crew. For those taking connecting flights, entertainment options are seamlessly joined up; passengers can continue watching their movies from where they left off even after changing planes. In-flight shopping has also been revolutionized, allowing passengers to choose from a broader inventory stored at the airport and receive their purchases as they disembark.[15]

Other aspects of customer experience have also improved through digitalization. The Internet of Things (IoT) is being used to enhance reliability by predicting maintenance issues, and the airline combines external data sources with its own to anticipate potential schedule disruptions, such as those caused by weather conditions. The digital transformation of Singapore Airlines provides an illustrative example of how firms can use data as a key resource to create a data-driven business model. By leveraging data to understand and anticipate customer needs, the airline can enhance its customer relationship management, personalized services and operational efficiency, demonstrating the powerful impact of data-driven strategies in a competitive industry.[16]

Data-driven business models (DDBMs)

For today's businesses, the effective use of data is essential not only for competitiveness but also for survival. This necessity has led to the development of data-driven business models (DDBMs), which are crucial for firms to thrive in the current digital era. To remain competitive, businesses must capitalize on the abundance of data available from various systems and service interactions. Failure to do so can result in a loss of market share and revenue.[17]

For example, Zara – the clothes shopping retailer – exemplifies a DDBM by monitoring fashion trends through data analysis. By leveraging internal data sources like supply chain and inventory records, as well as external data from social media, Zara creates a highly responsive supply chain that aligns with the latest fashions and trends. The company actively engages with consumers to understand their preferences and ensure timely clothing delivery. This data-driven approach enables Zara to achieve remarkably short product launch cycles, ranging from a few days to a maximum of one month. The key to this model is the two-way communication between consumers and manufacturers, where data is crucial for identifying consumer demand signals. Through this data-driven approach, Zara significantly improves the customer experience, supply responsiveness and overall business growth.[18]

However, implementing data-driven practices can be challenging, particularly for large established firms that must navigate existing company structures, cultures and traditional revenue streams. The potential competitive advantage associated with effective big data utilization is driving mainstream businesses to become more data-driven. Creating such models presents three main challenges:[19]

- **Extracting data from various sources:** Extracting data from customer interactions, social media platforms and other sources of big data can be challenging. The sheer volume and diversity of available data can be overwhelming, making it crucial to identify the most relevant and valuable data for the organization's needs.

- **Refining the data properly:** Raw data is often complex and unstructured, requiring cleaning, processing and organizing to make it useful for analysis, even with models such as LLM and GenAI. Refining data requires advanced machine learning models and techniques, as well as skilled data scientists who can identify patterns, trends and insights that inform business decisions.

- **Maximizing data usefulness:** Even after extracting and refining data, it's crucial to ensure it is used effectively to drive business value. This involves translating insights generated by the data into actionable steps that can improve business processes, create new products and services, and enhance customer experiences.

To better understand data-driven business models (DDBMs) and the elements that enable them, we will examine a comprehensive framework together. As shown in Figure 12.1, this framework outlines specific attributes for each dimension of a DDBM, including target outcome, offerings, data sources, key activities, revenue model and inhibitors. It provides a clear structure illustrating how data can be utilized as a foundational element to drive a coherent and effective business model.[20]

Value creation elements

DATA SOURCES

To create value, companies require resources, such as assets, capabilities, knowledge and information. These resources are essential for the success of a business. In the case of a DDBM, data is a key resource, although it may not be the only one. To develop a framework for DDBMs, it is necessary to have a clear understanding of the different types of data sources used. Companies can use eight types of data sources to create a DDBM. These sources can be categorized in two groups,[21] internal and external.

- **Internal:** Companies have access to a wealth of data from their *existing IT systems*, such as enterprise resource planning (ERP) systems, customer relationship management (CRM) systems, and financial management systems. However, not all of this data is effectively used, and some may not be utilized at all. This data includes customer purchase history, sales data and operational data.

    This might include data from systems that *self-generate data through tracking*. By capturing web navigation, sensor and user behaviour data, companies can better understand how customers interact with their products or services. This information can be used to enhance customer experience and optimize business operations.

- **External:** Companies can access data from a variety of sources. They can acquire data, obtain data from customers or business partners, or utilize

FIGURE 12.1 DDBM innovation blueprint

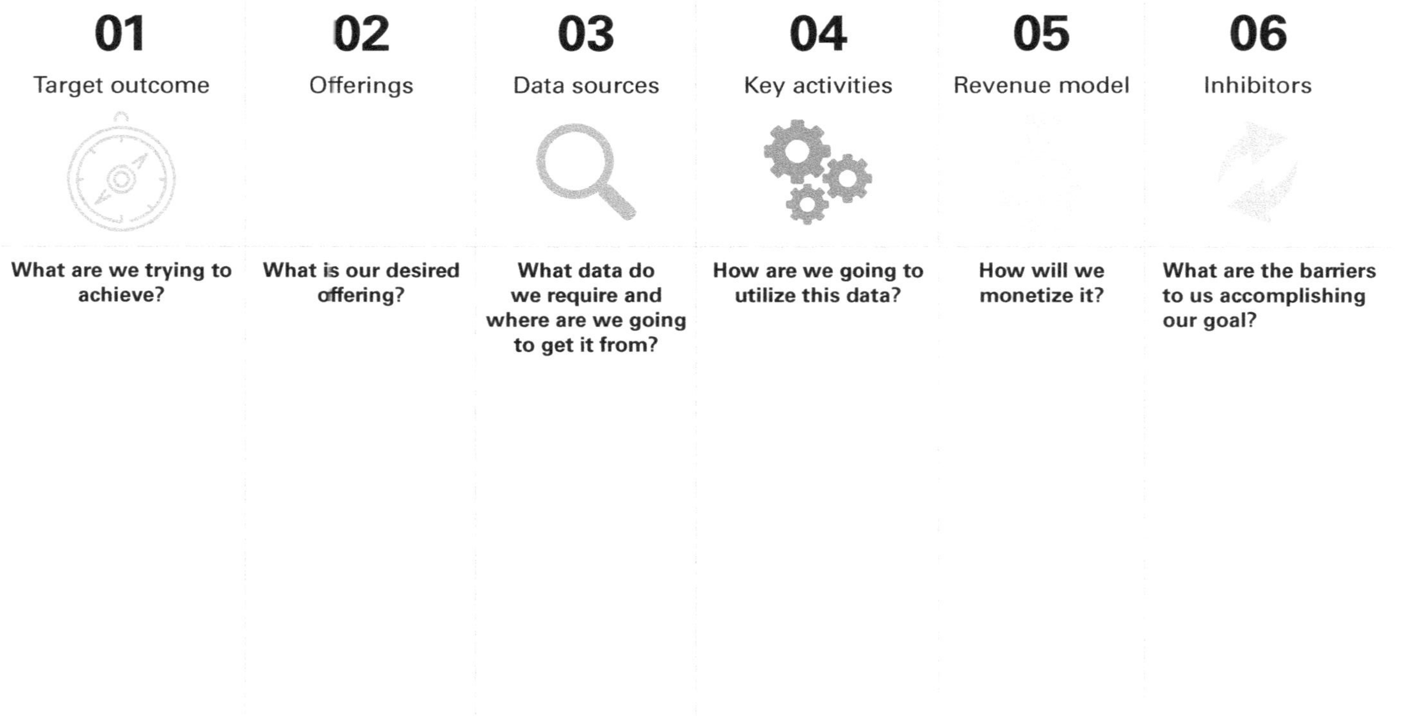

01 Target outcome	**02** Offerings	**03** Data sources	**04** Key activities	**05** Revenue model	**06** Inhibitors
What are we trying to achieve?	What is our desired offering?	What data do we require and where are we going to get it from?	How are we going to utilize this data?	How will we monetize it?	What are the barriers to us accomplishing our goal?

freely available data, such as open data, social media data or web-crawled data.

o **Acquired data** can be purchased from data providers. For example, a marketing firm may purchase consumer behaviour data from a market research company to better understand its target audience and tailor the advertising campaigns accordingly.

o **Data from customers or business partners** is another valuable external source. This data is provided by customers or partners and is not generally available to the public. For example, a company may collect data on customer demographics or preferences through surveys or feedback forms, providing invaluable information for market analysis and product development.

o **Freely available data** is publicly accessible without direct cost and can be divided into three sub-categories: open data, social media data and web-crawled data.

  – **Open data** is downloadable, machine-readable, and structured without prior processing. For example, a government agency may release open data on crime rates or population demographics.

  – **Social media data** is obtained from social media websites such as Facebook or X (Twitter). For instance, a company might analyse social media data to monitor brand reputation or track consumer sentiment towards their products.

  – Finally, **web-crawled data** is publicly available but needs to be gathered electronically. For example, a company may use web-crawling tools to collect data on competitor pricing or product reviews.

Each of these data sources presents unique opportunities for companies to create robust data-driven business models (DDBMs). By harnessing the power of internal and external data, businesses can unlock new possibilities, make informed decisions, and thrive in today's competitive landscape.

KEY ACTIVITIES

Each company carries out various activities to produce and deliver its offerings, and for data-driven business models (DDBMs), these activities must be related to the key resource: data. The key activities section of the DDBM framework combines various viewpoints from the literature and includes tasks such as gathering, organizing, selecting, synthesizing, generating and distributing data.[22]

KEY ACTIVITIES

- **Acquisition:** Data sources can be obtained from external sources, using social media data, open data, or data acquired through third parties.

- **Processing:** Once data has been obtained, it may need to be processed to prepare it for analysis. This could involve tasks such as cleaning the data to remove errors or inconsistencies.

- **Aggregation:** Once cleaned, the data can be aggregated from different sources. This might involve transforming the data into a different format or structure and collating data from multiple sources.

- **Analytics:** Once data has been aggregated, it can be analysed to generate insights or make predictions. This could involve tasks such as identifying patterns or correlations in the data, building models to predict future outcomes, or using machine learning algorithms to automatically classify or cluster data. These actions can be categorized into descriptive analytics (explaining the past), predictive analytics (forecasting future outcomes), and prescriptive analytics (predicting future outcomes and suggesting decisions).

- **Generation:** Data can be generated through systems such as chatbot conversational systems.

- **Visualization:** The data and the insights can be visualized to facilitate communication. This could involve creating visualizations (e.g. charts or graphs) to help stakeholders understand the data or creating interactive dashboards that allow users to explore the data in more detail.

- **Distribution:** With the visualizations in place, the business can communicate the insights to stakeholders clearly and understandably. This could involve publishing reports or dashboards on a web portal, sending automated emails or alerts to stakeholders when certain conditions are met, or integrating the insights into existing business processes (e.g. by automatically generating recommendations for sales reps based on customer data).

OFFERING

The offering, also known as the value proposition, is a critical aspect of any business model. It represents a product's or service's value to the customer and is central to various business model frameworks. The value proposition encapsulates the customer experience that a supplier offers. A company's offering can be categorized into data, information or knowledge, and non-data products or services. The following interaction contains more information on these offerings.[23]

OFFERING

- **Data** is considered a set of facts without inherent meaning. It must be processed to yield meaningful information. For example, companies like Nielsen provide market research data to clients. Nielsen collects data through various sources such as surveys, panels and other methods. Their offering lies in this raw data, which is then aggregated and presented to clients in the form of reports or data visualization tools.

- **Information or knowledge** is derived from interpreting data, involving analytics to provide meaning. For instance, Google Analytics is a web analytics service that helps website owners and marketers understand how their websites perform. Their value proposition is based on the service's insights, such as information on website traffic, user behaviour and performance metrics. By analysing this data, website owners can identify which pages are most popular, which products drive the most traffic, and how long visitors stay on the site. These insights enable data-driven decisions to optimize website content and design and to adjust marketing strategies to target the right audience.

- **Non-data products or services** refer to offerings that are not virtual. A good example is a company like Starbucks, which provides a physical product (coffee) and a service (in-store experience). While Starbucks does collect data on customer purchases and preferences, its primary offering is not data-driven. Instead, it focuses on delivering a physical product and a unique in-store experience leveraging data analytics.

Value capture elements

TARGET CUSTOMER

Every business model is designed to cater to a specific set of customers, making the target customer element an essential aspect of any business model. The most common and generic approach in business model frameworks is to classify customers into two categories: businesses (business-to-business (B2B)) and individual consumers (business-to-consumer (B2C)).[24]

Some companies may target both B2B and B2C customers. For example, Amazon provides B2B services by selling products in bulk to businesses and B2C services by offering retail sales to individual customers.

Another example is the public service sector, which caters to the needs of citizens in a specific geographic region, with services such as healthcare, education and law enforcement provided by governments. The following sections explain how target customers would benefit from each service.

In the public service sector, data-driven business models (DDBMs) can be used to improve the efficiency and effectiveness of service delivery to citizens. For example, in healthcare, electronic health records (EHRs) can be used to collect and analyse patient data to identify patterns and trends, which can inform decision-making and improve patient outcomes. EHRs can also enhance communication and co-ordination between healthcare providers, reducing medical errors and improving patient safety.

In education, DDBMs can improve student learning outcomes by providing personalized learning experiences based on individual student data. For instance, adaptive learning platforms can use student data to identify knowledge gaps and tailor learning activities to meet each student's needs. Student data can also identify at-risk students and provide early interventions to improve academic performance.

In law enforcement, DDBMs can enhance public safety by analysing crime data to identify patterns and trends. This information can be used to allocate resources to high-crime areas and to develop targeted crime prevention strategies. Data-driven approaches can also improve police accountability and transparency by collecting and analysing data on police activities and citizen complaints.

In each of these examples, DDBMs involve the collection, analysis and use of data to inform decision-making and improve outcomes. By leveraging data in this way, public service organizations can improve service delivery, increase efficiency and enhance the overall customer experience for citizens.

REVENUE MODEL

In the long run, it's crucial for any company to have at least one source of revenue. The literature proposes seven distinct revenue streams, which are incorporated into our data-driven business model (DDBM) framework.[25] These are:

- **Asset sales** (e.g. Apple sells its iPhones, MacBooks and other devices to customers).

- **Lending/renting/leasing** assets temporarily (e.g. Zipcar allows customers to rent cars for short periods).

- **Licensing** intellectual property for a fee (e.g. Microsoft licenses its Windows operating system to computer manufacturers who install it on their devices).

- **A fee per use** of a particular service (e.g. Uber charges customers for each ride they take using the platform).

- **A subscription fee** for service usage (e.g. Netflix charges customers a monthly fee to access its streaming service).
- **A brokerage fee** for intermediary services (e.g. Airbnb charges hosts a fee for connecting them with guests who want to rent their homes).
- **Advertising** and generating revenue through ads (e.g. Google earns revenue by displaying ads to users of its search engine and other products).

Developing a revenue model can be challenging, particularly for startups, as they need to identify the most suitable revenue streams for their business model. The choice of revenue model depends on several factors, such as the industry, target customer segment, nature of the product or service, and the competitive landscape.

Companies may encounter difficulties in determining the optimal pricing strategy, setting the appropriate price point, and ensuring the sustainability of their revenue streams over the long term. Additionally, some revenue models may not be suitable for certain industries or products, complicating the process of identifying the most appropriate revenue stream.

Furthermore, in today's rapidly changing business environment, firms must be agile in their revenue model strategies and adapt quickly to new market trends and customer preferences. This necessitates continuous monitoring and evaluation of their revenue models to ensure they remain relevant and competitive in the market.

Cost structure

To provide value to customers, companies typically incur costs for labour, materials and other expenses. However, for a data-driven business model (DDBM), the cost structure is less significant than having a specific advantage in the use of data. This advantage occurs when the data used in a product or service is generated independently of the offering. For example, X (Twitter) can use its own data without additional costs to provide an analytical service, whereas Brandwatch, a social media analytics company, must have a commercial deal to access and analyse data from social media platforms like X and TikTok.

Types of DDBMs

We identified six elements that companies can consider while introducing their data-driven models. Here, we will discuss six different types of DDBMs that companies can consider when launching data-driven services.[26] The categories are ranked from Type A to Type F.

Type A: Free data collection and aggregation

In this data-driven business model (DDBM), companies generate value by gathering and combining data from numerous free data sources and distributing it through an application programming interface (API), which facilitates communication between multiple computer programs. These companies primarily engage in data crawling and visualization. They predominantly use freely available data, with social media data being the most prevalent. However, some of these firms also aggregate proprietary acquired data or crowdsourced data.

There is a notable presence of companies offering this type of service to consumers. For instance, AVUXI gathers data from various sources on local businesses, including restaurants and bars, and makes it available to consumers. Similar companies generate income through revenue models such as advertising, brokerage fees, subscription fees and usage fees.[27]

A B2B firm that exemplifies this approach is Brandwatch, which gathers data from various social media platforms, standardizes the formats, and allows users to filter the data before providing access to the raw data via an API. Brandwatch not only utilizes freely available social media sources but is also a premium reseller of X (Twitter) data. The main value proposition of Brandwatch is providing a single API for easy and dependable access to a wide range of data sources. Subscription and usage fees are the primary sources of revenue for Brandwatch.[28]

Type B: Analytics as a service

Companies offering this type of data-driven business model (DDBM) conduct data analytics on data provided by their clients. They also focus on data distribution, primarily providing access to analytical results through an API and visualizing these results. Additionally, some companies incorporate other data sources to enhance their analytics, in addition to customer-provided data. Type B companies offer analytics services to their customers. They analyse client-provided data alongside other data sources to improve the accuracy of their results. The key activities of these companies include data distribution and visualization of analytics results.[29]

These companies provide a wide range of analytic services to improve various business functions such as marketing, customer service, sales and general data analysis. They primarily target business customers, with revenue models based on subscription or usage fees. Some examples of Type B companies are listed below.

- **Sift** focuses on fraud detection, identifying and preventing fraudulent activities. This service is beneficial for businesses with online transactions, such as e-commerce platforms, to minimize fraud and ensure the smooth processing of legitimate transactions.[30]

- **7signal** optimizes enterprise Wi-Fi networks, which are crucial for businesses that rely heavily on Wi-Fi, such as hospitals or airports. By providing insights, control and performance improvements, 7signal ensures reliable Wi-Fi connectivity, enhancing productivity and user experience.[31]

- **Sendify** offers logistics solutions by searching and comparing shipping options from major companies like DHL, DSV, UPS and FedEx before booking a shipment. This service helps businesses get the best rates and services for their shipping and logistics needs.[32]

- **Granify**, which Bazaarvoice recently acquired, focuses on increasing sales for businesses using machine learning algorithms to analyse customer behaviour and provide insights to optimize the customer journey and improve conversion rates. By helping businesses understand their customers better, Granify helps increase sales and revenue.[33]

- **innex.ai** is a startup in the healthcare sector that developed a platform leveraging RAG (retrieval-augmented generation) and data analytics approaches. Dr Jan Bluemel – CTO of innex.ai – stated that this technology enables users on the platform to efficiently search through vast amounts of data, retrieve relevant information quickly, and enhance decision-making accuracy for non-clinical healthcare professionals. This streamlined access to information improves productivity and ensures compliance with up-to-date guidelines and standards. The platform further uses advanced data analytics on interaction data within its platform to extract actionable insights. By aggregating and analysing data from user interactions, innex.ai identifies emerging topics and pressing issues. This proactive approach enables staff to anticipate and address potential challenges before they escalate, significantly enhancing operational efficiency. By continuously learning from user interactions, innex.ai refines its service offerings, ensuring that healthcare facilities are equipped with the most effective tools for managing their operations and staff.

Type C: Data generation and analysis

Companies of this type generate data instead of relying on pre-existing data. They can be further classified into three categories based on their method of data generation: crowdsourcing, web analytics and smartphone/physical sensor data. Many Type C companies also conduct analytics on the data they generate.[34] Some examples of Type C companies are listed below:

- **Foursquare** generates data through a smartphone application where users can check in to locations and leave tips and recommendations (crowdsourcing). Foursquare aggregates this data to provide users with recommendations about nearby places to eat, drink or visit. They also create features like city guides. Foursquare's business model is based on advertising and partnerships with businesses looking to promote their locations to Foursquare users.[35]

- **GoSquared** offers web analytics services. They use a tracking code embedded in their clients' websites to collect data, which is then analysed. Customers can access reports or raw data through a web-based dashboard or other interfaces. GoSquared provides insights into visitor behaviour and website performance, helping businesses make data-driven decisions about website optimization, marketing strategies and customer engagement. They offer features such as real-time visitor analytics, live chat support, email campaigns and marketing automation, all accessible through a web-based dashboard.[36]

- **Fitbit,** now acquired by Google, generates data through physical devices like wearable technology. These devices use sensors to collect data on activities such as steps taken, calories burned and sleep quality, syncing this data to a smartphone or computer. Fitbit analyses this data to provide insights into fitness and health habits, offering personalized recommendations for improvement. Fitbit generates revenue through the sale of its devices and subscription services. Additionally, it offers a B2B service called Fitbit Health Solutions, which allows companies and healthcare providers to use Fitbit data to promote employee wellness and enhance patient outcomes.[37]

Type D: Free data knowledge and discovery

Companies derive value from performing analytics on freely available data and from crawling data from the web, as this data may not be readily available in a machine-readable format.

The companies in this category share similar data sources and activities, but their offerings vary significantly. Type D encompasses various revenue models. In addition to subscription or usage fee-based models, companies targeting consumers often generate revenue from advertising or brokerage fees. Both B2B and B2C business models are present in this group. The types of analytics performed by Type D companies range from basic descriptive analytics to more advanced techniques.[38] Some examples of Type D companies are listed below:

- **CodeSignal** provides a service to facilitate developer recruitment. CodeSignal automatically evaluates published code on open-source sites like GitHub and coders' contributions on Q&A websites like Stack Overflow to identify hidden talents. A scoring mechanism ranks developers based on their skills and abilities.[39]

- **Olery** offers automated monitoring of review sites for the hospitality industry.[40]

- **Hopper** recommends hotel deals by analysing different booking websites and receives a commission from booking websites.[41]

- **Traackr** and **PeerIndex** (later acquired by Brandwatch) identify relevant social media influencers.[42]

- **Talkwalker** applies predictive analytics to identify emerging trends on real-time data streams like X (formerly Twitter) or Facebook before they become widely known.[43]

Type E: Data aggregation as a service

Companies do not create or analyse data themselves. Instead, they add value by aggregating data from various internal sources for their clients. Once the data is aggregated, these companies deliver it to their customers through various distribution and/or visualization interfaces.

The primary application areas focus on aggregating customer data from diverse sources for individuals and organizations. Some companies in this group may also specialize in particular sectors or address specific issues, such as education. Similar to Type B companies, which offer analytics as a service, Type E companies generally rely on subscription-based revenue models and mainly target business customers.[44] Below are some examples of Type E companies:

- **Segment** offers a platform that enables businesses to collect, unify and send customer data to various tools and analytics services. The platform is integrated with over 300 different data sources and destinations, facilitating easy customer data management and enabling businesses to derive insights and enhance operations. Segment operates on a subscription-based revenue model, with pricing determined by the number of monthly tracked users.[45]

- **Clearbit**, acquired by HubSpot, operates a data aggregation platform that provides extensive information about individual consumers or companies. It aggregates data from multiple sources, including social media, company websites and public databases, to create detailed profiles useful for sales, marketing and lead generation. Clearbit specializes in integrating data from multiple sources within an organization and delivering it to its customers through various interfaces.[46]

- **Edmentum** is an educational technology company that offers online learning programs and services for K-12 students. Their offerings include adaptive assessments, personalized learning paths and interactive content designed to support customized instruction. They also provide data analytics tools for educators to track student progress and identify areas for improvement, enhancing educational outcomes.[47]

Type F: Multi-source data mash-up and analysis

This type of data-driven business model (DDBM) generates value by aggregating and analysing data from multiple sources, including external sources. Companies operating under this model enhance their customer data by benchmarking it against other external data sources. These companies primarily serve business customers and typically utilize subscription-based revenue models.[48] Below are some examples of Type F companies.

- **Chartmetric** integrates proprietary data with external data sources such as YouTube view counts and Facebook Likes to provide comprehensive music analytics.[49]

- **Dataminr** offers a platform that merges real-time public data from social media, news sources and other external sources with internal customer data. The platform employs machine learning algorithms to detect and alert customers in the finance, public sector and media industries about significant events and trends as they occur, enabling them to make quicker and more informed decisions.[50]

- **Tactful AI** exemplifies a data-driven business model that leverages advanced AI to analyse and utilize data from multiple sources, providing a comprehensive solution that empowers B2B businesses to deliver superior customer experience and engagement and achieve operational excellence. It operates as a cutting-edge customer engagement platform that leverages AI and machine learning to enhance the quality and efficiency of customer service across various communication channels (e.g. ticketing data, social media data, conversational data, voice calls). Tactful AI uses a subscription-based revenue model, offering different plans tailored to the needs of diverse businesses, from small enterprises to large corporations.[51]

The DDBM innovation blueprint

Let me introduce a DDBM blueprint toolbox,[52] which comprises six key questions essential for developing a data-driven business and provides a structured approach to customizing DDBMs to align with specific goals, organizational structures, available resources, skills and industry contexts. This integrated approach serves as a roadmap for organizations aspiring to become more data-driven, guiding them in developing their own DDBM by addressing six fundamental questions for a data-driven business.

The six fundamental questions for data-driven business

1 TARGET OUTCOME: WHAT DO WE WANT TO ACHIEVE BY USING BIG DATA?

Businesses must set clear and achievable goals to utilize data effectively. Many organizations recognize the value of data, yet a significant number overlook the importance of establishing specific objectives prior to investing time and money into data acquisition and analysis.

Setting a predetermined target sharpens focus on realistic and desired outcomes. Utilizing the power of data allows firms to gain a competitive advantage in various operational areas. These include optimizing supply chains to minimize inefficiencies, facilitating expansion and consolidation, enhancing processing speeds, differentiating products in the marketplace, and strengthening brand recognition. Companies can significantly improve their business results by employing data-driven strategies in these key areas.

For example, the UK online fashion retailer ASOS prioritizes differentiation as its competitive edge. Leveraging data to monitor industry trends, ASOS offers a broad selection of products. Unlike traditional brick-and-mortar stores constrained by physical space, ASOS can provide its customers with a wider variety of items.[53]

2 OFFERING: WHAT IS OUR DESIRED OFFERING?

To capitalize on a data-driven business model (DDBM), a business must decide how to enhance its existing offerings or create new ones. Established businesses often leverage data to improve their value propositions. On its own, raw data is just a collection of facts, but when processed through analytics, it transforms into meaningful knowledge, insights or applications.

Companies have numerous options regarding their offerings, as they are not restricted to a single product or service. Typically, established organizations provide multiple customer offerings. Most have at least one non-data product or service, while others offer information services, and some provide data services. Non-data products or services are particularly prevalent in sectors such as publishing, finance, retail and insurance sectors.

Publishers may collect data on reader engagement or content performance, but their core business revolves around the production and distribution of books, magazines and newspapers, making their primary offering a non-data product or service.

For instance, a company like Penguin Random House primarily produces and distributes books and audiobooks across a variety of genres and authors. It uses data to guide decisions on title acquisitions and marketing strategies, yet its fundamental product remains the physical or digital book.

The finance sector primarily relies on non-data offerings. Banks, for example, mainly provide financial services such as loans, credit cards and savings accounts, with data analysis supporting risk assessment, fraud detection and customer profiling.

Even financial technology companies such as PayPal and Square, which utilize data to facilitate electronic payments and financial tracking, ultimately offer a non-data product or service – the capability to conduct financial transactions securely and efficiently.

In the insurance sector, companies like Progressive Corporation in the US utilize telematics data from customers' vehicles to analyse driving behaviour and calculate personalized insurance premiums. This data may include metrics such as vehicle speed, acceleration, braking patterns and the times when the vehicle is driven.

By analysing this data, insurance companies can better understand individual drivers' risk profiles and adjust their premiums accordingly. This not only allows insurance companies to price their products more accurately but also benefits customers who may receive lower premiums for demonstrating safe driving habits.

3 DATA SOURCES: WHAT DATA DO WE REQUIRE AND HOW ARE WE GOING TO ACQUIRE IT?

The development of a data-driven business model (DDBM) heavily relies on the careful selection and acquisition of data. Established businesses benefit from having a broad customer base, which provides a rich source of customer-provided data that can be integrated with other data sources. This extensive use of all available data underlines organizations' recognition of data's value and their movement towards a data-driven approach.

Customer-provided data is invaluable, yet self-generated data is often viewed as the most crucial source, particularly in retail, telecommunications and financial services. Telecommunications and retail, in particular, emphasize this due to their direct customer interactions.

For startups, building a DDBM presents the challenge of fewer customer interaction points to gather data. However, starting from scratch can be advantageous, as it often requires reliance on external data sources. The following examples are from established businesses across different sectors.[54]

Topshop, now part of ASOS, is a UK fashion retailer that leverages a mix of data sources. It employs predictive and descriptive analytics to spot trends in the competitive clothing industry. The company's data comes from customer interactions, publicly available information from fashion blogs and social media, and its existing internal databases. By utilizing these data sources, Topshop can extract valuable insights into customer preferences and behaviours, helping it stay competitive and seize opportunities for increased revenue. This example highlights the significance of effective data management and utilization in driving retail industry success.[55]

Orbital Insight is a geospatial analytics company that specializes in analysing satellite and aerial imagery and various other external data sources such as mobile phone geolocation and automatic identification system (AIS) ship tracking. The company delivers insights for multiple industries, including finance, energy, defence and real estate. Rather than deploying satellites, Orbital Insight uses satellite images from external providers like DigitalGlobe and Airbus. They apply machine learning and computer vision technologies to these images to detect changes and identify patterns on a global scale. For instance, they can estimate oil storage levels, monitor deforestation, track traffic in retail parking lots, and assess global agricultural production. Orbital Insight's core offering transforms extensive, complex external data into actionable insights that assist customers in decision-making.[56]

4 KEY ACTIVITIES: IN WHAT WAYS ARE WE GOING TO PROCESS AND APPLY THIS DATA?

For businesses to fully capitalize on the value of data, it's crucial to understand how to process it effectively. This involves identifying key activities in the virtual value chain and ensuring the availability of the necessary resources and skills to execute these activities. The approach may vary between established organizations and startups, as outlined in the following sections.

Established companies often prioritize data acquisition and generation, leveraging their market position to utilize these activities effectively. Data can be sourced internally or externally, with generation methods including manual collection by staff, automated collection through sensors and tracking tools, and crowdsourcing. Analytical techniques are employed to derive insights, categorized into descriptive analytics for understanding past events, predictive analytics for forecasting future scenarios, and prescriptive analytics for suggesting actions based on predictions. Established businesses leverage their data internally to enhance their operations and offerings without necessarily sharing it externally.[57]

Consider an established bank with a large customer base and extensive internal data. This data, such as customer transaction histories, can be analysed to identify spending patterns and to offer personalized product recommendations. Additionally, customer feedback can be used to improve service quality. Here, the focus is on internal data generation and acquisition to bolster the business model and create value internally.

Startups, on the other hand, often focus on data distribution, especially if they operate on a subscription fee model and offer their services as a product. This leads to a different perception of data and its value, with a more outward-focused approach.

A startup offering a software-as-a-service (SaaS) project management tool might collect data on user interactions with the tool. This data is then analysed to provide insights and analytics to customers. The startup likely charges a subscription fee to access the insights derived from the data. In this model, the startup's business relies on distributing data and creating value through analytics shared with customers.

5 REVENUE MODEL: HOW ARE WE GOING TO MONETIZE THE DATA?

A business must demonstrate quantifiable benefits to justify constructing and implementing a data-driven business model (DDBM). Incorporating a suitable revenue model within the DDBM is key to its operational success.

As discussed, we have identified seven potential revenue streams: asset sale, lending/renting/leasing, licensing, usage fee, subscription fee, brokerage fee and advertising. The appropriate revenue model depends on the specific business and its circumstances, as the choice can vary widely between sectors and even within the same industry. Below are some examples of how different sectors apply these revenue streams.[58]

In the publishing industry, advertising often serves as the primary revenue model. For instance, CNN has adapted to shifting market dynamics by leveraging its high-quality readership, which is attractive to advertisers. CNN offers its content online for free, employing descriptive analytics to develop unique reader profiles. These profiles enable advertisers to target their advertisements more precisely, often at a premium. Also, CNN emphasizes the importance of syndication and revenue-sharing models, where content is shared or hosted on different sites, generating ad revenue that is split among content owners and platforms. Video content is particularly suited for these models due to its engaging nature.[59]

Startups frequently depend on usage fees or subscription fees for revenue. A case in point is fitness apps like MyFitnessPal, which typify startups that utilize subscription fees.[60] These apps charge users for premium features or full access to the application's capabilities.

6 INHIBITORS: WHAT ARE THE BARRIERS TO US ACCOMPLISHING OUR GOAL?

We uncovered a significant correlation between challenges in implementing a data-driven business model (DDBM) and the lack of data-oriented personnel. The findings indicate that *personnel issues* might be the most significant barriers to adopting DDBM practices for both new and established businesses, often intertwined with other obstacles:[61]

- 100 per cent of respondents reported *cultural issues* (83 per cent strongly agreed, 17 per cent agreed) when implementing a DDBM.
- 86 per cent encountered obstacles related to *internal value perceptions* when implementing a DDBM.
- 71 per cent experienced issues with *data quality or integrity*.

A shortage of experienced, data-oriented personnel can lead to a company culture that does not support the development and implementation of a DDBM, leading to negative internal perceptions of the model. However, equipping staff with the necessary knowledge about the values and principles of DDBM can mitigate these challenges.

Businesses could organize training seminars or courses to educate employees on the benefits and methods of DDBMs and to address personnel resistance. Firms should emphasize the importance of fostering a culture supporting effective data-oriented initiatives.

Examples of applying the DDBM blueprint

Let's apply the blueprint and six dimensions in different industries.

Automotive

Consider an automotive company that specializes in electric vehicles and clean energy – the company is well regarded for its integration of data and technology to enhance its offerings and create new data-driven business models.

- **Target outcome:** This company aims to establish a competitive edge in autonomous driving technology and advance its battery technology to dominate the mobility experience market.

- **Desired offering:** The firm is focused on delivering data-driven electric vehicles.

- **Data sources:** This company gathers essential customer vehicle usage and battery performance data through in-car sensors, digital platforms and customer feedback.

- **Key activities:** The company utilizes this data to refine its autonomous driving technology, optimize manufacturing processes and advance battery technology. For instance, the company employs predictive analytics to monitor battery charging and discharging patterns, enhancing battery performance and longevity. Additionally, the firm can use AI to predict battery replacement times and to improve the efficiency of its battery storage systems.

- **Revenue model:** The automotive firm can leverage this data-driven approach to boost electric vehicle sales.

- **Inhibitors:** Challenges for this automotive firm include:

  o **Data privacy:** Protecting sensitive data gathered from vehicle usage and battery performance from unauthorized access.

o **Product complexity:** The complex nature of products, which necessitates extensive data to optimize performance and complicates data analysis and insight generation.

o **Legal challenges:** The development of the future of autonomous driving technology faces numerous legal hurdles, such as liability in accidents involving self-driving cars and regulatory and insurance considerations. The firm must actively engage with regulators and legislators to navigate these issues.

Healthcare

Let's take healthcare providers committed to delivering comprehensive and patient-centred care. They focus on innovation, incorporating advanced technology and data-driven methodologies to enhance patient experiences. Over the years, many medical companies have had access to a substantial amount of data, which holds the potential to be leveraged into a new business model aimed at personalizing care and improving patient outcomes.

- **Target outcomes:**
  o Enhancing patient outcomes.
  o Reducing healthcare costs through data utilization.
  o Identifying high-risk patients who might need expensive hospital stays or emergency services.
  o Providing proactive care to prevent such issues.
- **Desired offerings:**
  o Provide personalized care plans for each patient.
  o Focus on preventive measures and early intervention.
  o Avoid costly hospitalizations.
- **Data sources:**
  o Electronic health records (EHRs).
  o Patient surveys.
  o Wearables, like fitness trackers or blood glucose monitors.
- **Key activities:**
  o Employ analytical tools to identify patterns and trends using predictive modelling or machine learning.
  o Uncover insights into patient behaviour and health outcomes.

- **Revenue model:**
  - Sell insights to insurance companies.
  - Partner with pharmaceutical companies to develop treatments.
- **Inhibitors:**
  - Resistance from staff unfamiliar with data analytics.
  - Scepticism about the value of a data-driven approach.
  - Concerns over data privacy and data quality.
  - Regulatory compliance challenges necessitate investments in secure data storage and ensuring that patient data is anonymized and protected according to regulations like GDPR or HIPAA.

B2B service

Let's consider a maintenance B2B service company specializing in building and facilities maintenance for commercial and industrial clients. They offer a comprehensive suite of maintenance services, including HVAC (heating, ventilation and air-conditioning), plumbing, electrical and janitorial services, ensuring optimal functionality and safety of client facilities. The company aims to reshape its business model using the client data collected over the years to provide more reliable and efficient maintenance solutions.

- **Target outcomes:**
  - Enhance the efficiency and quality of its maintenance services using data-driven insights.
  - Increase customer satisfaction.
  - Reduce downtime.
  - Expand its business.
- **Desired offerings:**
  - HVAC.
  - Plumbing.
  - Electrical.
  - Janitorial services.
  - Using data to optimize service delivery, tailor services to specific client needs, and improve response times.

- **Data sources:**
  - Work orders.
  - Maintenance logs.
  - Customer feedback.
  - IoT sensors embedded in buildings and equipment.
- **Key activities:**
  - Optimize maintenance schedules.
  - Predict equipment failures.
  - Proactively address potential issues before they escalate.
- **Revenue model:**
  - Offering premium maintenance services that are more comprehensive and data-driven.
  - Using data to identify upsell and cross-sell opportunities.
  - Optimizing pricing and service packages.
- **Inhibitors:**
  - Data security and privacy concerns.
  - Data silos.
  - Resistance to change from employees and clients.

To overcome these, the company could invest in robust data security measures, promote data sharing across departments, and train employees and clients on the benefits of data-driven maintenance solutions.

Public service

Consider a city looking to reinvent its transportation department by adopting a data-driven approach to improve transportation planning. By leveraging state-of-the-art technologies and harnessing the power of data analytics, the city aims to optimize traffic flow, reduce congestion and enhance overall mobility for its residents and commuters. Through the implementation of real-time data collection, predictive modelling and advanced traffic analysis, the city transportation department is set to transform urban mobility, ensuring efficient and sustainable transportation systems well into the future.

- **Target outcomes:**
  - Improve transportation planning and reduce congestion.
  - Enhance the accessibility of transit.
  - Increase road safety.
- **Desired offerings:**
  - The department seeks to implement a sophisticated, data-driven transportation planning model that utilizes real-time data on traffic flow, public transit usage and road incidents to fine-tune transportation networks and alleviate congestion.
- **Data sources:**
  - Public transit usage statistics.
  - GPS data from ride-sharing services.
  - Real-time traffic data from sensors and cameras.
  - Accident reports.
- **Key activities:**
  - Identify and anticipate traffic patterns and potential road incidents.
  - Implement proactive traffic management strategies.
  - Reduce congestion and enhance road safety.
- **Revenue model:**
  - The economic benefits derived from improved transportation efficiency and effectiveness can serve as a form of monetization, enhancing the city's infrastructure and improving the citizen experience.
- **Inhibitors:**
  - Concerns over data privacy.
  - Technical difficulties related to data integration from various sources.
  - Resistance from stakeholders affected by changes in transportation infrastructure.

To overcome these obstacles, the city government will need to ensure that it has the appropriate resources, such as skilled personnel and technological infrastructure, to address these barriers effectively.

KEY TAKEAWAYS

In this final chapter, we explored business models and the transformative potential of data in creating new revenue streams. We focused on data-driven business models (DDBMs) and offered a structured framework to help professionals and business leaders design DDBMs that align with the evolving business landscape. We introduced a toolkit for developing DDBMs and discussed six main types, providing numerous examples across sectors like B2B, B2C, startups and public services.

Key takeaways include:

- A growing number of firms are exploring DDBMs to innovate their business models.

- The DDBM blueprint equips you with the necessary tools to leverage data as a pivotal resource for generating new revenue streams.

- Organizations that neglect to integrate data-driven practices risk losing competitive edge, market share and revenue.

Notes

1 OpenAI (2024) Our approach to data and AI. https://openai.com/index/approach-to-data-and-ai/ (archived at https://perma.cc/3XUN-URTQ)

2 ibid.

3 Race, M (2024) What went wrong for online car retailer Cazoo?, BBC News, 22 May. www.bbc.co.uk/news/articles/cjq55333xg9o (archived at https://perma.cc/PW2Y-UN8A)

4 Cazoo (2024) About us. www.cazoo.co.uk/about-us/ (archived at https://perma.cc/RZ6M-R32U)

5 Race, M (2024) What went wrong for online car retailer Cazoo?, BBC News, 22 May. www.bbc.co.uk/news/articles/cjq55333xg9o (archived at https://perma.cc/5PDN-JHHE)

6 ibid.

7 Hartmann, P M, Zaki, M, Feldmann, N and Neely, A (2016) Capturing value from big data: A taxonomy of data-driven business models used by start-up firms, *International Journal of Operations & Production Management*, 36 (10), 1382–406

8 Hedman, J and Kalling, T (2002) The business model concept: Theoretical underpinnings and empirical illustrations, *European Journal of Information Systems*, 12, 49–59. https://doi.org/10.1057/palgrave.ejis.3000446 (archived at https://perma.cc/P28Q-3HB9); Johnson, M W, Christensen, C M and Kagermann, H (2008) Reinventing your business model, *Harvard Business Review,* December. https://hbr.org/2008/12/reinventing-your-business-model (archived at https://perma.cc/BX7T-URF4); Bouwman, H, Faber, E, Haaker, T, Kijil, B and De Reuver, M (2008) Conceptualizing the STOF model, in Bouwman, H, Vos, H and Haaker, T (eds), *Mobile Service Innovation and Business Models*, Springer. https://doi.org/10.1007/978-3-540-79238-3_2 (archived at https://perma.cc/D3NL-A36X); Heikkila, J, Heikkila, M and Tinnilä, M (2005) The role of business models in developing business networks, in Saarinen, T, Tinnilä, M and Tseng, A (eds), *Managing Business in a Multi-Channel World: Success factors for e-business*, IGI Global. https://doi.org/10.4018/978-1-59140-629-7.ch016 (archived at https://perma.cc/67P9-PNAM); Baden-Fuller, C and Haefliger, S (2013) Business models and technological innovation, *Long Range Planning*, 46 (6), 419–26. https://doi.org/10.1016/j.lrp.2013.08.023 (archived at https://perma.cc/7NFY-3Q2Z)

9 Chesbrough, H and Rosenbloom, R (2002) The role of the business model in capturing value from innovation: Evidence from Xerox Corporation's technology spin-off companies, *Industrial and Corporate Change*, 11 (3), 529–55

10 Osterwalder, A (2004) The business model ontology: A proposition in design science research, thesis, Ecole des Hautes Etudes Commerciales de l'Université de Lausanne. www.researchgate.net/publication/33681401_The_Business_Model_Ontology_-_A_Proposition_in_a_Design_Science_Approach (archived at https://perma.cc/BF9T-AMBZ)

11 ibid.

12 Singapore Airlines (2024) *Annual Report FY2023/24.* www.singaporeair.com/content/dam/sia/web-assets/pdfs/about-us/information-for-investors/annual-report/annualreport2324.pdf (archived at https://perma.cc/Q8CB-T3D7)

13 Cambridge Service Alliance (2019) Service Week 2019. https://cambridgeservicealliance.eng.cam.ac.uk/IndustryDay/serviceweek2019 (archived at https://perma.cc/U8X8-38DG)

14 ibid.

15 ibid.

16 Singapore Airlines (2022) Singapore Airlines adopts AI solution from KLM-BCG partnership. www.singaporeair.com/en_UK/pt/media-centre/press-release/article/?q=en_UK/2022/January-March/jr0122-220110 (archived at https://perma.cc/B746-ZE9P)

17 Brownlow, J, Zaki, M, Neely, A and Urmetzer, F (2015) Business models: A blueprint for innovation, Cambridge Alliance Working Paper. https://cambridgeservicealliance.eng.cam.ac.uk/system/files/documents/2015March PaperTheDDBMInnovationBlueprint.pdf (archived at https://perma.cc/Z9ZJ-HGHD)

18 Zaki, M (2019) Digital transformation: Harnessing digital technologies for the next generation of services, *Journal of Services Marketing*, 33 (4), 429–35. https://doi.org/10.1108/JSM-01-2019-0034 (archived at https://perma. cc/44SZ-6RMJ)

19 Brownlow, J, Zaki, M, Neely, A and Urmetzer, F (2015) Business models: A blueprint for innovation, Cambridge Alliance Working Paper. https:// cambridgeservicealliance.eng.cam.ac.uk/system/files/documents/2015March PaperTheDDBMInnovationBlueprint.pdf (archived at https://perma. cc/8XXW-HNMX)

20 Hartmann, P M, Zaki, M, Feldmann, N and Neely, A (2016) Capturing value from big data: A taxonomy of data-driven business models used by start-up firms, *International Journal of Operations & Production Management*, 36 (10), 1382–406

21 ibid.

22 ibid.

23 ibid.

24 ibid.

25 ibid.

26 ibid.

27 AVUXI (2024) AVUXI: Location context for travel and real estate. www.avuxi. com (archived at https://perma.cc/ZRU8-W7UZ)

28 Brandwatch (2024) Brandwatch: Consumer intelligence and social media listening platform. www.brandwatch.com (archived at https://perma.cc/7X4N-R5MT)

29 Hartmann, P M, Zaki, M, Feldmann, N and Neely, A (2016) Capturing value from big data: A taxonomy of data-driven business models used by start-up firms, *International Journal of Operations & Production Management*, 36 (10), 1382–406

30 Sift (2024) Sift: Digital trust & safety solutions. https://sift.com (archived at https://perma.cc/YLL4-XCHM)

31 7signal (2024) 7signal: Wireless network monitoring solutions. www.7signal. com (archived at https://perma.cc/JU9C-SBLN)

32 Sendify (2024) Sendify: Simplified shipping for businesses. www.sendify.se/en/ (archived at https://perma.cc/R56P-NAAE)

33 Bazaarvoice (2024) Contextual commerce. www.bazaarvoice.com/products/ contextual-commerce/ (archived at https://perma.cc/T3Y4-ZCT2)

34 Hartmann, P M, Zaki, M, Feldmann, N and Neely, A (2016) Capturing value from big data: A taxonomy of data-driven business models used by start-up firms, *International Journal of Operations & Production Management*, 36 (10), 1382–406

35 Foursquare (2024) Foursquare: Location technology platform. https://foursquare. com (archived at https://perma.cc/C8TT-8J5D)

36 GoSquared (2024) GoSquared: Real-time analytics and customer engagement. www.gosquared.com (archived at https://perma.cc/2C5J-CNTK)

37 Fitbit (2024) Fitbit: Health and fitness tracking. www.fitbit.com/global/us/home (archived at https://perma.cc/2D9X-48M4)

38 Hartmann, P M, Zaki, M, Feldmann, N and Neely, A (2016) Capturing value from big data: A taxonomy of data-driven business models used by start-up firms, *International Journal of Operations & Production Management*, 36 (10), 1382–406

39 CodeSignal (2024) CodeSignal: Technical interview and assessment platform. https://codesignal.com (archived at https://perma.cc/DY9E-G2ST)

40 Olery (2024) Olery: Reputation and guest experience management for hospitality. https://olery.com (archived at https://perma.cc/KF2T-HJHK)

41 Hopper (2024) Hopper: Travel booking and price prediction. https://hopper.com (archived at https://perma.cc/YHS7-L5DW)

42 Traackr (2024) Traackr: Influencer marketing platform. www.traackr.com (archived at https://perma.cc/ES5Q-736T)

43 Talkwalker (2024) Talkwalker: Consumer intelligence and social listening platform. www.talkwalker.com (archived at https://perma.cc/GU6E-XADL)

44 Hartmann, P M, Zaki, M, Feldmann, N and Neely, A (2016) Capturing value from big data: A taxonomy of data-driven business models used by start-up firms, *International Journal of Operations & Production Management*, 36 (10), 1382–406

45 Segment (2024) Segment: Customer data platform. https://segment.com (archived at https://perma.cc/WG6X-TBM2)

46 Clearbit (2024) Clearbit: Data enrichment and intelligence platform. https://clearbit.com (archived at https://perma.cc/PFC7-NS32)

47 Edmentum (2024) Edmentum: International education solutions. www.edmentum.com/intl/ (archived at https://perma.cc/3Y62-6STV)

48 Hartmann, P M, Zaki, M, Feldmann, N and Neely, A (2016) Capturing value from big data: A taxonomy of data-driven business models used by start-up firms, *International Journal of Operations & Production Management*, 36 (10), 1382–406

49 Chartmetric (2024) Chartmetric: Music analytics and data platform. https://chartmetric.com (archived at https://perma.cc/G9PA-VASN)

50 Dataminr (2024) Dataminr: Real-time information discovery platform. www.dataminr.com (archived at https://perma.cc/9RNQ-CNAE)

51 Tactful AI (2024) Tactful AI: Customer experience and engagement solutions. https://tactful.ai (archived at https://perma.cc/29V4-WV74)

52 Brownlow, J, Zaki, M, Neely, A and Urmetzer, F (2015) Business models: A blueprint for innovation, Cambridge Alliance Working Paper. https://cambridgeservicealliance.eng.cam.ac.uk/system/files/documents/2015March PaperTheDDBMInnovationBlueprint.pdf (archived at https://perma.cc/546T-BJSU)

53 ibid.

54 ibid.

55 ibid.

56 Orbital Insight (2024) Orbital Insight: Geospatial analytics platform. www.orbitalinsight.com (archived at https://perma.cc/RYH9-BDZ8)

57 Zaki, M (2019) Digital transformation: Harnessing digital technologies for the next generation of services, *Journal of Services Marketing*, 33 (4), 429–35. https://doi.org/10.1108/JSM-01-2019-0034 (archived at https://perma.cc/P8B6-QL8M)

58 Hartmann, P M, Zaki, M, Feldmann, N and Neely, A (2016) Capturing value from big data: A taxonomy of data-driven business models used by start-up firms, *International Journal of Operations & Production Management*, 36 (10), 1382–406. https://doi.org/10.1108/IJOPM-02-2014-0098 (archived at https://perma.cc/M6TE-KVBC)

59 CNN Newsource (2018) Digital revenue models: Part 2. www.cnnnewsource.com/wp-content/uploads/2018/06/2018-POV_Digital-Revenue-Models_Part-2.pdf (archived at https://perma.cc/8ZD2-HZ8X)

60 MyFitnessPal (2024) MyFitnessPal: Calorie counter and diet tracker. www.myfitnesspal.com (archived at https://perma.cc/3N7K-VLT3)

61 Brownlow, J, Zaki, M, Neely, A and Urmetzer, F (2015) Business models: A blueprint for innovation, Cambridge Alliance Working Paper. https://cambridgeservicealliance.eng.cam.ac.uk/system/files/documents/2015March PaperTheDDBMInnovationBlueprint.pdf (archived at https://perma.cc/LYV9-D8HR)

Conclusion and future outlook

Over the course of these 12 chapters, we have explored how digital technologies, particularly AI, can transform customer experiences and journeys in ways that truly delight. In today's experience-driven world, businesses require professionals like you who can harness data to design, manage and deliver consistent and compelling customer experiences across all channels. As you reach the end of this book, I hope you are inspired to become one of those champions of customer experience within your organization, driving innovation with data and AI to create new business models and optimize the entire customer journey.

Throughout this book, we have discussed what makes customers delighted and frustrated and how data and AI can help sustain positive experiences, fix friction points, and open new revenue streams. We shared examples of digital service transformations across various industries, demonstrating how embedding digital solutions can secure a competitive edge, generate long-term revenue, and create new market opportunities.

We've seen that service delivery is not static; it continuously evolves with technological advancements, transforming organizational capabilities and enhancing customer expectations in B2B, B2C and public sectors. This ever-increasing demand for seamless, superior interactions is driven by continuous innovation from new and existing organizations aiming to enhance their services.

You have also learnt how to navigate the digital, physical and social realms, utilizing a multidimensional framework to understand and shape customer experiences across various channels.

With the knowledge and tools gained, you are now equipped to assess your organization's position and strategize where it wants to be in the digital landscape. By embracing this knowledge, you can help your organization deliver consistent value at every customer touchpoint, from designing effective customer journeys to generating actionable insights from AI and developing data-driven business models.

As discussed in this book, this new era of digital transformation is unlike anything that has come before. It offers endless opportunities for those ready to innovate and adapt. As you move forward, remember that the journey does not end here. The future belongs to those who are willing to learn, adapt and lead in creating memorable and valuable customer experiences.

I hope this book has provided you with the insights and inspiration to take these lessons forward, innovate in your practices, and lead your organization towards excellence in customer experience. Remember, the power to delight customers is in your hands – use it wisely and creatively to shape the future of your business.

Future outlook

I have invited two senior industry leaders to share their perspectives on the future of customer experience and how they envision these changes impacting their sector.

Potential applications

Dr Franziska Bell, *a visionary tech executive previously at Uber, Toyota and BP* stated that there are two potential applications of AI in customer experience:

AGENTIC SYSTEMS FOR CUSTOMER EXPERIENCE AND CUSTOMER CARE

AI-based agentic systems, characterized by their autonomy and goal-oriented design, hold immense potential to transform the landscape of customer care and customer experience. Agentic systems not only are capable of understanding customer intent and responding to customer queries but are also able to break down and execute complex tasks autonomously. This represents a significant departure from traditional hard-coded automated processes and rules, ushering in a new era of autonomy providing immediate, personalized responses, significantly reducing wait times and enhancing satisfaction.

In digital environments, agentic AI can manage real-time customer service via chatbots and virtual assistants. These AI systems can independently resolve complex issues, offer personalized recommendations, and adapt to customer behaviour, significantly reducing wait times and improving satisfaction. For example, an AI assistant could autonomously track a customer's order, identify a delay, and proactively offer a discount or expedited shipping without human intervention.

Socially, agentic AI can monitor and respond to customer feedback on social media platforms in real time, autonomously addressing concerns and engaging with customers to maintain brand reputation. By leveraging agentic AI, businesses can create seamless, proactive, and personalized experiences that exceed customer expectations across all channels.

APPLICATIONS OF GENERATIVE AI FOR USER RESEARCH

User research plays a pivotal role in understanding consumer behaviour, preferences and pain points. By gathering insights from real users, companies can develop products and services that truly meet their customers' needs. However, traditional user research methods can be time-consuming and resource intensive.

Recent advancements in generative AI have opened up innovative avenues for user research, such as augmenting human focus groups with digital twins of existing and potential target customers.

New York-based design agency Fantasy has been a pioneer in the field of so-called synthetic humans, earning the 2023 Fast Company's World Changing Ideas Award in the experimental category. Synthetic humans involve building models based on more than 100 customizable traits, capturing attributes of existing and target customers and overarching market trends. Marketers, user researchers and product managers can then query these models using a natural language interface as if they were a focus group member and test new product concepts, product feature ideas and marketing materials. In collaboration with product and design experts, these synthetic humans can also help co-generate and subsequently prioritize new ideas within seconds.

This novel approach allows at scale, on-demand, faster and cheaper user research and customer-centric ideation. For example, a collaboration between Fantasy and bp, documented by Harvard Business School, found that using synthetic humans reduced research costs by around 66 per cent. Early applications indicate that augmentation of human focus groups with synthetic humans can also lead to more well-rounded insights, as synthetic humans can simulate a broader and more diverse range of customer segments.

The models are being continuously refined and improved to capture user needs and market dynamics even better. Importantly, humans remain in the loop to ensure quality and accuracy.

But even in these early days it is clear that by leveraging the power of human–AI collaboration, companies can revolutionize their user research process, and as AI capabilities continue to evolve, the potential applications of synthetic humans will likely expand.

Key trends

Ashish K Gupta, Chief Growth Officer, Europe and Africa, Diversified Industries, HCLTech, stated that he works for a large technology company and often gets a ringside view into how the technology industry has enabled companies and industries to evolve. At the very core, almost all industries are digitizing and becoming more connected in real time with data, and now AI – or its more popular form, generative AI (what ChatGPT uses) – is bringing a level of speed and innovation which can create massive disruption for industries, companies, societies and people.

I discuss the eight key trends below.

TECHNOLOGY AND DIGITIZATION

The power of what technology and digitization are unleashing came powerfully to me, in a chat with the CFO of one of the largest steel companies in Europe. He described in 2010 how his focus was on competing with Chinese steel bought by their customers using Alibaba. They were facing stiff competition at the commodity end of steel with small customers buying directly from small manufacturers in China.

If steel, which is a very physical industry, can be disrupted through tech platforms, *what industry is safe*? Having seen this evolution in music first hand in 2005, over time I have seen this disruption only increase from newspapers to almost all industries getting reshaped by technology and companies that are using technology for competitive advantage.

Rapid digitization across industries and value chains provides opportunities to create value for customers through multiple ways:

- Improving the way customers buy existing products and services and how close you can become to these customers from the data these interactions generate online.

- Responding to competitors in days, not months or years.

- Creating completely new products, services or experiences offered through existing or completely new business models, channels and platforms.

What separates the winners in digitization is not the technology but, as I have realized working with multiple customers, customer context or how well the business understands why it exists, how it creates value for its customers, and how digitization helps them to become much better at predicting a fast-evolving customer choice environment and providing products, services and experiences which most closely match these choices. This almost always aids adoption.

One illustration of this can be seen in our collaboration with *various police forces in the UK*, perhaps the most challenging environment to create a lasting impact because of security, ingrained processes and legacy environments.

Mobile solutions aimed at aiding street officers have typically been challenging to implement and even harder to achieve broad acceptance – forget delight – at the hands of officers. Most of these initiatives often focused on technology with the purpose of monitoring how time was spent by officers on patrol and digitizing current processes.

A new initiative aimed at improving officers' daily tasks through mobile technology significantly enhanced their work experience. It automated manual data entry to prefilled forms, minimized repetitive tasks, and introduced a user-friendly interface. This approach saved officers about two hours per day on non-productive activities, lessened the frequency of trips from the field to the office, improved policing efficiency by 30 per cent, and saw extensive adoption.

The broad acceptance of this technology eventually led to the collection of real-time data from mobile devices used by patrol officers. This data was gathered in areas with high crime rates during specific times and days. Such information enabled the development of an **AI-driven prediction engine** for proactive policing and community crime-reduction initiatives.

These advancements were made possible by experienced officers with three decades of street experience, who understood the officers' needs, had empathy, and sought a solution that street officers appreciated, empowered by achievable technology. This highlights an important lesson for businesses: **while technology is essential, adopting a technology-first mindset often results in failures.** Studies show that 70 per cent of digital transformation initiatives do not meet their objectives, primarily because they overlook user needs and context and focus too much on the technology aspects of the solution.

CUSTOMER CONTEXT: THE NEW BATTLEGROUND

Digitization and the consequent emergence of an online world have significantly transformed the customer context. No longer is a great product or service at the right price enough.

Companies now need to deal with the following:

- Greater access to information shapes customer choice and leads to more discerning and critical purchasing decisions.
- Influencers increasingly play a massive role in shaping choices.
- When an experience goes bad, irate customers tell millions of customers and not just a few, and bad news becomes viral.
- Customers expect to be served with a consistent experience across all touchpoints, whether online or offline, all seamlessly blended into a new product or service.
- Comparison of experiences is not just within a category but across what is available across categories and brands.

Generation Z, growing up with the internet, social media and devices like iPads or smartphones from an early age, are true digital natives. They now represent about 32 per cent of the world's population, making them a significant demographic group. Their buying habits and influences have led to rapid changes in the market. Trends on TikTok, Instagram and the like and virality, both positive and negative, shape the choices that customers make.

THE RISE OF THE EXPERIENCE ECONOMY

Navigating customer preferences in the omnichannel era with social media and influencers is challenging, but those who succeed are now enhancing their offerings by incorporating experiences along with their products and services. Studies show that 76 per cent of consumers prefer to spend money on experiences rather than material items. This shift is particularly pronounced among millennials and Generation Z, with 72 per cent prioritizing experiences over possessions.

Fast forward 25 years, and this notion rings increasingly true.

Today, experiences are not just add-ons; they're the main event, and whole industries are getting reshaped by this phenomenon. For instance, an automobile company might reposition itself as a provider of mobility experiences, being able to charge a premium for the experience – or an admission fee. Scaling this to make it a significant part of the business model is where the real test of a good business strategy lies.

It's impossible not to think about Costco as a brilliant example of this approach. The Costco subscription (which is not easy to get) makes almost 72 per cent of the annual profits of Costco – and shows that experience need not be premium, as sometimes the word 'experience' suggests. All it requires is alignment with your value proposition and a relentless focus on delivering it.

Although it often goes unrecognized within the broader services sector, its impact spans almost every part of the economy. Notable examples include live events, theatre and travel experiences, where growth is driven by consumer demand for unique experiences. However, we can find examples everywhere. This thinking creates loyalty and connection far beyond the product and the service being transformed through experience.

An example is a Chevrolet dealership, which invites Manchester United fans to watch Premier League games on a big screen while having their cars serviced. By charging a premium for this service, the dealership illustrates how innovative thinking can create additional value and customer loyalty, turning routine tasks into memorable experiences and additional profit. There are examples like this across almost all industries.

Many companies, across industries, today recognize that covering the extra distance from your product and service to how it is experienced by the customer really is the holy grail on which future businesses need to be built.

Done right, it will help businesses build lasting relationships and loyalty. Done wrong, it will almost always result in a substantially weakened position in your industry.

HARNESSING TECHNOLOGY FOR BETTER INSIGHTS

We have discussed that the route to experiences which delight, create loyalty and profit lies first and foremost in knowing what value you deliver to your customers and a maniacal focus on delivering it. This is easiest to do by being so close to your customers that you can predict their needs and what brings a smile to their face when they interact with your product, services or experiences.

Strategies which focus on technology and ignore closeness to client needs and context almost always never work; **however, technology is a massive multiplier which needs to be leveraged to create the insights and choices that create great experiences.** Some technology areas creating impact are discussed here.

Given that experience is about predicting choice, the better the quantity and quality of data and the better the algorithm underpinning this data, the better the chance that predictions will be good. We see leading companies across all sectors, physical and digital, leveraging artificial intelligence (AI) and machine learning to analyse customer data and predict what customers will like, or shaping customer choices by integrating these insights with their marketing and social channels, creating a virtuous cycle of more targeted data and choice leading to better predictions. Shien, the Chinese fast fashion brand, and Zara are good examples of leveraging technology to predict demand and choices and use that for shaping products, services and experiences for customers.

Emerging technologies like **augmented reality** (AR) and **virtual reality** (VR) are set to take customer experiences to the next level. For instance, IKEA's AR app lets customers visualize how furniture will look in their homes before making a purchase, leading to a 35 per cent increase in sales for products featured in these settings. With generative AI integrated into AR/VR experiences, we anticipate a new area of experiencing a product, service or place digitally and under different contexts/simulations before experiencing them physically, or a mix of physical and virtual; all melded into one experience like we have seen in gaming.

These technologies, individually and built together, have helped businesses create offerings which delight – the key remains imagination and context.

THE IMPORTANCE OF AN OMNICHANNEL APPROACH

Consumers today expect a seamless experience across all channels. Start a transaction or information search on the web, pick it up on your mobile to compare with what some influencers say on Instagram, transact on the stores app, and pick and try/return in a store – these need to all meld into one seamless experience to drive conversion and growth.

Disney gets this right with its MagicBand technology, which acts as a hotel room key, park ticket and payment method all in one. This seamless integration improves experience, reduces entry wait times by 70 per cent and increases customer spending. Hotel chains, retail outlets and sports teams all understand and leverage this technology for a great experience.

PERSONALIZATION: THE KEY TO LOYALTY

Personalization done the right way with first-party data and a regard for privacy can help move from traditional market segmentation and personas to real-time, individual-level personalization. Amazon's recommendation engine is a prime example, generating 35 per cent of its revenue by suggesting products based on past purchases and browsing behaviour. Netflix's recommendation engine, which drives 80 per cent of content watched on the platform, exemplifies this shift.

CREATING A CULTURE TO EMBED CUSTOMER-CENTRICITY

Ultimately, experience is not what you design but what a customer experiences and how they feel about it in the instance that they experience it.

I strongly believe experience is a human and intuition thing as much as it's about science, process, data, tools and technology – the art of bringing all these insights, processes and tools together to create a 'wow' is a creative process which, ultimately, people with the right motivations do.

Creating a culture that prioritizes customer experience requires dedication and a willingness to go above and beyond and it's not a target but a journey, where each day you can become a little bit better by reading signals from your customers better and continuing to improvise and evolve.

Companies like Disney, Zappos, Starbucks, Ritz-Carlton and Amazon demonstrate that when businesses embed customer-centric values into their culture, the results are transformative. By focusing on personalization, empowerment and attention to detail, these organizations not only meet customer expectations but also create lasting memories that foster loyalty and advocacy. In a world where consumers have countless choices, delivering magical experiences is the key to standing out and thriving.

Building a culture that prioritizes customer experience requires constant reinforcement.

Key strategies include:

- **Lead by example:** Leaders shape organizational culture significantly. Vineet Nayar of HCL Technologies championed Employees First, Customer Second, which led to happier employees and rapid company growth.

- **Embrace transparency and authenticity:** Fakeness is easily noticed. Genuine experiences and transparency during setbacks are crucial for extraordinary customer interactions.

- **Embed customer-centricity as an organizational obsession:** Jeff Bezos made Amazon highly customer-centric through his relentless focus on customer satisfaction.

- **Empower employees to make decisions:** Decentralizing decision-making enables better customer interactions by allowing employees to act in the moment.

- **Develop comprehensive training programmes:** Empowerment works only if new hires receive thorough training and cultural reinforcement.

- **Foster continuous improvement:** Prioritizing customer experience means constantly seeking improvements. Top companies have staff spend time solving real customer issues to build empathy.

- **Measure and reward customer experience champions:** Consistent positive experiences require measurement and management. Many companies use detailed experience scorecards to track customer and service provider interactions and do annual audits of customer satisfaction from which company performance is built.

Done right, each one of these helps build a solid foundation and culture which creates, sustains and drive experiences that bring customers back to the business for more.

EXPERIENCE-CENTRICITY IS A JOURNEY, NOT A TARGET

Experience-centricity requires a continuous commitment to understand and anticipate customer needs, preferences and behaviours.

As companies navigate complexities of an ever-changing market, a culture that prioritizes customer experience wins. This requires fostering an environment where employees are empowered to innovate, adapt and create memorable interactions driven by an obsession on delivering the best experience in the context of the consumer and the value you deliver to them.

Experience not only gets embedded in the products and services that are delivered to customers but, most critically, the products and services evolve to deliver an experience which people are willing to pay a premium for. Technology and culture play an important role in achieving this outcome.

By viewing customer experience as an ongoing journey, businesses can cultivate lasting relationships, drive loyalty, and ultimately thrive in a competitive landscape. The pursuit of excellence in customer experience is not a destination but a dynamic process that evolves with each customer interaction, which enriches the next interaction.

Great businesses are built on the foundation of delivering exceptional experiences to the customers they serve. They stand for something meaningful and provide their users with value and association that resonate deeply, creating lasting loyalty and admiration. They do this in a manner which anticipates user needs and understand the context of how they use the business's products or services better than customers can expect. I believe in Steve Jobs' insight: **'Get closer than ever to your customers. So close that you tell them what they need well before they realize it themselves.'**

This obsession with customer experience shows both in market share and more so in profit share that these businesses enjoy in their industries. A great example is Apple and the smartphone industry – while the smartphone market has reached almost $0.50 trillion/year in 2024, what has remained constant is that Apple, with an 18 per cent market share, continues to monopolize the profit share, earning around 83 per cent of the industry profits. Amazon and its founder's obsession with customer experience has led to the reinvention of retail as we know it. There are examples across all industries, from Disney to Zappos to the dabbawallas in Mumbai and your 30-year-old corner shop, which continues to delight you every time you walk into it. All of these are built on providing an experience that customers love and that enables businesses to remain profitable over a very long period.

I hope you find the insights from Dr Franziska Bell and Ashish Gupta on the future of customer experience and digitalization enlightening as you reach the end of this book. Thank you for joining me on this journey. I am excited to see the impact you will make in the dynamic field of customer experience.

INDEX

The index is filed in alphabetical, word-by-word order. Acronyms and 'Mc' are filed as presented. Numbers within main headings are filed as spelt out.

Looking for another book?

Explore our award-winning
books from global business
experts in Marketing and Sales

Scan the code to browse

www.koganpage.com/marketing

From 4 December 2025 the EU Responsible Person (GPSR) is:
eucomply oU, Pärnu mnt. 139b – 14, 11317 Tallinn, Estonia
www.eucompliancepartner.com